CONTENTS

Introduction

Mission Accomplished
... 30 Years On!

As I sat on a boulder, eating my lunch in the October sunshine, halfway up the steep-sided gouge in the fellside that is Arten Gill, I was at just about the same level as the railway track as it crossed the viaduct, whose tall piers rose from the valley floor below me.

Viewed from this elevation, the viaduct at Arten Gill is not merely taller, but also more dramatically located than its more famous cousin, the celebrated 24-arch structure at Ribblehead. The shimmering black of the fossil-rich 'Dent marble' from which it, like its near neighbour at Dent Head, was constructed, gives it an aura of authority and longevity.

Ribblehead Viaduct – which carries the Settle–Carlisle railway (S&C) across the peaty headwaters of the rivers Ribble and Doe – is the most emblematic and most photographed of the 21 viaducts on the 116km of track that are the finest legacy of the once mighty Midland Railway. But Arten Gill is my favourite, for the way it so lightly shrugs off the challenge posed by the gap to soar more than 30m above the beck below.

It's a view that you never get to see, should you rely solely on the train to take the strain of travelling from Settle to Carlisle. For it is self-evident that, while a railway journey may unfold fine scenic vistas, it can never afford the best vantage from which to study and admire the railway itself.

Of course, many – perhaps most – railways hold few surprises and are somewhat prosaic. But when a line attracts such epithets as 'England's greatest scenic line' or even 'the world's most iconic railway', as Network Rail described it in a 2017 press release, then it is clearly deserving of the same kind of attention as the countryside through which it passes.

The enduring S&C was built by the Midland Railway between 1869 and 1876, as part of its quest to forge its own independent route to Scotland. It is, uniquely for a railway in the UK, a Conservation Area in its own right: besides the 21 viaducts, its 14 tunnels and its bridges (325 of them, when first built) enjoy special conservation status. So too do its stations, trackside structures and railway workers' cottages, extending all the way from the magnificent glazed canopies of Hellifeld station, actually nine kilometres south of Settle, right into Carlisle's Citadel station.

By walking from Settle to Carlisle, you get the chance to get up close to the railway's magnificent architecture and to understand just why the Midland's surveyors chose precisely the route that they did to carry their tracks across the lonely and lofty fells.

For me, this walk meant I finally got to fulfil an ambition that had been nagging me for the best part of 30 years, ever since I first spotted the potential for creating a highly sustainable long-distance walk through magnificent country, using the railway as both the walk's primary theme and as a way of avoiding unnecessary use of a car. I had driven the creation of the Settle–Carlisle Way walking route, loosely following the path of the railway, and yet had only walked sections of it myself.

In finally getting my boots muddy and walking every inch of the route in 2019 and 2020, the adventure came to be so much more: I found myself more deeply immersed in the history of the line – from its unusual inception to its unexpected reprieve from closure in 1989 and, now, its potential new future – than I had ever been when writing about it in years gone by.

Mission Accomplished

The adventure opened the door to stories that pre-dated the line by many centuries, as well as to tales of the lives of the mercurial men who built it, or of the people whose remote rural lives were changed by it.

It also, rather unexpectedly, increasingly took me around the unexpected twists and turns of memory lane. I had lived in the Yorkshire Dales for a significant period of my life but had rather pushed many of the memories to one side after leaving the area more than 20 years ago. The reasons for my departure were both personal and professional and it was the action of walking alone with my thoughts that proved capable of unlocking these recollections.

* * *

It is difficult to think of another railway that lends itself quite so well to acting as the backbone to a long-distance walk. Some routes, it is true, follow country branch lines and pass through fine countryside. But country branch lines were built without the extravagance that made the S&C so very special. For this was no quaint little branch – it was conceived and built as a railway 'super-highway', striding straight and level across the high fells, leaping gills and gorges on towering viaducts and burrowing beneath the highest summits and other awkward obstructions.

It is the magnificence of the most level section of the line – from Ribblehead to its summit, at Ais Gill, in the upper Eden Valley – that makes this part of the journey stand out, and I dare say it shall always remain my favourite part of the walk. But that is not to diminish the manner in which the line travels down the course of the Eden, to the Solway Firth, at the edge of the Irish Sea. Even today, the valley retains the distinctive culture and features that make it something of a world apart.

Walking the Line

It nestles beneath the towering Pennine escarpment, to its east, and the Lakeland massif, to the west; its sleepy villages oozing history and intrigue and its more ancient relics reminding us of a pre-history of which we now have to guess more than we can know.

The railway cuts through the northern edge of limestone country, recently absorbed, as the Westmorland Dales, into the Yorkshire Dales National Park. As it gets nearer to Carlisle, it must find a route above the deep gorge carved by the sometimes tempestuous Eden.

It is a land of heroes and heroines; of nomadic Romani and of families who have farmed their land for generations; of the only wind in the British Isles to have been given its own name.

So it seems only fitting that the line's own place in this landscape and its traditions should, therefore, have received appropriate recognition, when it acquired its special conservation status in 1991. This was in the wake of the long but ultimately successful battle to save it from closure, proposed as part of a British Rail response to progressively diminishing government support.

I was personally involved in this long skirmish rather by accident. In 1983, I moved to Hawes, in Upper Wensleydale, where I embarked on a freelance journalism career, writing features for the national and regional media. So, when the formal notice of closure was announced in December of that year, I found that I was 'the man on the spot', attracting commissions to write about the railway and, through my swiftly bulging contacts book, stumbling upon successive scoops as the bizarre closure saga unfolded over six years – coincidentally, the same period of time that it had taken an army of up to 6,000 navvies to build the line in the first place.

As the dust settled on the ultimate U-turn, in late 1989, that finally saved the line for future generations, I teamed up with Alan Whitehouse, of the *Yorkshire Post* and, latterly, the BBC's

North of England transport correspondent, to write an account of the whole saga. *The Line That Refused To Die* was a sequel to my earlier work, *To Kill A Railway*, and ran to two editions, in 1990 and 1994.[1]

By this time I was running a small publishing business in Wensleydale, with a list of 50-plus non-fiction titles, including a series of books dubbed RailTrail, which featured country walks from railway stations throughout the UK and beyond. The line's salvation prompted us to add to this series a book based on the S&C, with the idea of creating a walking route along its entire length. This book, *Settle–Carlisle Country*, included a complete guide to the new walking route, the first of which, with an extraordinary leap of the imagination, we called the Settle–Carlisle Way. My friends and colleagues – the photographer John Morrison and the celebrated writer on the Dales and other things Yorkshire, Colin Speakman – embarked upon researching the route I had sketched out on OS maps.

Unbeknown to us, Ian and Andrew Gordon were also busy walking from Settle to Carlisle, and their account was published by the venerable Dalesman publishing house shortly after our own, in 1990. Their book was a travelogue, rather than a guide, and the route they took stuck closely to the railway itself and was 130km long: ours was driven by the desire to reflect the most interesting walking possibilities, which might be further from the tracks, and so it ran to at least 150km, with the option to start out from Leeds, via the Leeds & Liverpool Canal and add a further 72km.

The singer-comedian Mike Harding, then President of the Ramblers' Association (now simply The Ramblers), snipped a ribbon to launch the route and our book sold out its 5,000-copy print run quite quickly. Many walkers applied to us for the completion certificates we designed, so I explored with colleagues at the Yorkshire Dales National Park the possibility of a formal designation as a Long Distance Walk. It was an idea that never really gained traction – local authorities were not then (and certainly aren't now) looking for the extra expense of specially waymarking and maintaining extra stretches of rights of way.

Nonetheless, Harvey Maps produced its own dedicated 156km route, subsequently modified by Rucksack Readers in a more recent publication, and now generally recognised by the Long Distance Walkers Association (LDWA) as 'the route', should such a definitive thing exist. Just for good measure, the LDWA offers another, far more challenging route, modestly called a 'hill walk', of more than 170km, taking in some of the highest peaks in the Dales, the Howgills and the eastern fringes of the Lake District and with 6,700m of climbing.

For my own part, I've become very lukewarm about the whole concept of such prescribed long-distance routes as they can encourage overuse, and this in turn may necessitate expensive and intrusive footpath repairs that can despoil the very country-side that people set out on foot to enjoy.

The whole point of creating a Settle–Carlisle Way was that it would be a low-impact footpath, as the train would always be there, both to reach the start of the walk and to enable the weary walker to bale out at any intermediate station. So my new 'rule' for walkers who choose to hike from Settle to Carlisle, or to and from any stations in between, is a very simple one: your route should ensure that you visit each intermediate station, with the proviso that you may miss out a maximum of two stations, providing that you at least pass within sight of both of them.

Beyond that, you can follow the routes described in any of the four publications already mentioned or you can devise your own, while sticking, of course, to rights of way or other permissive routes.

* * *

Mission Accomplished

As I've said, it had rather niggled me in the years since devising the Settle–Carlisle Way, that – while I had walked much of the route – I had never systematically set out from Settle, bound for Carlisle: I'd only ever walked some of the individual stages, albeit some more than once. Then, in 2009, an old pal and I set up base camp in an Appleby hotel, intent on using the train to help us walk three one-day stages, from Garsdale to Kirkby Stephen, Kirkby Stephen to Appleby and, finally, Appleby to Langwathby.

Day One went well and the walk along the High Way, on the flanks of Mallerstang, with its commanding views across to the railway at the head of the Eden Valley, surpassed my expectations. Day Two revealed the delights of Smardale and the fine limestone pavements of the old county of Westmorland, recently incorporated into the Yorkshire Dales National Park, and saw us mingling with Coast-to-Coast walkers for a time. Then my pal suffered an injury, leaving me to set out on Day Three, towards Dufton, on my own. Writers I know, who specialise in producing self-guided trails, have told me often enough that their work requires annual checks and updates, and I soon understood why: a forest had been planted on the described route and I was soon lost. My compass was of little use and – having walked in a near circle – I eventually ended up back at Appleby. I never imagined it would be more than a decade before I would finally complete the entire route from Settle to Carlisle.

In writing this book, I have declined responsibility for ensuring that readers can navigate 150-something kilometres without getting lost. That task is for those who write walkers' guides. Nor do I really mind if readers are happy to share my experience from the comfort of their armchair without walking any of the route for themselves. It is, after all, only the story of how I, eventually, completed the entire walk myself, and of some of my adventures along the way.

Walking the Line

I've always found that there are few better ways than walking to set my imagination roving: even when walking in a group, I often find that my default is to walk slightly apart and lose myself in my own thoughts. That is despite rarely making a conscious choice to avoid engaging in conversation.

So, walking through the Yorkshire Dales and the Eden Valley became something of a nostalgia fest: not so much because I was revisiting specific places, but because the journey rekindled in my mind a subconscious record of so many adventures. I really hadn't appreciated just how indelibly embedded into my own psyche the land, its lore and my own place in it all had become.

I share with readers, therefore, not just the trek itself, but also the gentle voyage of discovery that I made into my own recollections and the process of then setting out to satisfy my curiosity as to what might have become of people I used to know; and how they might have helped shape both places I visited, and the lens through which I now saw these locations.

When I set out in autumn 2019 on the first two stages of the walk, it was with some confidence: earlier that year I had a hip replaced after doggedly resisting it for some time. Pain is a strange companion and one it is tempting to deny when the remedy is radical – it was only when I found myself taking five hours struggling to descend Skiddaw in the summer of 2018 that I finally found myself conceding that, yes, I was in pain and yes, it was affecting my quality of life.

Acquiring my new hip proved a liberation. Not only was I now back to actually wanting to walk long distances but I was playing football again, albeit the so-called 'walking' variety, in which players of a certain age are not allowed to run. Or that's the theory, anyway. Not only that, but now sporting two legs of the same length for probably the first time in my life, I could actually play better than I ever could before.

However, I don't want this book to be a dedication to the merits of hip replacement or of any kind of triumph over medical or other adversity. I could just as easily have written it all in my youth, when I first started walking long distances, though it would have been without the knowledge and, dare I say, wisdom, of more senior years. I hope those of all ages may find in it something of interest to them.

Besides the stories that are based in quite specific locations, there are themes that connect long sections of this linear route. The Midland engineers were not the first to discern a south–north opportunity through the fells and one of my companions on a good stretch of the walk was the redoubtable Lady Anne Clifford who, having fought for the right to her inheritance, then set about bringing all her properties back up to scratch.

For anyone wanting to understand more about this dogged 17th century defender of women's rights, the place to start is Skipton Castle, among the best preserved of medieval castles. You might indeed choose then to arrive in Settle on foot, by walking from Skipton along the towpath of the Leeds & Liverpool Canal, as far as the watershed, near Gargrave, and then by rights of way as you enter the limestone Dales.

The route from Settle northwards is comfortably completed by division into the same stages that we created back in 1990 and I made it my own rule to stick to those divisions, while also being alive to alternative possibilities. I also initially decided that my staging posts should, where possible, be pubs with rooms – near the stations the route passed by, and the more local the better. Then, of course, COVID intervened, though I did do my best to maintain the basic principle of local pubs once lockdown lifted.

Others may prefer a single base, using the train daily to return to a familiar bed. Those not averse to carrying a heavier load might choose to camp, but I sought to travel as light as possible, gauging my top layer according to the weather forecast and carrying no more than the most basic toilet kit and a change of undies when on the trail for more than one night.

Like the finer details of the route itself, these are matters of personal choice, and I hope that some readers will feel motivated to make those choices, while respecting the fundamental ethos of the walk and seeking to minimise their impact in all ways they can.

I shall return to the inevitable subject of COVID in later chapters and in my postscript – I might have preferred to ignore it altogether, but to do so would have been false and would have been to fancifully wish out of existence an event that already has changed, and shall further change, all our lives in some way.

Happy hiking!

Stan

Chapter 1

Restoration, Bad Navigation and All that Jazz

From Settle to Ribblehead

Earth, sweet Earth, sweet landscape, with leav's throng
And louch'd low grass, heaven that dost appeal
To, with no tongue to plead, no heart to feel;
That canst but only be, but dost that long –
From 'Ribblesdale' by Gerard Manley Hopkins

There can be few better ways to jolt your mind into the universe that is the S&C than to arrive at Settle station and head for Mark Rand's water tower.

The tower that once filled the tanks that fed the boilers of loco-motives as they readied for the Long Drag up to Blea Moor, 15 miles to the north, is arguably the most famous railway water tower in the world. Such status is thanks to Channel 4's *Restoration* programme, on which the tower and its occupants, Mark and his wife, Pat, were among the first stars.

Mark had also been, for some time, something of a shining light among the Friends of the Settle–Carlisle Line (FoSCL), occupying at various times the roles of chairman, vice-chairman and press officer.

I'd previously found him a convivial and welcoming host, but knew little of his life before the Friends. Our meeting today would take us from *Restoration* to ambitious ideas about the railway's future, via his previous life as a senior policeman, in Bradford, at the time of the infamous fire at Bradford City's football ground, and how he had, since our previous meeting, broken his neck in a fall at the water tower.

Arriving in Settle, it is dull, but still dry, and I'm hoping that the latest forecast Atlantic front will pass through before I have to set off walking in the morning. Negotiating my way past telltale signs of new building projects, to the water tower's rear door, I greet Mark with the observation that, even in October, the train down was alive with a mix of walkers and both British and overseas visitors – alongside a pretty solid core of passengers with more prosaic reasons for travelling: work, study, visiting friends, and so on.

'I had a headmaster from Zimbabwe turn up at the door one day,' smiles Mark, who somehow never seems to tire of showing off the water tower to anyone who might be interested. And with *Restoration* having been sold to countless overseas TV stations, there are many of them.

Mark and Pat love living in the water tower almost as much as living in Settle, which Mark believes is as close to the perfect little town as anyone can get. 'We are very happy here, and every facility you can think of, short of an A&E hospital, is within walking distance.'

An A&E hospital might have been quite useful, it turns out, as he shares with me the details of the 'little accident' he had when he fell badly on the water tower stairs. In fact, the X-ray of his broken and misplaced vertebrae is the wallpaper on his mobile phone and he's not shy about sharing it. Ditto the large dent in the wall, created by his head.

'It seems I fainted and then fell,' he says, nonchalantly. 'The paramedics suspected a broken neck and so it took them two and half hours to get me out and into the ambulance. I wasn't too worried, as I remembered as a medical student trying to cut a spinal cord just how tough it was, so I knew that if it wasn't already broken, it would take a lot to break it.'

Mark ended up in the regional spinal unit at Preston, where various titanium accessories were inserted, so his neck now has more metal in it than Frankenstein's monster. These days he uses the lift to go up and down the tower and he carries his head just a little awkwardly, which, I reflect, is better than not being able to carry it at all.

I knew little of Mark's background before this meeting and, if challenged to guess what his career had been before retirement, would probably have struggled to pin the label of senior policeman on his lapel. Ex-policemen tend to have a certain look and it's not one that Mark shares: he's altogether more the convivial, grey-haired uncle than Knacker of the Yard. He had been, in fact, Chief Superintendent with West Yorkshire Police, and one day in 1985 he received a phone call in the early hours. A few hours later, he found himself working with the coroner on the identification of victims of the fire at Valley Parade football ground. At a time when modern methods of identification were not available, Mark and his team established a methodology for reconciling the identification of victims with missing person reports, and his experience was subsequently deployed by Interpol.

Mark and Pat's first home at Settle, after his retirement from the police, was a 17th century Grade I listed building, which they eventually sold to the trustees of the Museum of North Craven Life. As a result, the couple were able to finance the water tower project.

This may be as good a moment as any to recommend a visit to said museum as a suitable prelude to embarking on the long walk to Carlisle. It's what you might call a 'small but perfectly formed' attraction, housing as it does a somewhat esoteric collection of photographs and artefacts, including farm implements. You may marvel at aspects of its single most extensive collection – of medical memorabilia and descriptions of 19th century remedies. There's a smallish room dedicated to introducing you to the railway line, although on my own visit, the excellent interactive map[2] was out of action. The café next door is also run by the museum trust and offers nice homemade fare in pleasant surroundings.

But back to Mark and Pat – just how did they get the crazy idea that a redundant water tower might make a nice, or indeed any kind of, practical home?

'It was our son-in-law, Alan – an American for whom anything older than 1910 is ancient history,' Mark tells me. 'He kept pestering us about the tower and was a real pain in the arse. It turned out that the chap who ended up as our architect had also wanted to buy it, only his wife-to-be put her foot down, so he came to us with a head full of ideas. He pleaded to be our architect and though we thought we didn't need one, as it already came with planning permission to be a dwelling, we brought him on board.'

The architect was Stuart Green, whose avant-garde inspiration, from the 1920s, was 'a lot more imaginative than the end result, as the planners clipped our wings along the way'. The plans for the conversion involved installing three floors in the tower and hoisting up a glazed rooftop conservatory to sit inside the old water tank itself. 'The actual building work was only about six months, but buggering about with planners took years,' he reflects.

Upon completion, an album featuring milestones in the restoration was presented by 'Restoration Man' George Clarke, and it now enjoys pride of place in the large open-plan sitting room on the first floor of the tower, where Mark pours an unusually passable glass of home-made red wine. Then we're joined by another Settle resident and Settle–Carlisle expert, Martin Pearson. It was

Martin's diligent posing of countless Freedom of Information requests that cast so much light on the government machinations that preceded the famous 1989 U-turn and reprieve for the S&C, which had been under threat of closure for six years.

I could spend a long time talking to Mark and Martin and not get bored, but my digs, just up the road at the Royal Oak, are beckoning...

There's only one person in the bar when I go in: the man at the pumps, Simon, shows me to my plain but comfortable room. I opt for a short stroll around town before returning for supper and an evening of live jazz, which looks like it could be interesting. I ask Simon when the jazz will start and receive the confusing response of 'Eight o'clock, give or take 17 minutes', accompanied by a slightly manic chuckle from a woman on a bar stool. 'And the raffle will be at 18 minutes to ten!' he adds, as I head out of the door.

A short distance down the high street, I spot Bar 13, which I assume to be Settle's response to the growing trend for independent micro-pubs. I don't remember it from the last time I stayed in town, back in 2014. That was when I was giving a talk at Victoria Hall, on the fight to save the S&C, as part of the town's innovative Storytelling Festival.

'We've been here 14 years,' the barman tells me, confirming just how far ahead of the game this wee town is, for this is a 20-teens micro-pub in all but age, boasting a fine array of some very local ales, some with notable railway themes, like the Kirkby Lonsdale Singletrack.

In my imagination this trip is going to be typified by my rubbing shoulders with new acquaintances in every pub I visit, but I'm suddenly gripped by shyness and choose a table on my own, nonetheless close enough to the neighbouring one for me to earwig their conversation.

'Okay,' says the guy returning with the drinks: 'Give me songs with parentheses in the title...'

'*(Don't Fear) The Reaper*!' ventures his female companion. 'Blue Oyster Cult.'

'Good one! How about *Sittin' On (The Dock Of The Bay)*? The Otis Redding classic.'

There follows a short debate about whether the latter has parentheses or not, before the man with the drinks comes up with *If You Are Going To San Francisco (Be Sure To Wear Some Flowers In Your Hair)*. 'It's also possibly the longest song title ever,' he adds. No one is arguing. I want to shout out The Beatles' *Revolution (Number Nine)*, but that would only show I've been listening in and, anyway, I'm still feeling shy.

Back at the Royal Oak, I walk into the function room and am conscious that the average age of those in the room has fallen – something that rarely happens when I walk into anywhere, these days. It quickly rises again when an old lady with a wide smile and a severe shake somehow gets all the way from the bar with her drink without spilling a drop.

A chap takes a call on his mobile and, in something of a stage whisper, starts talking about 'hairy backs who like jazz'. I'm unsure what a 'hairy back' is, though guess it may be associated with the process of hair departing the male head in middle age and relocating to parts of the body where it is unwanted. And then his conversation moves on to illness among mature people: someone has died...

I'm relieved when the arrival of a) my enormous pie supper, and b) the Black Horse Jazzmen mean I no longer have to listen to this gloomy chatter. The latter has a neutral impact on the average age of the room, but a very positive impact on the levels of joy: they're a truly wonderful trad jazz quartet.

* * *

It is raining: steadily. That wet rain that no one really wants to walk in. I'm thinking I'll buy a sandwich for lunch at Ye Olde Naked Man Café, which was a favourite rendezvous for various caving trips, back in my 20s. There were only about four of these trips: three involved getting lost, getting caught in a flood, and my then wife getting stuck in the entrance to Gaping Gill. But I digress from the question of the moment, which is 'Why is Ye Olde Naked Man so called?' As with the similar question as to why the Durham suburb of Pity Me is so called, the answer is that no one knows for sure. But the building's been here since the 17th century, when it was first a funeral parlour and later a pub. Some suggest the moniker may have come from the idea of folk shuffling off this mortal coil as naked as the day they were born.

None of which will make Ye Olde Naked Man any more open than it isn't at half past eight on a wet October morning. The Copper Kettle rises to my challenge in its stead, and – hefty ham and cheese sandwich in my day bag – I set forth along the little ginnel that takes me from Victoria Hall to where the railway exits the town on the first of its many viaducts.

Crossing the road bridge over the Ribble I'm soon heading for open country, but something is strangely missing. There is not a bird to be seen or heard, and I find my mind straying to that Douglas Adams book, *So Long, and Thanks For All The Fish*, in which the dolphins have decided to leave Earth. Have the birds now followed the lead of our aquatic cousins? Just for the record, a lone wren and a scrawny, rain-soaked crow will represent my total avian sightings all the way to Stainforth.

This is virgin territory for me: I am on the western bank of the Ribble, on the waymarked Ribble Way, which is also the route of our original Settle–Carlisle Way and of all subsequent routes, excluding the early Dalesman walk.

The first settlement of any note after leaving Settle is Stackhouse, an attractive collection of terraced houses, separated by unmade lanes and almost entirely enclosed by a dry-stone wall. It seems a fittingly rustic point at which to be entering the Yorkshire Dales National Park.

I re-cross the Ribble, muddy brown and slightly swollen, near the weir and the salmon ladders, and soon reach the railway again, before taking a field path, called Stack Lane. The path conceals the faint remains of brick steps that suggest the field might once have been filled with terraces of cottages, perhaps for workers at the nearby mills or quarries.

In a few weeks' time, I float this idea with Miles Johnson, Senior Historic Environment Officer (archaeologist, to you and me) at the national park. He suggests, rather, that they are all that's left of former allotments.

My route takes me to a low summit, from where it's a gentle descent towards one of the line's most interesting industrial relics, the Hoffmann lime kiln, built adjacent to the railway in 1873 by the Craven Lime Company. This was what was known as a 'continuous process' lime kiln, meaning that each of its many furnaces could be lit in turn, with coal and lime added from the top. It's what the park calls a 'low-key interpretation site', which basically means there are a few explanatory signs and then you're on your own.

Miles will tell me that there's a new management plan for the site in the making, and there are concerns about its vulnerability because it lost its roof many decades ago and the water's getting in. I'm pleased, on arrival at the kilns, to take advantage of the shelter they do still offer for perhaps a hundred yards or so, as I stumble across the uneven floor the length of its lugubrious tunnels.

It's an immensely impressive structure – a veritable cathedral to the mortar of Victorian masonry. I can imagine the bats and spiders roosting in the murky heights of its chambers. Apparently, however, it was a couple of metal Spencer kilns that produced the best lime and they were still in use as recently as the Second World War.

Once upon a time, people had grand designs upon this entire site: having begun to accept that the S&C would not be closed, the government was, during the 1980s, feverishly encouraging private initiatives that might help to stimulate a new tourist economy along the line.

One of these was an idea conjured up by the Manpower Services Commission (MSC), which used to help to provide employment and a way into work for young school leavers, back in the 1980s. The plan was to make the kilns a major tourist attraction, with much more fancy interpretation than exists now and an aspiration to attract visitors on a similar scale to Beamish, County Durham's 'living history' museum. But the MSC, Edward Heath's baby, was effectively killed off by the Thatcher government in 1987, and the plan died with it.

Exiting the kiln site, I arrive shortly in the village of Stainforth. I recall writing about the place back in the days when I wrote a regular column for the *Yorkshire Post*, featuring cameos of villages all across God's Own County, and each illustrated by a nice pen and ink drawing. I'm tempted to call this a picture-postcard kind of a place, but my cliché alarm is bonging dangerously. So let's find some real evidence of its attractiveness, beginning with the Craven Heifer. I like this pub's scale: not quite miniature, but certainly not big and brash. It's shiny and whitewashed and the Thwaites sign stands for good beer and occasional visits by dray horses. It was a winner in 2019's Hospitality Awards.

There are a number of Craven Heifer pubs around Skipton, and the name refers to a specific cow in the early 19th century. She weighed in at comfortably over a ton, after her owner, the Rev William Carr, of Bolton Abbey, effectively force-fed her.

Unsurprisingly, she died, aged just five, and remains to this day the heaviest cow ever known in England. The sign on the pub is based on an oil painting from the period.

All of which is immaterial, as, today, it is not open yet. But I reflect that for those for whom the bright city lights of Settle may be all too much, this could make a gentle alternative overnight stop. Arrive in Settle in the afternoon and just get the walking muscles fired up to arrive in Stainforth in time for supper. But that would be for another time.

I like the scale of Stainforth: just a few more-imposing houses, among the more traditional cottages. You need to detour west to see the village's most celebrated monument, the graceful 17th century packhorse bridge across the River Ribble to Little Stainforth, just upstream of the 'rapids' of Stainforth Force. It's still open to vehicles, but really shouldn't be. I wonder if it could be the longest single-span packhorse bridge in the country, but to test this theory requires defining a packhorse bridge and then sifting out all the multi-span ones. Anyway, it is a rather fine bridge.

When Colin Speakman did his original research for the Settle–Carlisle Way, he recommended a diversion to Catrigg Force, a smaller but apparently very pretty waterfall, demanding a steep climb up out of the village. But the rain is still falling and the clock is ticking, so I pause instead to look at a rather prosaic little feature in the centre of the village, called The Pinfold. Technically, a pinfold was a structure in which stray sheep were held until their owners came to reclaim them. But an interpretation board suggests it was more likely a pigsty. It was gifted to the village in 1980 and restored by the local environmental group some 19 years later. All in all, it's a peaceful little village and there could be worse places than The Pinfold to stop for a sandwich but, as I say, time presses.

The next hour or two will provide as clear an illustration as any as to why I am, these days, resolute that writing guidebooks of the 'turn left at the third cow past the byre' variety shall not be my métier. I study Colin's instructions carefully and exit the village, as appears to be required, by the path that starts 'just east of Stainforth church', and soon find it tracking uphill. I have some doubts as to whether this is the right path, as it seems too insignificant to be the Ribble Way, but then I spot a notch in the field wall on the horizon, which must be a stile.

It's only on arriving at the 'stile' that I realise it has been blocked up with large stones. I try to reconcile my position with the OS map: there's a tumbling stream in a gully on the other side of the wall and it looks, from the map, as though the path should follow its bank. I elect to climb the wall – an activity that is definitely not encouraged in the Countryside Code. I place my rucksack atop the coping stones and slowly and very carefully clamber on top of the filled-in portion, where the stile once was, and drop down safely on the other side – only to discover that my rucksack has somehow journeyed in the opposite direction.

The drop on this side is higher than side I climbed and I am reluctant to risk toppling the wall on top of myself, remembering the consequences when an old Scoutmaster of mine did precisely that, back in my youth. So I painstakingly and systematically remove all the stones used to block the old stile and retrieve my rucksack. Such activities are not featured in the Countryside Code either, but I do carefully replace all the stones previously removed, before setting off up the gill. And then I am confronted by a choice of edging across the head of the gill by a narrow ledge, or climbing another wall. I am getting close to being dismissed from membership of both the Countryside Code Society and the Guild of Mapreaders.

Finally, I am confident that, upon gaining the skyline, I shall find my correct route opening up before me in all its clarity. If only. Instead I am soon plodding across an endless marsh, ruing the fact that I have opted for walking shoes, rather than boots, and that they are shipping water with each step. It must be the best part of an hour later that I finally intercept the Ribble Way – a broad strand of a bridleway, confident of its place in the landscape. I have been walking well to the west of the correct route and I can only conclude that the original route description was wrong.

On a more optimistic note, I spot crows and seagulls sharing a thermal, suggesting there is at last some movement in the morning's dank air. I turn to look south-west and see blue sky approaching from the Irish Sea. Things get even better as the lane begins its descent to Helwith Bridge, allowing me to increase my pace and regain some lost time. The pub at Helwith Bridge is a large, quite dramatic building at the edge of the river, and I toy with making an unscheduled stop, but I am still a little nervous as to how accurate my estimated timings are likely to be, so press on, passing Hotel Paradiso, a bunk barn for four, fashioned from an old garage behind the pub.

Behind Helwith Bridge, decades of quarrying have hewn a huge hole in the end of the escarpment. It's not just the flanks of the hill that are being gobbled up, but the actual styling. Yet I recall from my time working with the national park that many quarry permissions have immense longevity, including the dormant ones, and even the park's protected status can not enable such activity to be easily stopped. Its impacts can, however, be mitigated, and the quarry at Helwith Bridge is a dramatic example of how this can be done to significant effect.

The construction of new railway sidings here came out of negotiations to reopen one of two quarries at the site. The quarry operator, Tarmac-Lafarge, agreed to a plan to install new rail infrastructure and thereby transfer 16,000 lorry movements a year to the railway. It represents a very significant environmental benefit and I'm fortunate enough to witness the arrival of an immense quarry train shunting its 75-tonne wagons into the three new sidings. It will shortly depart with a full load up the line to Blea Moor, the locomotive using the sidings there to reverse around the train so as to begin its return journey south to depots in Leeds and Manchester.

There seems to be a slight irony in the fact that the bulk of the stone quarried here is destined for roadbuilding. For anyone who fancies a closer look at what goes on in these immense holes in the ground, the quarry company has actually created a public trail, with viewing platforms.

My route to Horton-in-Ribblesdale continues on level ground between the railway and river. Horton-in-Ribblesdale is a rather unremarkable Dales village, but one that once enjoyed an important place in my career path. During my time as a freelance journalist and small-time publisher in Hawes, the Yorkshire Dales National Park had what we might call a bit of an image problem. Yorkshire folk are not keen on others coming in and telling them how to run, or not to run, their lives: things like requiring people not to demolish old field barns or replace slate roofs with corrugated iron. Or not to build suburbia-style houses, or erect flashing neon signs.

So, when the park announced a plan to build a car park extension at Horton on unspoiled meadowland, cries of hypocrisy rang loud. The villagers managed to create a bit of folklore about the land intended for the development as it had belonged to a lady from the village who had been, if I recall correctly, a bit of a character. The car park would not only despoil a meadow but it would also offend her legacy, they asserted.

The *Yorkshire Post* sent me to investigate and I met up with Peter Bayes, whom I knew as the owner of the celebrated Pen-y-ghent Café in the village. He gave me the low-down on the meadow saga: he was not overly impressed with the national park, though I do recall that the owner of the (rival) pub up the road was a member of the National Park Committee at the time, which may have had something to do with it. In any event, I'm afraid the park came in for a bit of a beating in my coverage of the issue – but the whole affair had an unexpected result for me personally when I met John Baker. He was the Assistant National Park Officer and invited me to his offices at the park's southern HQ, at Grassington (the main, northern one was in Bainbridge, in Wensleydale). I was more than a little trepidatious, as John's reputation went before him and he was known as a bit of an ogre by some of the staff I knew.

These days, however, people will know of John as the man whose end-of-life is the main storyline in the film and stage show, *Calendar Girls*. The Calendar Girls, of course, were members of the Women's Institute, in Upper Wharfedale, who were the first to have the bright idea of posing nude for a fundraising calendar. Now everyone does it, but back then, it really was groundbreaking. John had sadly been diagnosed with non-Hodgkins lymphoma in February 1998. Apparently, John knew that his wife, Angela, had had the idea of the calendar, but never thought she would actually dare to make it happen. After his death in July of that year, she determined to go ahead with the project, with the aim of raising £5,000 for blood cancer research. The rest, as they say, is history: the alternative WI calendar came out in April 1999 and the women, aged from 45 to 65, became international stars and ultimately, directly and indirectly, raised 1,000 times their original target, and helped create the relaunched charity, Bloodwise.

All that came about more than a decade after the day I first met up with John, when, I have to say, he was charm itself. His idea was to convert me from poacher to gamekeeper, thus launching my new career in media relations, which I managed to sustain, alongside my separate journalistic work. I was well respected in both local and national media and it was a relatively easy job to transform the way the park was projected in print and on TV, as the focus shifted towards all the good, but formerly unsung, works that it was engaged in.

In the late 1980s I became editor of *National Parks Today*, a newspaper published by the then Countryside Commission on behalf of the national parks in England and Wales. I became involved in the organisation of the annual conference of all these parks, writing and publishing a journalistic report on proceedings after each, on behalf of each host park. My company also produced a nifty little magazine for the Commission, called *Enjoying the Countryside*. It did what it said on the tin, or at least aimed to help people 'get out more'. Much of this success I owe to the late John Baker.

The other key player in the Horton-in-Ribblesdale accident that launched all this is, at the time of writing, not in a good place. The Pen-y-ghent Café has been a traditional refreshment stop on the Three Peaks Walk, which some of my friends and I have tackled every year since the beginning of time. Latterly I have tended to do just one or two peaks, or none at all since my hip got bad. In 2019, the first peak, Ingleborough, became my first major summit since my hip replacement. But the Pen-y-ghent Café, which had latterly been run by Peter's son, Matthew, closed in 2018. Matthew took the decision to shut up shop to enable him to care for Peter, who had become quite ill. This remains the case on the day of my walk: it feels very much like the end of an era.

* * *

I mentioned that Horton was an unremarkable village. It is essentially a ribbon development, without a focal point, such as a village green. The S&C climbs at a steady gradient of 1:100

from the moment it leaves Settle, all the way to Blea Moor, so the line is already elevated above the valley floor by the time it reaches Horton, whose station is therefore perched at the top of the settlement. On my way down on the train the previous day, I'd noticed that the highest structure in the village was not the church, as might have been expected, but an exceptionally tall and slender flagpole, with a union flag hanging limply from its crest. The village is neither Everest nor the South Pole, so I struggled with the concept that it had, somehow, only just been conquered by a British expeditionary force.

Now, as I approach Horton on foot, I'm a little unsure precisely where to branch away from the riverbank and into the village. I reach a small grassy field, bearing tyre tracks that slope gently up from the riverbank, and judge that this must be the correct route.

As I reach the top of the field, there is a gate, leading into a smaller paddock, in which there's a rather decrepit polytunnel, an old camper van and the remains of one of those 1960s corrugated Citroën trucks – the kind that says 'baguette delivery vehicle' and was once synonymous with 2CVs and Gitanes. It appears to have been heavily cannibalised for spares. The mysterious flagpole I'd seen from the train rises from the centre of the paddock. It must be at least 50ft high. I exit the paddock into a short cul-de-sac, via a gate alongside a tumbledown open-sided garage, in which, I note, a sign imploring people to Vote Leave in the EU referendum lies discarded on a pile of timber. On reaching the end of the little lane, an officious-looking notice tells me that it is private and that there is strictly no access to the riverbank. The little paddock, the *Keep Out* sign, the rusty van and all the other shambolic accessories have a whiff of metaphor about them.

At this point it is my plan to part company with the Ribble Way and stick to the route that Colin and I devised, which will take me up onto the limestone, on the footpath up Ingleborough, before turning at a high crossroads to follow the Pennine Bridleway around the slower slopes of Ingleborough's northern shoulder, Simon Fell. I'll cross the railway and the main road near Selside and rejoin the Ribble Way, eventually arriving at the road that runs from Ribblehead to Hawes. The first part of my route will afford loftier views than sticking to the Ribble Way and it will, I believe, also be drier underfoot. To begin the ascent requires that I cross the railway at the station. I'm already familiar with every inch of my planned route as far as the 'crossroads' but have previously always been descending towards Horton, rather than climbing the fell.

As I approach the station, a sign on the railings implores me to visit an exhibition in the southbound waiting room, called *Collections: Three Peaks Arts Trail*. It feels a little improbable that I'll find anybody in attendance on a Wednesday afternoon in October. So, imagine my delight upon finding artist Hester Cox, sitting behind a desk, surrounded by a colourful collection of artworks. She offers me a cup of tea and I take the opportunity to swap my socks for a dry spare pair. It's been only half a day, but it's already nice to have someone else to talk to. And Hester has an interesting story to tell.

Previously she'd been living on the other side of Dales, near Masham, but she and her partner moved to Horton, as houses were more affordable. Some of her friends suggested they had opted for isolation, but Horton, unlike Masham, is on a railway and Hester feels the move has been a win-win on the accessibility front.

Hester is a printmaker and leading light in the Three Peaks Art Trail, whose core rule is 'if you can see one of the three peaks from your studio or house and earn a living from art, you can join'. There are 26 artists, which seems like a pretty fair tally for a thinly populated area. Hester's exhibition is a joint one with Charlotte

Morrison, a ceramicist from Hester's old stomping ground at Masham. Many of Hester's works on display look, for all the world, like those Victorian glass cabinets filled with moths and butterflies mounted on pins. They are, however, a bit of a visual deceit. Each 'insect' is actually made of patterned paper and the origin of these patterns is interesting.

Hester tells me that the inspiration comes from century-old wallpapers uncovered at Spout House, an old thatched cruck house coaching inn, at Rosedale, on the North York Moors. These have been lovingly restored by the National Trust and fragments are now at Ryedale Folk Museum.

'My moths are based on the patterns, which are 100-year-old block printed papers,' Hester says, as our conversation somehow segues to large-scale artworks in Sweden, just as you might expect it would.

'I had a residency at Ålgården, near Borås, in southern Sweden, in 2012, and now I go every year for a couple of weeks to try new ideas and use equipment I don't have at home, or just to have uninterrupted time,' Hester says. She explains that her primary interest is in printmaking, and specifically collagraphy, which means printing from a stiff base, covered in different materials, to create a kind of collage. The resultant surface is then covered in the printing ink, which is then transferred to paper to complete the artwork.

Hester's exhibition has rather whet my appetite for her work – it's not going to be practical for me to take anything with me today, beyond a nice postcard, so a visit to her studio will have to be for another day. I am not aware at this stage that Hester will be popping up again later in this narrative.

* * *

The tea and clean socks have worked wonders, albeit the latter remain inside wet shoes, and it is with renewed vigour that I cross the tracks and begin my ascent onto the limestone plateau. I begin by traversing an undulating meadow, before a short clamber up the limestone crag that makes the spring line. Beyond this point, I had expected that the shallow layer of topsoil on the porous limestone would make for easy walking, but I'm wrong. In fact, what I am now traversing is a thin lake of mud, smeared across a base of well-polished rock, and I find myself wishing I'd troubled to bring at least one walking pole.

There's a bit of a natural landmark on this route, called Sulber Nick, which, when descending and seen from a distance on the horizon, bears an uncanny resemblance to an intimate part of the female anatomy. For some years I think all my Three Peaks crowd had noted this similarity but been embarrassed to share their private thoughts – until the day somebody mentioned it and everyone said 'Oh, I'm glad I'm not the only one who thinks that!' I idly wonder if Stone Age people may have flocked to Sulber Nick to indulge in fertility rites and ask myself why they never built a stone circle nearby.

I'm hoping that, beyond this point, where the ground levels out further, the going may become easier. It does not, and it's not long before I make an inelegant lateral slide and end up caked in mud. It's with relief that I finally reach the crossroads and, having made my right turn, I am on the excellent Pennine Bridleway. It sits on a dry shelf as it contours the mid flanks of Simon Fell and is a veritable motorway, compared with what has gone before.

Simon – now there's another name from my time working with the national park. Simon Rose joined the park authority to run its Three Peaks Project. This involved the restoration and consolidation of overused walking routes, specifically the

Pennine Way and the Three Peaks walk, the complication with the latter being that much of it was not, and still is not, on formal rights of way.

There've been many different techniques applied in the field of footpath restoration, as different bodies have striven to find an optimum repair method. One fix has been to erect rather unsightly boardwalks to cross the boggiest stretches while, at the other end of the spectrum, Hadrian's Wall Heritage (which accomplished so much in its short life before being abolished by the coalition government) – mindful of extensive archaeology beneath the surface – preferred the non-intrusive 'green sward' method, by which walkers use a wider, unmade route, which may be moved in response to overuse. The most extensively used method of 'permanent' repair these days, however, involves large quantities of imported rock, usually air-dropped by helicopter. This can be either in the form of aggregate, to be compacted on top of a membrane, or large paving slabs. The latter often come from the demolition of old mills in Yorkshire or Lancashire. They can look tidy and quite natural, even if the sandstone is at odds with a limestone environment. Hitching a ride in the chopper on one of these drops, back in my national park PR days, was one of the perks of the job.

When Simon first arrived at the national park, however, it was a still a time of experimentation. One particular such experiment was the use of what we dubbed 'magic powder', which – when mixed with soggy soil – had the property of setting like concrete. Or so the theory went. I have a distinct recollection of this experiment having taken place further up Ingleborough, on the first long steady descent towards Horton. However, other Three Peaks colleagues assure me that I am wrong about this detail and this prompts me to track down Simon again, now retired and living in Ilkley. This is what he tells me in an email:

The 'magic powder' was a product sold in the UK under the name SOLIDRY and was conventionally used in the civil engineering works as an additive to sub-soils to help improve their strength and load-bearing capacity. We only ran the one trial of it in February and March 1987, on the Pennine Way ascent of Pen-y-ghent, in the immediate vicinity of a sinkhole called Churn Milk Hole.

"Initially, it seemed that a really good and firm walking surface was easily created simply by removing any remaining turkeys [sic], and then Rotavating (using a powered cultivator) the SOLIDRY into the top 150mm, and then compacting it with a vibrating plate or roller.

However, the problems started as soon as severe frosts arrived. While the ground was actually frozen everything continued to look good. But the moment the thaw set in, the entire surface (and, in fact, the 150mm layer we'd treated) became an incredibly sticky, gooey mess which I always thought resembled walking through a molten Mars bar, but your memory of 'walking in moon-boots made of mud' is equally graphic. It was disgusting and wholly unsuited for any self-respecting footpath.

So we rectified it (or covered it up, both literally and metaphorically) using a more conventional method, by installing a geo-textile, and then covering that with 150mm of black (used solely for its colour) limestone, which was then compacted.

I went back to the site, some 30 years later (and for the first time since I left the national park) during June 2017, and was pleasantly amazed that the footpath was still in remarkably good condition, and appeared to have had or required very little maintenance. But best of all was that the vegetation (which had previously resembled a World War One battlefield) had almost fully recovered.

Walking the Line

I should reassure readers that not a single turkey or any other animal was ever harmed during the entire Three Peaks Project: in its infinite wisdom, Microsoft Outlook's spellchecker had preferred 'turkey' to Simon's intended 'turf or turves'.

But I digress… so, back to my contour walk along the Pennine Bridleway. The sky has cleared and Pen-y-ghent's craggy gritstone scarp rises from the now softly glinting limestone on the gently inclined fells opposite me, in sharp relief against a blue sky streaked with a long white-grey street of cumulus cloud. My foreground is open pasture punctuated by strips of off-white limestone. I love the way limestone changes colour with the light and humidity: it can be all shades, from shining white beneath a summer sun to jet black on sunless winter's day. The smallish brown cows enjoying its lush green grass are a native breed: they're part of the management plan for the Ingleborough National Nature Reserve.

Infused with enthusiasm for the new Settle–Carlisle Way 'rules' that I have come up with, I begin to toy with the idea of extending my time within the reserve, west of the road and the railway. Checking the map, I realise that I can veer off the bridleway shortly before Selside, to hit the Ribblehead road, to the north of the hamlet. It will then require just a short walk on Tarmac until I can ascend again onto the plateau. Thereafter, only the final few hundred metres of my day shall then demand that I plod a metalled surface.

I like this plan: my Three Peaks history has been defined by trying to find ways of mitigating the 'boring bit' between Pen-y-ghent – 'hill of the winds', in the old Brittonic tongue – and Ribblehead. However you address this, it's either too samey, too much on the road, or too long and hilly, should you elect to try what we did for a few years and miss Ribblehead altogether, to go instead via Gearstones, a mile or so to the north-east of the viaduct. This stretch of the Three Peaks walk is also home to the infamous Black Dub Moss. This bottomless pit of deep, soggy peat sits in a drumlin field and used to be directly traversed by the then 'official route' of the Three Peaks walk – it had been known, in wetter conditions, to swallow living beasts whole. I remember one year when we struggled to find a way across. One of our number, Angharad, took a long run-up, hurtling towards a seemingly feasible crossing, only to forget to actually jump. She sank, waist-deep and had to complete the walk, as I remember, barely half dressed.

A few minutes later, having milked our vocal chords of every last echo of laughter, we realised that Angharad's partner, Gordon, had vanished. We shouted for him and a distant, plaintive cry of 'help' found its way across the fetid waters and through the tangled reeds. We eventually located him, almost wholly immersed in peat, just his head and one arm extant. In this hand he was clutching my copy of Wainwright's *Walks in Limestone Country*, or was it *Swimming the Three Peaks with Wainwright*? I recall that even two washes in the launderette at Kirkby Lonsdale couldn't restore their clothes.

I think the route avoids Black Dub Moss these days and, indeed, the dreaded swamp may all have dried out somewhat, with successive dry winters and summers. But memory is a sound predictor of current behaviour and I shall today stay west of the railway.

It also occurs to me that it would be possible to add a bit more of a challenge to the walk from Settle, while still observing my new rules. You could, if you wished, continue all the way to the summit of Ingleborough and then make the steep descent to Chapel-le-Dale, where the Old Hill Inn has rooms and a campsite. In our earlier Three Peaks days it was the venue for our celebratory completion banquet, though this became more difficult, as ageing joints made completing the walk in comfortably less than

12 hours ever more challenging. The bar at the Old Hill Inn still has a large cartwheel hanging from its ceiling. When I look at it now I struggle to comprehend how my then girlfriend rose to a challenge issued by some off-duty soldiers to squeeze between two of its spokes. She ended up black and blue, but ten pounds better off.

Now, if you were to stay at the Old Hill Inn, you could, the following day, walk the spring line to Ribblehead Viaduct and rejoin the 'core route'; or you might, if suitably masochistic, even ascend Whernside and rejoin the Settle–Carlisle Way at the southern end of Blea Moor Tunnel. Either way, you'd be in sight of Ribblehead station and thus in compliance with my 'rules'. You could also pay homage to the lives lost in building the railway by visiting the eponymous church at Chapel-le-Dale. Here, a commemorative plaque erected by the Midland Railway recalls those who died building the line, some from injury, but rather more of smallpox and other illnesses that were at times endemic in the shanty towns that housed the navvies. Of all this – and J.M.W. Turner's time in the area – more later.

Another alternative route could see you ascend Ingleborough, but then take the ridge route all the way down, via Simon Fell and Park Fell, to Ribblehead. This is not, technically, a right of way, but is nonetheless well walked. Another day, perhaps.

* * *

Returning to the present, I feel buoyed by my decision to keep west and, having made the short climb up from the road, beyond Selside, I go through the scrubby woodland that tops a low limestone escarpment and through a gate that warns of both *Cows with Calves*, and *Bull in Field*. I see only the former, minus calves, and arrive at farm buildings, which turn out to be home to the team that manages the nature reserve. An ancient dry-stone wall, slumbering beneath a luscious green quilt of moss, poses for a picture as I begin the easy descent, passing a gnarled limestone pavement, where mountain ash and other hardy saplings seek to clamber out of the deep grykes between the limestone blocks, or clints. As I near the railway, old quarry ponds have been permitted to return to nature. I can imagine dragonfly and pond skaters, perhaps the odd reed bunting among the birch trees. But it is October and nature is winding down for winter. I turn to cross the railway in its deep cutting and join the road for the final stretch of today's journey.

Approaching Ribblehead, at Gauber bunk barn, the headwaters of the river open into a gently undulating plain. It is here, to the south of the junction with the former turnpike from Ingleton to Hawes, that the navvy camp of Batty Wife Hole was built. It had a population of more than 300 in 1871, but you need to look hard for any trace. The national park has carried out extensive archaeological surveys here and at Sebastopol, which was the more 'industrial' settlement, just to the north of the road. Earlier excavation work nearby, in the 1970s, revealed the floor plan of a large farmstead, of either Anglian or Viking origin, along with a number of small artefacts – raising the intriguing possibility that the Vikings may have ventured inland, via watercourses draining to the Irish Sea, earlier than their arrival in Yorkshire from the North Sea.

As ephemeral as all these remains were, the railway navvies themselves appear to have left few footprints on their departure for other projects elsewhere. There are plenty of records about the townships themselves, but personal details of individual navvies or their families are hard to find, as are any diaries or other accounts of the brutality of life in these shanties. I have a future appointment with Miles, the archaeologist, to find out more.

The Station Inn, at Ribblehead, is warm and welcoming. It's tended to be one of those up-and-down kind of pubs, at turns lovely and at others, a little scratty. It appears now to be in an 'up' phase and the current owners have spent real money on freshening the place up and installing a rather fine traditional range, which is ablaze and inviting.

I get chatting with Kacper, the barman, who arrived from Poland some years ago, aged eight. His parents live in Barnoldswick, in Lancashire, and run a care home in Settle. His sister, in Ilkley, works in a nursery. It is not Kacper, however, who commands the room, but Richard, a large, dishevelled man in shorts, with a big voice and many stories, mostly involving rugby and his own opinions on a range of subjects on which I'd probably prefer to differ. He dubs himself 'Head Monkey' and says he rarely works at any one pub for more than two years. I think I can understand why.

I eat well by the fireside and sleep the sleep of the dead, punctuated only by a coal train, idling on the track above the pub in the wee small hours. I don't resent the disturbance: it's good to know that, once again, this is a working railway with a true sense of purpose.

Chapter 2

The Line's Lofty Bit
and a Curious Tale of Slavery

From Ribblehead to Garsdale

Down there below tall trees
where shadows creep
and blackbirds call
beyond hallowed stones
the mossed green mound
secret and apart
is their mass grave
        From 'Chapel-le-Dale Churchyard',
        by Averil King-Wilkinson

The portents for the day are good: a gently warming early morning autumn sun is casting long shadows as I pop my belongings into the car boot ahead of breakfast. And it is a repast fit to fuel a long day's walk.

My breakfast companions are a mother and son up from London on a short adventure. They are discussing the ins and outs of their day's intended walking route, which involves walking to Chapel-le-Dale and then up onto Ingleborough summit. I hear them discussing the plan and I ask if they intend to walk down from the tops to Horton and catch the train the one stop back to Ribblehead. No: they're going to walk back, Mum says.

'That's a long walk,' I venture.

'What do you think, Chris?' she asks her son.

'Aha,' I say. 'Chris and the mum?'

'Chrysanthemum?! Very droll,' she sighs, inviting me to take a closer look at their map with her. I suggest they might cut a corner by following a similar route to my own of the day before, heading north around the eastern flank of Ingleborough. Then I study the map more closely and all falls into place: the recommended route is to backtrack from the summit of Ingleborough and then follow the fence line along the ridge all the way back to Ribblehead. This is the very high-level route that I mooted in the previous chapter but now, over breakfast, is the first time I am aware of it being actively promoted. This is, I guess, a consequence of the presumption of there now being a general right to roam on uncultivated higher ground in England. This is since the implementation of the Countryside and Rights of Way Act (2000), which brought England and Wales broadly into line with Nordic and other countries. Scotland followed suit in 2003.

Our generous packed lunches are delivered by the ever-ebullient Richard, who's been holding forth this morning about his 'pal', the folk singer and comedian Mike Harding, who was also the public face of the Ramblers' Association in the 1990s.

'We don't see quite eye to eye on politics,' booms Richard, adding something to the effect that this shouldn't come between them. This is an unsurprising revelation to me: I have long been aware of Mike's political persuasions and Richard wears his own contrasting ones like a badge. I am not hugely tempted to seek to convert this monologue into a conversation, but I'm curious as to Mike's current whereabouts, having pretty much lost touch with him since I left the Dales more than 20 years ago.

In those days, Mike lived in the little village of Gawthrop, which sits above Dent, on the steep road over into Barbondale. I recall the day he proudly showed me his recording studio, in a converted barn adjoining his traditional Dales home. This was no ordinary studio: it was right at the cutting edge for its time, being wholly driven by Apple Mac, in the days when Macs were becoming fashionable but had yet to evict the traditional PC from the creative sectors.

'So, is Mike still in the area?' I ask Richard.

'Oh yes, he lives at Langcliffe now and he plays with his band at the Royal, in Settle, on the fourth Thursday of the month and here on the fifth.'

'Here, at the Station Inn, on the FIFTH Thursday of the month? You mean maybe two or three times a year?'

'Well, it depends, but let's say it's an occasional gig.'

I make a mental note to attend one of these and catch up with the one-time maestro of Buxton Opera House. Just for the record, there were four fifth Thursdays in 2019 and five in 2020. Well, that's a sight more frequent than a Preston Guild, I reflect.

* * *

Wary of the unfortunate wet feet experience, I don the walking boots I'd deliberately left in the car at Ribblehead station ahead of yesterday's adventures, and slip round the back of the pub and out across the former industrial landscape that is Ribblehead. I would guess that, if you drew a three-kilometre circle round the Station Inn, it would enclose perhaps 100 folk. Yet Ribblehead station, since the restoration of its demolished second (north-bound) platform sees a similar number of passengers to those at the other stations that reopened to traffic back in the 1990s. This may, in part, be because it offers an alternative railhead for people heading south from places like Hawes, but it is, I suspect, mostly because it is a fine disembarkation point for walkers and for those looking to explore. And much is there indeed to explore.

Walking the Line

Suppose you were to choose to spend not just one but two nights at the Station Inn. Well, you might walk beneath Ribblehead Viaduct and five km or so along the spring line, before dropping down to Chapel-le-Dale. The dale used to be called Waesdale, which apparently derives from the Anglo-Saxon word for pasture. In the 18th century, the small chapel of rest I mentioned in the last chapter was built, close by Weathercote Cave. Entry to the cave is from private land and is discouraged today, for safety reasons, but back in Victorian or even earlier times, it was accessible to tourists via Weathercote House. It's a shame it's so inaccessible as its principal feature is a 25m cascading fall of water as it makes its way into a subterranean passageway. I originally found it almost by accident when exploring for another of those little village features for the *Yorkshire Post*.

Perhaps the cave's greatest claim to fame is having featured in sketches and watercolours by J.M.W. Turner, who visited at least twice. One such visit was in 1816, when the artist was sketching illustrations for *Whitaker's Richmondshire*. His journey is described in David Hill's 1984 book, *In Turner's Footsteps*, which is a collection of Turner's sketches and other works from across the North of England. According to the British Museum, Turner's Whitaker commission earned him 25 guineas for each water-colour, while the engravers who printed them received three times as much. It was a very wet July, and while he had been able to enter Weathercote Cave on a previous visit, on this occasion he found it half full of water. His sketch, now in the Tate's Turner Bequest, depicts what he saw, but – in the Romantic tradition – when he went on to complete the watercolour, he added a few flourishes, including a dramatic rainbow, and 'achieved some striking effects in the foliage by scratching with a blade, and scraping the wet paint with the blunt end of his brush'. The work is entitled, helpfully, *Weathercote Cave, near Ingleton,*

When Half-filled With Water And The Entrance Impassable.

It was a very wet and weary Turner who eventually arrived in Askrigg, having trudged the turnpike over the moors, to stay at the King's Arms, where he received 'the kindest attention from the landlord and his two amiable daughters'. Later in my journey I shall be reminded of Turner by another great sketcher, the late Alfred Wainwright, who also trudged 30 or more kilometres a day across the North in foul weather.

Getting on for a century and a half post-Turner, the neighbourhood received visitors in far greater numbers. There are few records to suggest that they counted sketching or watercolouring among their pastimes, but evidence of their extended presence can be found both inside and outside the little chapel. Inside, the commemorative plaque on the west wall, which I also mentioned earlier, reads: 'To the memory of those who through accidents lost their lives in constructing the railway works between Settle and Dent Head. This tablet was erected at the joint expense of their fellow workmen and the Midland Railway Company, 1869 to 1876.'

Outside, in the churchyard, the only clue to the fact that 100 or so victims of smallpox are buried in a mass grave beneath a grassy mound, is a second memorial plaque, this one installed by parishioners as recently as 2000. This was the nearest consecrated ground to the largest concentration of the hutted shanty towns, which housed the army of navvies who built the S&C early in the second half of the 19th century. There is immense interest these days in this aspect of Victorian industrial archaeology, in part perhaps because we know surprisingly little about it. The S&C is dubbed 'the last great navvy-built line', as greater mechanisation became increasingly more economic later in the century. Anything up to about 6,000 navvies worked on the S&C, excavating cuttings, digging tunnels and building embankments and viaducts, like the mighty 24-arch structure at Ribblehead. There is no formal record of just how many died during six years of construction, but – given that memorials up and down the line each commemorate a few score victims – it might easily have been between 300 and 500, or between five and eight per cent of the total workforce.

These men (and, in some cases, their families) came and lived in temporary homes of wood and felt bearing intriguing names, some drawn from Crimean battles and other exotica, perhaps with a sense of irony. A peak of more than 2,000 were engaged on building the viaduct and excavating the tunnel beneath Blea Moor – at 2.4km, the longest on the line. It was immensely dangerous work, handling dynamite, using heavy tools and working at height on wooden scaffolding. Terry Coleman, whose 1965 work, *The Railway Navvies*, remains perhaps the most authoritative work on the subject, says these veritable mules of men were a class apart from locally recruited labour. Drawn from other parts of Yorkshire and as far away as Ireland, they owed their origins to the earlier canal building era and gambled their safety on the altar of earning more money more quickly.

The passage of decades since Coleman's work seems to have permitted a degree of reassessment in some respects. Coleman did not state that all the navvies were Irish: far from it. But there has been a generalised lazy assumption, epitomised by the coupling of the words 'Irish' and 'navvy' in popular speech. Yes, men from Ireland did work on the line, but they were neither necessarily the most numerous group, nor the most riotously behaved. Further north, in Mallerstang, a local man, Ian Murray, did his own research and found that none of the navvies there was Welsh and only one was Irish. Many lodged with local families and brought their own families with them and attended church. Only a third of them lived in shanty towns at Ais Gill and Birkett. My own research of parish records from Dentdale has uncovered modest evidence of quite locally sourced labour at camps there.

The exhibition at Ribblehead station chronicles the construction of the S&C. It is a modest collection that nevertheless provides a perfect introduction to the railway, just the job for anyone in need of fast-tracking their knowledge about the line and its history. I especially enjoyed 'building my own viaduct arch' using wooden blocks and exploring the route on the interactive map. This is the same map as the one that I found to be out of order at the Museum of North Craven Life, in Settle.

* * *

Quite a few people have written quite a lot about the shanty towns near Ribblehead and elsewhere. Bill Mitchell, of *Dalesman* magazine fame, springs particularly to mind, as does the aforementioned Terry Coleman, for painting a picture of these driven men.

'What sort of men became navvies,' asks Coleman rhetorically, 'and where did they come from? First, they must never be confused with the rabble of steady, common labourers, who they out-worked, out-drank, out-rioted, and despised. A navvy was not a mere labourer, though a labourer might become a navvy. The first navvies came from the bankers, the fenmen of Lincolnshire who had built the sea walls, and from the gangs who had built roads and canals. Many came from Scotland and Ireland, and from the dales of Yorkshire and Lancashire. The Irish were not nearly so wild as their reputation.'

I have no criticism of Coleman's or indeed of any other accounts: they translate good solid research into a graphic picture of how life must have been in these edgiest of communities. But the one real thing that seems to be missing is the kind of personal diaries that would so illuminate the stories of bravado, lawlessness, illness and danger.

When I meet the national park's Miles Johnson, he confirms that the navvies – and indeed their entire settlements – appear effectively to have evaporated once the railway was finished. The park's work has focused on creating a better understanding of who did what, and where, at the sites of Sebastopol and Batty Wife Hole, in particular. This has acquired some urgency, given the prevalence of wild camping and casual car parking across the area.

The National Park study, carried out by Northern Archaeological Associates in 1995[3], suggests that the Ribblehead shanties differed form the norm inasmuch as they appear to have been the subject of a degree of planning and coordination, more akin to that found in the later period when municipal reservoirs were constructed. The authors suggest that this may have been down to either the remoteness of the location or to the relative benevolence of Midland Railway. The sites were planned, rather than having evolved through market forces, and included schools, hospitals and the railway company offices.

No sooner was the viaduct completed in 1875, however, than demolition began and the schools and mission house had gone by 1878, although some railway workers remained on site for a few years. All trace of the settlements had disappeared by the time of the 1909 Ordnance Survey.

A notable exception to the general rule about the invisibility of the navvies, is one George Gibbs, who moved north to work on the railway as a tunneller, having found work in the tin mines of Cornwall. When the mining industry there collapsed, many miners emigrated to the 'New World', but George, his wife and children moved north and, by the time of the 1871 census, were settled in a navvy settlement on the flanks of Garsdale. Thanks in part to the fact that George was literate, his twice great grandson, Ken Lister, was able to research and assemble a short biography of him in 2019. This was written up by Sarah Lister and is included in the Settle-Carlisle Railway Conservation Area archive.[4] She writes:

He was described as a 'railway miner' and was helping to build the Black Moss Tunnel, also known as the Rise Hill tunnel, along with 120 other miners. This was one of the most challenging tunnels to be built. Despite the generalised perception of navvies being loud drinkers and fighters, George and Jane were trying to bring up their first four children. As in most huts, the host family provided lodging and food to unmarried navvies to supplement their income. The family would have been at one end of the hut, boarders at the other, and the central area for eating and cooking.

The birth places of the labourers on this census return show that many navvies came from Lancashire, Yorkshire and Derbyshire but also some from further afield, like George. On this part of the railway, there were less Irish navvies than usual. Several men were recorded as 'NK' birthplace – 'not known' – and a noticeably high number gave false names and/or were untraceable before and afterwards. Some gave incredible names – one of George's lodgers called himself Francis Frattlefarty from Lichfield; one wonders about his personal hygiene? Unsurprisingly, he can't be traced any further.

A navvy village was not the dream location for child rearing. Typically navvies and tunnellers were paid daily or weekly, sometimes in tokens, which had to be spent at the village stores, and notoriously on ale. George and Jane's boarder, James Smith, was fined five shillings for being drunk at Black Moss.

Perhaps alcohol got the better of James as he may have died in 1875, although there is a disparity with his age.

Another drunken episode involved the attack on Ellen Bowers by a drunken Levi Abbott in 1874. Levi, another miner and his wife Susan, both from Somerset, had recently arrived after working on a tunnel at Lazonby, north of Penrith, with their seven children. Levi's victim was Ellen, wife of miner Alfred Bowers, who lived in Railway Hut number five. Alfred was another railway miner from Wiltshire and the 'old and decrepit' witch of an Irish woman, Ellen, was 53 years old, and provided for seven boarders. He had been 'drinking for a week or a fortnight'.

George passed away in November 1895, aged 62, just six months after his son, also a tunneller and also called George, died aged just 25. They both died of tuberculosis. George had been working as a miner or tunneller for at least 40 years.

(In an interesting aside, as my meeting with Miles draws to a close, he sends me from his office to the point at which the A684 enters Bainbridge from the east. In a field beside the road, as it descends into the village, there's a wooden shack bearing old advertising hoardings. This particular portable building, Miles says, is strongly reminiscent of those which must have 'vanished into the mist' once the railway building was complete. This particular example comes not from the S&C but from a shanty camp at Gouthwaite reservoir, constructed by Bradford Corporation, in remote Nidderdale, early in the 20th century. It comprises an odd patchwork of corrugated iron sheets, rotten wooden windows and improvised repairs. It looks like something from the set of *All Creatures Great And Small*, thanks to the advertising boards affixed to it, proclaiming the virtues of Hazell's Roost B&B and the Cornmill Tea & Coffee House.)

Of course literature, like nature, abhors a vacuum, and into this factual vacuum may step fiction, of which there's been something of a flurry in recent years. *Batty Green*, by Dennis Bickles, apparently tells the story of a restless young farmer's wife, who finds herself drawn to the 'raw energy' of Batty Green. I need hardly tell you that she ends up having an affair with a contractor at the camp. Together they help two young women to 'escape' the shanty to London.

Then there's Diane Allen's *For a Mother's Sins*, whose main character is a navvy's wife who takes over the 'Welcome Inn', at Ribblehead – a hostelry based on today's Station Inn. The author lives close by, at Long Preston.

The Railway Girls has a cover illustration reminiscent of romantic fiction for teenage girls. Leah Fleming's tale of the change that the railway wreaks upon the Dales is set in the fictional village of Scarsbeck.

This proliferation of the written fictional word was, however, trumped, in January 2016, when the first episode of ITV drama *Jericho*, aired. I was more than a little disappointed when this lavish production failed to make it to a second series: created by *Doctor Who* and *Sherlock* writer, Steve Thompson, and directed by *Cilla*'s Paul Whittington, it boasted a set that comprised an entire shanty town. It ought to have done better, but audiences dwindled by 700,000 from three million across its eight episodes. In mitigation, it was up against *Death in Paradise*, over on the Beeb, but maybe the solution might have lain in rescheduling.

The location for the drama was a fictional shanty on a fictional railway, but the inspiration was obvious and there were a few innovative touches, including an African-American foreman. I had no problem with this, as the notion that Black people are unrealistically invisible in accounts of Victorian Britain is a widespread one. Of something tangentially related to this, a little more later.

But the S&C was already providing fertile ground for fiction more than 60 years previously. Peter Pickles, a Carlisle solicitor and long-standing family friend of my own, drew my attention in the 1990s to a series of four novels by the Cumbrian author Graham Sutton, who died in 1959. In one of the series, *Fleming of Honister*, published in 1953, the eponymous hero becomes embroiled in a tale of murder, intrigue and retribution, set against the backdrop of the building of the railway. Peter wanted to interest me in reviving the novels, which were, by then, all out of print, but (leaving aside questions of copyright) I had no expertise in publishing fiction and so the idea went no further.

* * *

I've walked from Ribblehead Inn to the start of the ascent of Whernside more times than I've enjoyed a stotty cake sandwich. The track from the pub to the viaduct now forms part of the 'official' Three Peaks route. I'm unsure precisely how many times I have walked the Three Peaks: I first did it back in the early 1970s with a housemate and his pals, but reprised it and turned it into a habit a few years later with the gang of mates, then in Leeds, who remain today my only enduring group of friends from my younger life.

In the early days, much of the route was neither on rights of way, nor waymarked or maintained. It was the national park authority which, ultimately, saved the Three Peaks route from itself, formalising a route and rescuing the worst bits from peat bog by means of sometimes ugly boardwalks (now almost all replaced by millstone grit slabs). In the early days, the way up Whernside was both direct and destructive: straight up the middle of this great slug of a mountain. You'd haul yourself up shifting scree by means of what remained of a boundary fence and wall. Ultimately, this killer of a climb was 'closed' and the route diverted via the northern end of the 'slug'. This removed the gradient but added about three kilometres to the walk.

For some of the years that our gang completed the walk annually, we rang the changes by setting out from Gearstones, a couple of kilometres or so along the road from Ribblehead towards Hawes. This necessitated striking out across moorland directly towards the start of the new route up Whernside. The idea was to reduce the amount of road walking and I think it may have been a little more direct. However, we ultimately concluded that the first stretch just about constituted a fourth peak and we switched to generally starting out from Chapel-le-Dale, or thereabouts. The downside of this is that you then have to end the long day by conquering Whernside, undertaking the long drag from the foot of the slug to its highest point. Now, as I ease myself back into the Three Peaks concept post-hip operation, I am happy to skip the final insult that is Whernside and keep my total distance each year comfortably below 30km.

I feel the wisdom of such an approach was vindicated in 2019 when one of the gang took a tumble atop Whernside when too weary and ended up in A&E.

But I digress: today I am on the 'conventional' Three Peaks route as far as Blea Moor, where the path up Whernside branches to the left. This route coincides with that of the 'official' Settle–Carlisle Way. Thanks to the work of Miles's team at the national park, there's a certain amount of interpretation alongside the route these days, helping visitors not just to admire the viaduct itself, but also to better understand how it was built. The signage gives context to what you might always have suspected was something to do with the immense civil engineering task, most notably the enduring embankments of the old tramways and the associated engine shed, at the old Sebastopol camp.

At the northern end of the viaduct, the path ascends the blunt end of the embankment, which carries the railway towards Blea Moor Tunnel. I recall once walking this way with a chap called

Neville Caygill, after I had the idea of writing an article about the man responsible for running 'England's most remote signal box'. Neville lived in the old railway cottages, at the end of Dandry Mire viaduct, which crosses the A684 from Hawes to Sedbergh, close to the county boundary between North Yorkshire and Cumbria. Just as an aside, pre-1974, this was the boundary between the North and West Ridings of Yorkshire, which is why you should be unsurprised to find so much of Cumbria in the 'Yorkshire Dales' National Park. London based local government reorganisation plonked the rural northern arm of the West Riding partly into the county of Cumbria and partly – Craven and Harrogate – into the new North Yorkshire. In just the last few years, the most northerly Dales, once in Westmorland, have also been absorbed into the national park.

I struggle to recall too much of the conversation I had with Neville or even, if I'm honest, to picture his face. I don't think he was a man of too many words. But I do remember that Neville's commute to work necessitated driving the 15km or so to Ribblehead and then taking the same walk as I am taking today.

The Blea Moor box is more than just one end of signal 'block' on the railway – it is the point at which the single-track stretch of line across the viaduct begins. The line was reduced from double track over nearly two kilometres across the viaduct, and at either end of it, as part of the programme to convert the viaduct from a supposedly life-expired liability to a rejuvenated structure that could look forward to many years of happy life. Converting the double track to a single one down the centre of the trackbed ensured that the forces radiating outwards when a train crossed would impose less stress on the structure. One of the defects identified when local authorities opposing the line's closure carried out their own survey, was that the so-called spandrel walls – the actual viaduct structure beneath the parapets

– were being forced outwards. The repair work saw the sides of the viaduct strapped together, but the track singling means that the forces are transmitted further down the structure, to where it is strongest.

So, Blea Moor box controls passage across the viaduct, but it now also enables the new quarry trains from Helwith Bridge to 'turn around' before creeping back across the viaduct at the designated 20mph limit for heavy goods trains.

As I pass the box today, all is quiet on the tracks. The box itself is neat and tidy but there's a raggle-taggle collection of old vehicles and machinery around it. A few metres further on, the old detached house is in a sorry state. Apparently, this once belonged to a terrace of three railway workers' cottages, two of them long since demolished. The last I knew it was owned by a school somewhere and was in use as a bunkhouse. It looks to have fallen out of use and into disrepair. Sitting at one of the most significant historic locations on the line, once close to the site of the Jericho township, it surely deserves better. After all, it is slap bang in the linear conservation area that is the railway.

Blea Moor marks the end of the so-called Long Drag – the 26km of continuous ascent at a steady gradient of one in 100 all the way up Ribblesdale, from Settle. Here, locomotives would have been able to pause and take on water, but the water tower, which once stood immediately north of the signal box, was demolished a few decades ago. I stride on from where post-industrial tat interrupts open moorland, my sights set firmly upon the line of the old tramway, which ascends Blea Moor on a direct path, slightly to my right. To my left, the Whernside route crosses the line by an aqueduct, carrying Force Gill, a tributary of the River Doe, which flows down into Chapel-le-Dale, before, ultimately, joining the Greta and then the River Lune, on its journey to the Irish Sea.

Walking the Line

I recall when my girls were young, walking this way and enjoying picnics beside the pool beneath a part-hidden waterfall at the foot of Whernside. How very long ago such enchanted, lazy days seem now, as both 'girls' are in their 30s. I reflect how rewarding it was to raise them in the Dales, on the doorstep of so many little secret wonders like this. A very young Hannah, the elder of the two, appears on a photograph taken when Mike Harding snipped the ribbon on the Settle–Carlisle Way.

I extricate my wandering mind from its reflections and turn to the matter in hand, which is the direct ascent of Blea Moor by a course that precisely follows the line of the railway, deep below. Just as Ribblehead Viaduct is the longest of the 21 viaducts on the railway, so Blea Moor, is the longest of its 14 tunnels. The path today follows the tramway route, built during the railway's construction to connect the five vertical shafts created by the tunnellers, and to ship building stone down from a quarry near the summit. Large spoil heaps still punctuate the course of the tramway to the top of the hill.

At the start of the climb, a fenced-off compound warns of the danger of an open shaft within its bounds. This was one of two shafts required for construction that were no longer needed for ventilation once the tunnelling was complete (the other is at the Dentdale end of the tunnel). Both of these construction shafts were filled after the tunnel was finished, but there has been a partial collapse at this one. The other three shafts were lined and topped with brick chimneys, which still stand proud. The scant remains of the buildings, which housed the winding gear that hauled the spoil to the surface, can also still be seen. As I near the first such chimney, I turn to see a northbound passenger train pass Blea Moor signal box and enter the cutting, which leads to the tunnel's mouth. A few seconds later and the sound of the train echoes eerily up the chimney from the track, perhaps 45m below me.

From Ribblehead to Garsdale

The climb to Blea Moor summit is about 200m, steep but steady. On cresting the shoulder of the hill, a short summit plateau opens up before me. I am, once again, completely alone, as I turn to look back towards Ribblehead. I can see all of the Three Peaks summits – Whernside above me to my right, Ingleborough around my two o'clock, beyond the viaduct, and Pen-y-ghent to the left of the railway as it disappears down Ribblesdale. The magnificence of the panorama is such that I wonder why I have never taken the trouble to make the ascent before. The answer, of course, is that I have spent too much of my walking time endlessly ascending big brother Whernside instead. Indeed, Blea Moor is sometimes described as a subsidiary summit to Whernside, but this really does not do it justice, for it is a fine hill in its own right.

I pause awhile at the summit before taking the modest number of strides necessary to swap my Ribblehead panorama for Dent Head. Dentdale is so much greener and gentler than the often windswept wilderness I am leaving behind. Below me, the railway emerges from the tunnel and goes straight across the viaduct at Dent Head. Its route northward is then etched on the fellside, as it crosses the magnificent viaduct at Arten Gill, and finally disappears below ground again, into Rise Hill Tunnel. From here to Garsdale and on to Ais Gill Summit, the Midland engineers succeeded in creating a pretty much near-level railway and one whose views are among the finest on the whole route.

The near silent majesty of the landscape is interrupted by the arrival of an RAF Tucano trainer, which climbs out of Dentdale and hugs the shoulder of Whernside, to eventually disappear beyond the south-western end of Ingleborough. Once upon a time, low-flying military aircraft blighted the Dales and other remote areas of the UK. They were training for a type of conflict that – it turned out – was rarely, if ever, going to happen in 'real life'. The idea was to fly unseen by an enemy by remaining below radar sight lines. It was the core of RAF and USAF training philosophy for decades. To be honest, it was a daily blight on living in the Yorkshire Dales, particularly given that most of these contour-hugging flights were made by much louder and faster aircraft, such as Tornado jets. Or even by aircraft that were not primarily designed to fly low and fast, such as the American-built Phantom, which dated back to the 1950s and the Vietnam War. I remember a Phantom flying into the flank of Great Whernside in January 1986 after losing control at low-level. It was one of a flight of four aircraft. Both crew escaped with their lives after ejection at high speed.

As a hang glider pilot at that time, there were additional worries for me: when flying in the Dales, or indeed anywhere, we would issue what's known as a NOTAM, or Notice to Airmen [sic]. This was intended to alert military pilots to our presence in particular locations, often at low altitudes. It was not always effective: American pilots particularly either ignored or were unaware of these alerts – and often actually got totally lost. I recall once a flight of USAF jets flying straight through the middle of a group of hang gliders above Wether Fell, near Hawes. They were also a potential threat to commercial airliners as many near misses were recorded, particularly in uncontrolled airspace between Newcastle and Manchester – a situation eventually alleviated by the creation of a new controlled Airway.

Low flying practice only eventually diminished when it was found, in conflict, to be not such a great idea, after all. In his 2006 book, *Lions, Donkeys and Dinosaurs: Waste and Blundering in the Military*, the respected military author Lewis Page describes how more than ten per cent of RAF Tornados on low-level wartime attacks on Iraqi airfields during the second Gulf War were shot down – which was not what was supposed to happen. 'If relatively feeble Iraqi point defences alone could shoot down more than one in ten of the Tornados operating against them, one can only imagine what the bristling weaponry of the Soviet Central Front would have done, he writes. Military Top Brass quietly dropped the tactic, and this is one reason why there are now far fewer military aircraft shattering the much vaunted 'quiet, peaceful enjoyment', which the enabling legislation said should be what our national parks are all about.

* * *

The descent from Blea Moor is very much steeper than the ascent was and it takes me through felled woodland, which has yet to return to any semblance of 'regular' moorland landscape. The path picks its way between stunted tree stumps and I can't help but think about the warning of *Macbeth*'s witches, of the fate that may await him should Birnam Wood up sticks, as it were, and somehow move to Dunsinane Hill. I imagine the wizened residual stumps are all that Birnam Wood has left behind, bar a few incongruously ignored dead pines dotted here and there amid the devastation. On one, two ravens are perched, in ominous portent.

As the descent steepens, the way has been eased by the addition of vertical wood shuttering to create a rough staircase. However, each step retains a puddle of muddy water and I reflect how hazardous this must become in winter.

Eventually, the path levels off and takes me through pleasant woodland, before emerging to cross a collection of long overgrown spoil heaps, passing close to a pretty little waterfall, and arriving in the yard of Dent Head Farm. I note that Colin's original walk description says that the farm is no longer lived in, but today it looks both inhabited and well kept. A flock of inquisitive geese and poultry are soon about my feet and a sign on the gate reminds walkers that they'll do them no harm.

The farm is not merely secluded, but astonishingly well hidden and, by the time I reach the road at Bridge End, there is no evidence at all of its existence. My arrival here coincides with that of the parcels van at a little terrace of Dales cottages and I reflect how home delivery has eased life in places like this. I am joining the Dales Way for a kilometre or two here and I note that my entire route today also matches that of the LWDA's 'official' Settle–Carlisle Way. This stretch is a road walk, although it is possible to make small detours to the banks of the River Dee, where a few attractive picnic areas have been installed.

I pass the rather fine looking Deeside House, once a youth hostel, and note that is up for sale. Indeed, the current owner's stated intention is to sell it to a suitable buyer who will keep the Grade II hostel and holiday cottage complex in the manner to which it is accustomed.

At Stone House Farm, I turn right to follow the bridleway up the valley of Artengill Beck, which passes beneath Arten Gill Viaduct and climbs to around 1,500ft to meet the old drovers' road, known as Galloway Gate. 'Gate' here comes from the Norse word, meaning a road or street, suggesting that it may have had its origins back in the days when the Vikings held sway in the northern Dales, and across the Lake District. It may have been either an old trade route, from Galloway, or, perhaps, Galloway cattle were driven this way. Or maybe both. Then again, it might refer to the now extinct Galloway pony breed. The fell ponies you come across grazing on some Pennine moors today are the modern descendants of the Galloway, the small but powerful little horse that became the breed of choice in the lead mining industry of Swaledale in the 18th and 19th centuries.

Climbing up the gill, I pass the remains of the old 'Dent Marble' quarry. This rock is a dark, fossil-rich limestone, which has not undergone the full metamorphosis of extreme heat or compression that is required to make 'true' marble. It is not unlike so-called Frosterley Marble, found in Weardale, and both feature decoratively on the floors and fireplaces of buildings in their respective areas. Dent Marble, however, can never have dreamt that it would ever be employed in a structure quite as magnificent as Arten Gill Viaduct, the tallest of all those on the railway, or indeed in the only slightly less impressive Dent Head Viaduct.

A short climb later, I encounter other walkers for the first time today. They are reading a plaque, which explains a little about the marble and, indeed, limestone in general. For this rock not only created the landscape of the Yorkshire Dales but also helped shape the early industrial landscape. The earlier remains of the modest lime kilns that dot the hillside here seem no more than a distant cousin of the huge Hoffmann works I explored yesterday.

I gaze up at the immensity of the viaduct and reflect that the tallest spans of the structure begin somewhat below where I now stand. The wonder of these structures is surely surpassed in this country only by that of the early cathedrals, or perhaps at Stonehenge. I decide to climb a little higher before taking lunch, so that I can see any train that may cross. I select a smooth rock, warmed by the midday sun. I have a fat green caterpillar for company – so different from the big hairy red-brown ones I saw earlier, up on the heather moorland. The hairy ones are very possibly those of the fox moths, but I'm unsure what the green ones will become.

This is the first time I have walked this route in this direction and I'm aware that there's quite a dogleg to the point at which I reach Galloway Gate. In an ill-judged act of impatience, amplified by the satisfaction of a good lunch, I allow myself to be lured by a set of tracks across the fell from a gate on my left. They were probably made by a quad bike and may lead nowhere, but I persuade myself that they will cut the corner and take me directly to the drove road as it contours round Great Knoutberry Fell. You might think I should have learned from yesterday's off-piste experiences, but clearly I have not.

It turns out to be quite some distance across to the drove road, which also, it seems, remains perhaps 30m above me. I'm glad to get through the long grass and boggy meadow, but only to find the gradient getting steeper and steeper. Worse, a local wind is blowing up out of nowhere and is pressing me down onto the slope so that walking upright is impossible and I have to resort to a crawling scramble. When I eventually reach Galloway Gate, I find that a sturdy wire fence has been erected atop the collapsed dry stone wall, which formerly demarcated the old road. I judge that it is not safely climbable. Eventually, I find a spot at which a little gill flows beneath the fence: there is just enough room, if I lie on my back, to wriggle under the wire. (Note, here, previous references to the Country Code and what one should or should not do.) I judge that I have gained no time whatsoever.

The earliest industrial visitations along the drove road exploited shallow seams of poor coal and there are more old lime kilns dotted along the way than you might shake a stick at. It is a magnificent walk: it begins by offering a commanding view down Dentdale, but as you round Great Knoutberry, a more distant vista unfolds until, ultimately, you can see the 'jaws' of Mallerstang, in the Upper Eden Valley, inviting the railway onward on its inevitable course through the Pennines.

Dent station, when it comes into view, is quite far below, to my left, but I am excused a formal visit under the 'rules' of the walk, described earlier. Suffice to say that, at 350m above sea level, it has earned the sobriquet of 'England's highest main line station'. The station was one of the locations that was 'asset-stripped' during the long years of the battle against the railway's planned closure and the station building itself became a quality bed and breakfast under the stewardship of Robin Hughes. The station was nicely restored, though not nicely enough to enable him to win Channel Four's *Four in a Bed*, in which other competitors found him overpriced. But then they would do, wouldn't they?

Later I learn that Robin is selling up and the Friends of the S&C are poised to buy it. It will become a self-catering holiday let, and where better could you ever choose to stay?

Robin also converted the nearby former snow huts, which once offered refuge to track workers struggling to keep the line open in the depths of winter. We once visited friends who'd rented one of these for a week, and they really are something special, with huge squashy sofas and views to die for. I remember glancing out of the kitchen window to see two peregrines hovering in the updraft just feet away. Today's bird of the day is the skylark, which might well make lunch for a peregrine.

* * *

Dentdale and the Upper Eden, to the north, were the remotest dales to be affected by the coming of the railway in the 19th century and the line's impact would have been felt the moment the first navvy cut the first sod. In 2016, the Rev. Peter Bowles, vicar at Cowgill, just below Dent station, conducted a ceremony to commemorate the 72 lives lost in Dentdale during the railway's construction, with the erection of an attractively carved commemorative stone at Cowgill Church. This followed his discovery of a similar number of unmarked graves in the churchyard. My subsequent research at the Dales Countryside Museum, in Hawes, suggests there may have been quite significant navvy settlements in the upper dale, near Cowgill and Kirkthwaite. Census data from 1871 reveals a series of settlements: Leayet Huts, Stone House

Huts, Pavilion Huts and the highly imaginatively named Railway Hut. And those who lived and died there came from as far afield as London, Berwick, Portland and Stratford. Or, closer to home, from Wennington (on the way to Lancaster) and Dewsbury. Their trades included marble mason, police officer and engine driver.

After the railway eventually opened for business, change became more profound. The S&C was built as a high-speed railway, capable of whisking passengers northward from Leeds to the Scottish border at 100mph. With its gentle gradients and curves it was a far better line in a technical sense than the LNWR's route over Shap Fell, to the west. But its original parliamentary approval drew upon earlier plans for local railways through the Dales, which it superseded. So there were always going to be local stations on the line, even if – like Dent, in particular – they might end up some distance from (or above) the settlements they served. And those local stations would prove transformative to the local economy and way of life.

Even today, Dentdale still feels rather a world apart from the much busier Dales east of the watershed, so it's not difficult to imagine just how isolated it must have felt a couple of hundred years ago. Isolated enough, perhaps, for practice to lag behind what might be expected in better-connected parts of the country. When the railway opened to goods traffic in 1875, and to passengers a year later, its arrival must have felt like a revolution: not only could people travel from these hitherto remote areas to big cities, but so too could goods. In the case of the S&C, 'goods' meant quarried stone and, perhaps more significantly in terms of how lives were affected, farm produce. Suddenly, fresh milk could leave the Dales and be in Leeds or Bradford for next day's breakfast. And animals for slaughter could equally arrive 'fresh' for the urban populace.

In his 1973 book, *Rails in the Fells*, the author, David Jenkinson, comments: 'It is probably not too fanciful to assert that many present-day farmers in the North West Pennines may have had no farm to operate had not the Settle–Carlisle provided the essential communication facilities for their fathers and grandfathers.' He backs up this assertion with evidence that the great majority of all livestock travelled to market by train and that the number of head of cattle carried grew by 65% during the line's heyday.

Such change could not pass by without also affecting society at large and, as I gaze down Dentdale from on high, I find myself reminded of a story I once read, citing the isolated valley as the possible inspiration for Emily Brontë's *Wuthering Heights*, and the occupant of a nearby farm, as the model for the wayward Heathcliff. More than that, I recall that the local historian Kim Lyon, who came up with the idea, also suggested that there may have been a rather unsavoury link with the transatlantic slave trade, a trade that had, theoretically, been abolished in this country more than a decade before *Wuthering Heights* was published.

Kim, a former occupant of Whernside Manor, which used to be the Yorkshire Dales National Park's caving centre, wrote about the history of the Sill family, who built the manor, originally known as West House, in a 1979 *Dalesman* article. Although privately persuaded that characters in the Sill family might well have inspired Emily Brontë, the article did not mention this, focusing rather on the Sills' links with the transatlantic slave trade. Records included an advertisement in a Liverpool newspaper, placed by Edmund Sill, of Dent, offering a reward for the return of an escaped enslaved person. Subsequent meetings with Brontë scholars, including Christopher Heywood, of Sheffield University, gave credence to her theory that Heathcliff had indeed been modelled on one Richard Sutton, a 'foundling', installed by Edmund Sill in High Rigg End, a kilometre from West House.

It's an intriguing story, and one that could fill a book on its own – and indeed it pretty much subsequently has. To be fair, other scholars point out that there are other potential inspirations for Emily's Heathcliff, but what is curious is the vehemence with which Kim Lyon's conclusions seem to be dismissed by those who disagree with her ideas – ideas endorsed by several learned scholars, it should be remembered.

Some of the events that took place in the Sill household were far from savoury and, when Kim did her research, there were actually Dent residents old enough to recount tales of the Sills based upon family lore. Some commentators today suggest that the Sills were Dentdale's guilty secret – one tale has it that the people enslaved by the family were slaughtered and their bodies dumped in the Dee, another that they were chained to the walls of the cellar at West House. Others suggest that links between the Sills and Adam Sedgwick, the 'father of modern geology' and the dale's most famous son, may have been an incentive to keep the truth about slavery quiet. Sedgwick, whose progressive views on geology got him into trouble with the Church, was somewhat less progressive with regard to female emancipation but, as a Whig, he was passionately in favour of the abolition of slavery. Paradoxically, however, as co-trustee of the will of Margaret Sill, in 1835, he received a significant sum of money, being half the government compensation for enslaved people freed on the Sill estate in Jamaica. Remember that we, the populace, only recently finishing paying off the bonds issued by the government to compensate the enslavers for their ill-gotten gains.

A new edition of *Wuthering Heights*, with commentary by Christopher Heywood, was published in 2001 and in it Heywood asserts: 'Kim Lyon identified beyond reasonable doubt the historical figures who provided the Dales story material in the first part of *WH*.' He continues: 'By identifying the extensive links between the Sills of Dent, their Caribbean estates, and the practice of plantation slavery in Yorkshire, Kim Lyon pioneered the insights which were found later, through independent reading of the text, by Andrea Dworkin and Maja-Lisa von Sneidern.' He goes on to hint that Kim was effectively 'got at' and persuaded not to include the Brontë link in her *Dalesman* article.

Heywood's edition also features a Black Heathcliff as its cover picture and, indeed, a 2011 film adaption of *Wuthering Heights* starred the Black actor, James Howson, as Heathcliff.

Looking at the debate and the Sedgwick story reminds me of my other link with the people of Dent when I lived in the Dales. Photographers John and Eliza Forder got in touch with me to ask if I might help them to promote their book *Open Fell, Hidden Dale*, a beautiful work of evocative black and white landscapes, portraits and subterranean views. They lived in Sedgwick Cottage, on Dent's main cobbled street, right next to the granite block that commemorates the geologist. Eliza had fled north to Dent with two young children to escape a bad marriage; John worked as a caving instructor at Whernside Manor, with Ben Lyon, husband of the aforementioned Kim.

After some digging I manage to track Eliza down, and she has quite a bit to say about Kim Lyon, now deceased, but whom she knew well at the time of the Sill debate. She believes there is potentially much truth in the notion that the local gene pool bears witness to the enslaved Black people brought to Dentdale by the Sills, and recalls Kim Lyon appealing to people to seek out any photographs they could find from the turn of the 20th century. 'You could very clearly see dark faces,' she tells me.

And this suggestion is backed up by Heather Boyles, who grew up in Dent and now works in Appleby. Writing in Bangor University students' union newspaper, in 2012, she commented: 'Dentdale still retains many secrets. Some of the older residents recall their grandparents remembering the slaves "wandering into Dent" after the Emancipation in 1833.'[5]

Even 150 years or so on, perhaps not everyone in Dentdale is comfortable with this suggestion. An old journalistic colleague, Roger Ratcliffe, writing about the 2011 *Wuthering Heights* film for the *Yorkshire Post*, recounts this tale: 'A woman who ran the Dentdale Heritage Centre was really unhelpful to the point of rudeness when I asked about the Sills. The reason, I later heard, was that people in Dentdale and the Sedbergh area, even to this day, don't like to acknowledge the Black slaves story because some of them are of mixed race and would rather the subject was dropped.'

However, the question of Black genes in Dentdale is interwoven with the seemingly equally controversial one of the provenance of Brontë heroes and locations. When I contact the Sedbergh and District Historic Society about the subject, I receive a reply from one Diane Elphick, who wrote to me in forthright terms: 'There is very little evidence to back up many of the stories promoted in the 1980s.'

I now realise it is the same Diane Elphick who is a leading proponent of alternative theories regarding Heathcliff's provenance. Well, Jan Bridget, whose four times great grandfather was the aforementioned Richard Sutton, has written a biography of Will Sutton, his grandson, who was a pioneer on Vancouver Island.[6] In it she carefully evaluates three possible models for Heathcliff, including her own ancestor and those more favoured by such as Diane Elphick. She suggests that some of Kim Lyon's dates appear a bit awry, having been researched by Diane Elphick, but concludes: 'Which of these three is the true model for Heathcliff: Richard Sutton? Hugh Brontë? Or Jack Sharp? Or is it a combination of all three or none? Reader, make your own decision.' Hugh Brunty, later Brontë, was Emily's grandfather in County Down before his son, Patrick, moved to Yorkshire. I recall the Heathcliff parallels from my own visit to the Brontë Homeland Centre, near Newry, more than 20 years ago. There are similar parallels to be found in Jack Sharp, the villainous one-time resident of Walterclough Hall, near Halifax.

So, if all three may be possible and, given that we cannot climb inside Emily's mind, I am left wondering, 'Why be so dogmatic?' Sometimes it appears that the less proven something is, the more passionate about it people become. And yet paradoxically, 'serious historians' can seem sniffy, to say the least, about oral history, passed down through the generations – even though, without oral history beneath it, there can be no written history. This kind of dogma sometimes seems to me like a disease that afflicts the 'uncertain sciences' of history, economics… even archaeology. Academics espouse their own pet beliefs and feel vulnerable if those beliefs are challenged. On the other hand, $E=mc^2$; the area of a circle IS πr^2; and water DOES (normally) freeze at $0°$ C.

I return to the subject in July 2020, with the aim of allowing Kim Lyon's widower, Ben, a final say on things. 'Academics have their own particular bees in their bonnets that they try to justify,' he chuckles. Given that the Brontës went to school just down the road at Catherton and were friends with the vicar of Dent, it would be more surprising if they had *not* drawn inspiration from their surroundings and the people they met, he says.

'I think Kim was right in the stuff she came up with, but there are hidden strands underneath.' The police murder of George Floyd and the subsequent focus on the Black Lives Matter movement have both happened since I first looked at slavery in Dentdale, and Ben comments: 'These days we are talking much more easily about slavery and everything to do with it. It was clearly something that shaped things in Dent: when we came to Dent there were historical people who pooh-poohed the idea of it all, even though it is plainly evidenced by the plaque in Dent church.' The plaque he refers to commemorates John Sill 'of Providence in the island of Jamaica'. Upon the death of Ann Sill, a further inscription was added, stating that she had been the last surviving member of the dynasty.

But Ben is a little wary of the idea that people in the old photographs appeared to be of mixed race. 'I used to laugh because I couldn't see it: they were black and white photographs!' He goes on to tell me how some have sought to jump on the bandwagon. One such was an artist who produced a supposedly contemporary picture of a slave market in Dent. But the street scene included a bay window on Ben and Kim's own house, which they knew to have been added quite recently. 'It was a total fraud!' he says. 'But there is no doubt that they did have Black slaves at West House.'

And further word on the same West House, later Whernside Manor. Shortly after local government reorganisation in 1974, the newly formed Yorkshire Dales National Park Committee resolved to take the caving centre over, only to find its 'parent', North Yorkshire County Council, vehemently opposed. It became an early test of conflicting powers and responsibilities of the supposedly autonomous national parks and local authorities, with the county council obliged, very much against its will, to execute the decision of the national park committee. However, in the the 1980s, it was clear to me that the national park did not want to own what could and should have been the country's premier centre to celebrate the underground limestone landscape, and it did ultimately get its way, when Whernside Manor was sold as a private home.

* * *

With Dent station receding from view, the drovers' route joins the metalled road, which descends to my left into the upper dale via the station. But I continue straight on along Galloway Gate, at this point more commonly known as the Coal Road, after the old scattered drifts and bell pits. Curiously, it was the arrival of the railway that effectively put paid to coal mining here in the latter half of the 19th century. Prior to that, people had dug coal for their own domestic use and for the relatively modest lime kilns, but now the railway was able to bring in high quality deep-mined coal, leaving the old workings to be gradually absorbed back into the landscape.

I've driven the Coal Road a few times, and in all kinds of weather: this is one of the highest roads in the North of England and it's a veritable switchback. In cloud, it commands your fullest attention as you're never quite sure which way it will turn after each shrouded crest. It can seem to go on forever, when you're driving blind like this. But today, it's hard to imagine such conditions, as the sky is clear October blue. As if to emphasise the point about the weather, I hear the drone of another, or perhaps the same Tucano, before I see it as it swoops up from Dentdale, behind me, and swings right down Wensleydale. I discover later that these two Tucano sightings are very nearly the aeroplane's swan song, as the type will be retired, and its base at Linton-on-Ouse closed, in a little over a week's time.

I'm not keen on road walking, but I feel I have made short work of the Coal Road today: far easier than driving the route in cloud. I rescue a few more crossing caterpillars from the occasional passing car or motorbike as the moorland gives way to a forestry plantation on my right, with Garsdale station now no distance ahead of me. I arrive on the platform, with 40 minutes or more to spare before the earlier of the two return trains I can catch.

I remember early morning drives from my home at Hawes to Garsdale to catch the train for a day's work in Leeds. I'd usually park near the back side of the southbound platform, where the Hawes branch used to join, leaving me with a bit of walk from the northbound, when returning in the evening. These days there's a generous overflow car park by the bridge, equidistant from both characteristically well tended platforms. There's plenty of colour left in the flowerbeds and Ruswarp's statue looks proud and smart.

Ruswarp first came to modest fame as the only one – among 32,000 who objected to the closure of the S&C in 1983 and 1984 – who was not human. He was a border collie, belonging to a prominent anti-closure campaigner, Graham Nuttall, from Colne, in Lancashire, who was the first secretary of the Friends of the Settle–Carlisle Line Association. Ruswarp was named after a station on the line to Whitby and his objection was deemed valid because his paw print was appended and he was, in those days, required to pay a fare, just like a human passenger.

Early in 1990, not long after the line was reprieved, Graham and Ruswarp went walking in Wales and failed to return. Eleven weeks later, an emaciated Ruswarp, aged 14, was found by a lone walker beside the remains of his master, on the bank of a remote upland river. He was too weak even to walk, but Ruswarp recovered and survived long enough to witness his master's funeral – and to receive a variety of different bravery awards from animal and canine charities.

Eight years later and thoughts turned towards making Ruswarp a symbol of the whole fight to save the line. Mark Rand, of the water tower in Settle, recalled to me that there was some reticence among the Friends of the line about funding the project, as to do so might have been unconstitutional. There were also colourful stories about Graham's personal life, which had nothing whatever to do with the price of fish, as it were.

Seeing these as irrelevant footnotes to many years grafting to save the line Graham loved, Mark launched a private appeal by the Friends to raise funds for a bronze statue to Ruswarp. Animal sculptress Joel Walker was commissioned and the life-size likeness was unveiled in 2009 by two key figures in the closure battle. Olive Clarke chaired the North West Transport Users Consultative Committee, which, with its North East counterpart, conducted the public hearings that ultimately recommended the line remain open. Ron Cotton was British Rail's Project Manager who, having been appointed to close the railway, ended up saving it instead.

A plaque tells the story of Ruswarp, concluding: 'Ruswarp's eyes look towards the hills and to a bench on the far platform, dedicated to Graham Nuttall. Garsdale was their favourite place.'

My day bookended by commemorative plaques, I go to sit in the waiting room – it's beautifully clean and stocked with leaflets and other sources of information, not least a complete collection of all volumes of the *Encyclopaedia Britannica*. They fill two windowsills – it would take a very long train delay indeed to tackle that lot. Another lone walker shares the room and I ought to engage with him, but I'm lost in my own reflections on having completed another stage of my journey – and looking forward to getting home to a hot bath in a couple of hours' time.

Chapter 3

Of Castles, Kings, Ladies
and a Vampire in Darkest Peru

From Garsdale to Kirkby Stephen

God save King Pendragon
May his reign long drag on,
God save the King.
Send him most glorious,
Great and uproarious
Horrible and hoarious,
God save our King.

From *The Sword in the Stone*, by T. H. White

It is a day for reunion and reminiscence. I've driven down to
the Moorcock Inn with my wife, Linda, for a book launch. The
Moorcock is my suggested staging point for the journey to Carlisle
and it's a 15-minute walk from Garsdale station. It would, I guess,
be rather less if you were bold or naughty enough to trespass on
the old branch line to Hawes and cut across the field.

In the 116km of track between Settle and Carlisle, the railway is crossed twice by the old North Eastern Railway's lines:
at Smardale and at Appleby. At the latter there was an awkward
connection between the two networks, which required complex
shunting to get from one to the other. This tricky link remained
in use by freight traffic to and from Warcop military ranges until
as recently as 1989. There were even two stations at Appleby,

almost next to each other, as parliament lived in terror of any cooperation between different companies, lest 'free competition' be compromised.

There were no such issues here at Garsdale: the branch to Hawes was constructed by the Midland Railway as one of the requirements of the Act of Parliament that enabled the S&C to be built in the first place. So the eight kilometres of track in Upper Wensleydale was something of an S&C in miniature. It was a single-track line but featured both a tunnel and two viaducts in its short length. At Hawes, it connected end-to-end with the North Eastern Railway, which already came up the dale from Northallerton, on the main East Coast line. Once upon a time you could catch a train from Hawes to places like Bradford.

So, the Moorcock Inn seemed to Paul Salveson a strategically good place to launch his new book about the S&C, those who built it, and those who worked on it over the years. It is called, imaginatively, *The Settle-Carlisle Railway*... but why not? It does what is says on the tin, as they say. In my mind I'm convinced I first met Paul, the socialist campaigner and writer, sometime during the long, hard battle to save the S&C. He thinks that may be the case and suggests the meeting perhaps took place on the platform at Garsdale. What is without doubt is that we did work together rather more recently. In 2017, Linda and I delivered a project in the Shropshire Hills and, as part of this, I was in close contact with Arriva Trains Wales, which at that time held the franchise to operate trains from Manchester and Shrewsbury to Hereford and Cardiff – and on the Heart of Wales line, from Craven Arms to Swansea. Paul ran the Community Rail Partnership for this lovely line, helping to promote its leisure use, including a newly devised walking trail from Craven Arms to Llanelli. He's a visiting professor at the universities of both Bolton and Huddersfield.

At that time Paul owned a house in Knighton, just over the Shropshire border, in Wales. However, as I was driving home from Shropshire, we agreed to meet at the rather soulless Buckshaw Parkway station, near Preston, and then chat about life and railways over a cuppa at the pretty little village of Croston, nearby. It's good to see him again today in a rather different context.

With no prior inkling as to who will be at today's little event, it is also both surprising and pleasing to see Colin Speakman, oft mentioned already in this book, and Roger Ratcliffe, likewise name-checked in the Dentdale Brontë anecdote. I have immense admiration for Colin, who can demonstrate a lifetime dedicated to the simple principles of public transport access to the countryside and of defending the rights of ramblers. At 78, he's looking great and is just as active as ever. It's an informal little gathering, which Paul opens by telling how a publisher got in touch with him to ask if there was 'anything new' that he might be able to write about the S&C.

'My own experience and quite a lot of very interesting social testimony,' was his response. That personal touch comes from having trained in Blackburn as a railwayman and worked on the line for some years back in the 1970s.

It turns out that quite a few of those gathered are former 'Midland' colleagues of his on the S&C, but it is a woman of perhaps a little over 70, towards the back of the room, who catches my eye. She begins by asking if I used to live in Hawes and, upon my response, says her daughter Andrea taught my daughter, Izzy, at Hawes School. And then the penny drops: she is Sylvia Caygill, widow of Neville Caygill, guardian of the remote signal box at Blea Moor. A small world indeed.

It turns out that generations of Sylvia's family have S&C blood flowing through their veins. 'My great grandfather, George Fawcett, helped build the line – he had a bit of a smallholding in Dent.

From Garsdale to Kirkby Stephen

'My grandfather was a signalman to start with and then became a stationmaster – at Dent, Garsdale and Settle. My mother, Daisy, was a little girl at Dent station and my father, Ted Ashton, worked at Ais Gill and Garsdale as a signalman. My father's father, Arthur Ashton, was a shepherd and first on the scene at the Ais Gill crash. And my brother, another Arthur Ashton, worked on it all his life... He's 92 now.

'It was my grandfather and a signalman called Jack Banks who relieved the signalman who caused the crash at Ais Gill,' she continues.

Ais Gill Summit is the highest point on the S&C and is just a short distance north of Garsdale. As Sylvia recalls, it was the site of the worst ever accident on the railway, although the one to which I'm sure she is referring was the second worst and occurred a bit to the south of the summit.

Notwithstanding the brief but horrendous reign of Railtrack, railway accidents through history have been, by and large, infrequent; and yet, as Paul's book describes, the few kilometres of track between Garsdale Station and Ais Gill Summit saw two terrible accidents within three years – and another fatal crash just a few years ago. Statistically, then, it is by quite some distance the most hazardous part of the entire line.

Paul tells the stories of all three crashes in his book, describing how Hawes Junction back then was more than just the joining of two lines: it was also the place where 'assisting engines' – extra locomotives that helped haul trains up the 1:100 slopes to south and north – would be decoupled and turned on the turntable. As an aside, the redundant turntable was controversially removed in 1988 after having been bought by the Keighley and Worth Valley Railway. But back to the story: on Christmas Eve 1910, Alfred Sutton, the signalman at Garsdale, had no fewer than five locos on his hands at the station, as well as a fast-approaching express for Glasgow and Edinburgh, when he inadvertently allowed two slow-moving assisting locomotives into the path of the express. The resultant collision was exacerbated by the gas from the lighting system on the express, which exploded when it came into contact with hot coals.

Sylvia was correct in saying that the signalman caused the accident and the subsequent inquiry said as much – but signalling systems then simply did not have the same number of failsafes that they have nowadays. In truth, like almost all accidents, the tragedy occurred because of the coming-together of a variety of different factors, some human and some systemic.

The September 1913 crash was similarly the consequence of the coincidence of several different events but, to cut a long story short, the leading train ran out of puff and ground to a halt just short of the summit at Ais Gill, and the following train ran through a signal at 'danger' and crashed into the back of it, killing 16 people.

The most recent accident, in 1995, was also the most recent fatal incident on the line, and Paul Salveson was travelling on the S&C the day it happened. He'd planned to travel to Garsdale and catch a bus to Hawes but, at Horton, the non-stop torrential rain had already partially flooded the track, so he cut his losses and took the next train south, anticipating that all services would soon be cancelled for safety reasons. They were not, and with tragic results. A southbound train was forced to return north from Ribblehead because of flooding, but in the short intervening time, a landslide had occurred at Ais Gill. The train was derailed and ended up across the other track, where it was hit by a southbound train. The conductor was killed and several passengers injured.

* * *

From Garsdale to Kirkby Stephen

On the walls of the Moorcock Inn are photographs of a newspaper report of a fatal fire at the pub in the 1970s, in which the landlord and landlady both perished. The circumstances surrounding the fire were mysterious, inasmuch as Ronald and Muriel Bucknell had just thrown a retirement party on what would have been their last night at the pub, as police had blocked the renewal of their licence. I believe the place had enjoyed a bit of a reputation for underage and out-of-hours drinking.

The cause of the blaze could not be established and there was a hint, but no proof, of arson. The place was already well ablaze and starting to collapse when the alarm was sounded and the part-time fire crew from Hawes was first on the scene.

Now, more than 40 years later, we take a short drive into Hawes to meet old friends. Curiously, our friend Andrew recalls how his father, a member of the part-time fire team at Hawes, helped to tackle the raging blaze. 'What my dad always said was that the family of the licensee were among those watching the pub burn down and they were desperate for the firemen to find a box, which must have contained their most precious possessions. I don't think they ever found out what was in that box.'

The inn was back in business a couple of years later, but it was in 2006, when new licensees took over, that the spirits of the late Ronald and Muriel seemingly made their presence felt, as bar furniture apparently began to move around at night. A few days later, according to *The Northern Echo*, a fire extinguisher salesman arrived at the pub and, as he walked across the bar, a framed newspaper clipping about the fire fell off the wall.

With a degree of understatement, Simon, the new licensee, said: 'We were both freaked out about that. Afterwards we had quiet words with the ghosts. I told them if they were there, I didn't mind as long as they didn't cause any trouble. We've not had any problems since.'

Walking the Line

That newspaper cutting remains in place today, and it never fell during our own stay. Let's hope Ronald and Muriel remain at peace, with or without that box of valuables.

After it was rebuilt, the Moorcock Inn remained for some years the venue of the Moorcock Show, one of the oldest sheep shows in the Dales. But, one day in 1986, I found Hawes rife with the gossip that none other than Prince Charles would be opening that September's show. I found the story pretty hard to believe, but, with the assurance of my local contacts, I was able to stand the story up for *The Northern Echo*.

Over the following few weeks, the Moorcock Show, once the preserve of dedicated sheep breeders, morphed into a quite different beast. It moved down Wensleydale a couple of kilometres to a larger site, at Mossdale, and acquired all the other attributes of much bigger shows, like Muker, Reeth, or the Wensleydale itself (held near Leyburn).

When the big day finally came, the heir to the throne was able to sample the dressed sticks, admire all the vegetables and witness all the sports. There remains an annual clue in the Moorcock Show programme each year as to how the HRH came to visit a hitherto little known and somewhat specialist event. It's the van Cutsem Cup, awarded for a prize sheep in memory of the late Hugh van Cutsem, a close friend of Charles's. The van Cutsem family owns a large (and not especially attractive) shooting lodge above the A684 and close to the old Hawes branch railway and Charles has been, over the years, a not infrequent visitor, enjoying shooting on the van Cutsem estate.

Followers of things royal will recognise the van Cutsem name. Hugh and his wife, Emilie, were neighbours of the Queen's at Sandringham, and Hugh's son Edward was Charles's godson, and a pageboy at his wedding to Diana. Prince William is god-father to Edward's daughter, Grace, and little Florence van

Cutsem was a bridesmaid at the wedding of Meghan and Harry, her godfather. My recollection is that Charles arrived in 1988 aboard the Royal Train and stayed on board in the sidings at Garsdale station, though I have struggled to substantiate this and may indeed be quite wrong.

David Stewart, a friend of mine who lives on the high fells above Kirkby Stephen, is a member of Kirkby Stephen Mountain Rescue team, and he recalls being called out to search for Hugh on the moors, near Garsdale, back in 2010. By then Hugh, 68, was not in the best of health. He had failed to return home after going out for a walk. He was only found alive, sheltering by a shooting butt, after an extensive all-night search.

The aforementioned branch to Hawes crosses the van Cutsem land, which is worth mentioning, as there are ambitions to reopen the line – a proposal that would necessitate the agreement of the van Cutsems. This idea has lately rather superseded older ambitions to reopen the entire missing section of the old Wensleydale Railway, between Redmire and Garsdale – a scheme in which I was once heavily involved, as chairman. My feeling now is that reinstating the short stretch from Hawes to Garsdale is both more realistic and, potentially, more useful, not least because a connection with the S&C is far, far easier than one with the busy East Coast Main Line at Northallerton.

One of the key advocates of the reinstatement idea is Ruth Annison, who runs Outhwaite's Ropeworks, beside the old station yard at Hawes. The day after our stay at the Moorcock, I meet up with Ruth for the first time in a quarter of a century, at the Christmas dinner of the Friends of the Settle–Carlisle Line, at the Golden Lion in Settle. Ruth was always high-energy, and a passionate advocate for the S&C, being a leading light in the Business Liaison Group, which pressed the case for local business during the long, hard battle to save the railway.

I was with her back at the very beginning of the idea of following the salvation of the S&C with the formation of the Wensleydale Railway Association, dedicated to reinstating the missing bits of railway to complete a link from the S&C all the way to the East Coast Main Line, 56 or so kilometres to the east. Ruth is no stranger to the idea of reviving things: she and her husband Peter came to Wensleydale from Nottingham in the 1970s to take over the old W. R. Outhwaite & Son rope business and create a living for themselves in the dale. Peter had been a textile chemist and was, at the time, recovering from stomach cancer, having received pioneering chemotherapy. I think you might well deem his treatment a success, given that he went on to live for another 43 years, until 2018. I guess I owe my own recovery from stomach cancer – through a combination of chemotherapy and surgery at the Northern Oesaphago-Gastric Unit, in Newcastle, in 2013 and 2014 – in part to trailblazers like Peter.

Together, Ruth and Peter reinvented the little ropeworks, transforming it from a one-product business to a highly successful enterprise, manufacturing everything from banister ropes to bell ropes, and progressively extending the little factory into Hawes station yard so it could produce longer and longer twines.

I remember Peter as extraordinarily laid-back; he was as laconic as his wife was (and remains) frenetic, and, notwithstanding his brush with death, had a pipe pretty much glued to his bottom lip.

So, I find Ruth, in Settle, as enthusiastic as ever, as she introduces me to Andrew Longworth, 'chairman designate' of the Upper Wensleydale Railway, which has, as I write, now been promised funds from the Department of Transport's Ideas Fund to enable the next stage of exploring the feasibility of reopening the line from Hawes to Garsdale. I'd love to think their ambition might be achieved in at least one of our lifetimes.

From Garsdale to Kirkby Stephen

* * *

I am back in Hawes, indeed in the station yard, just a little over two weeks later, following my meeting with Miles Johnson at the National Park offices, in Bainbridge. I am here to look through parish records and other archives at the Dales Countryside Museum to see if I can find out anything new about the lives of the railway navvies. I'm also curious to look at some of the diaries of the late Marie Hartley, whose tireless research and writing with her companion, Joan Ingilby, created a legacy testifying to the traditional way of life in the Dales, unrivalled by any similar folk collections elsewhere in the country.

One of the most celebrated pieces of work by Hartley and Ingilby was *The Old Hand Knitters of the Dales*, published by Dalesman, back in 1951. It proved a lasting testament to the Dales knitting tradition and, most especially, the so-called 'terrible knitters of Dent'. The word 'terrible' here refers to the speed of their knitting as the men and women of Dentdale were renowned for the adept use of traditional 'knitting sticks' attached to a belt, so they could actually knit while multi-tasking on other things. Their most celebrated product was gloves for troops in the Crimea. My friend Angharad has inspected the Hartley-Ingilby knitting collection at Hawes as part of her PhD research. She's travelled Europe and beyond in search of knitting traditions and patterns, especially gloves. As part of her work, she has knitted collector's item gloves for her friends. We have had ours framed for the wall.

What grabs my attention on this visit, though, is Marie Hartley's diaries and beautiful pencil sketches. The diaries are quite prosaic, but revelatory of the life she led in the cottage she shared with Joan Ingilby, near Askrigg. The diaries are written in a neat hand in a manner that shall, I reflect, doubtless be pretty much consigned to history, thanks to the advance of technology. I do sometimes fear that our Age shall become as dark as the Dark Ages for want of the right equipment a few hundred years from now, with which to read our copious online musings (remember what happened to that extensive BBC people's history record when the recording medium it used became obsolete).

There are all manner of notes and letters in the collection, including, coincidentally, a letter to Fleur Speakman, wife of the aforementioned Colin, as recently as 2000, when Joan was terminally ill. Perhaps most appealing, though, are the handwritten diaries, with their detailed observation of the ways in which life was lived. Here's a short extract written during a fortnight's stay in Wensleydale, in August 1935:

A very busy time, scarcely time to eat. We saw a good deal of Mr D Chapman, Mr Skidmore, Mr Skidmore Senior – clock repairer and descendant of clockmakers of Wensleydale. A thirty-hour clock about a hundred years ago cost £3. An eight-day clock about £5. It was one of the first things a newly married couple came to order. The clockmaker would take the case on his shoulder and the movement in a butter basket over his arm and so deliver the clock.

I take a lunch break in the station building itself, now attached to the 'goods shed' via a smart glass atrium. As I exit via the museum, the woman on reception clearly knows me, but I'm struggling: I really never have been great at recognising faces from the past. Eventually the penny drops: it's Janet, whose family used to run the camping and caravan site. She's aged rather better than I have, I fancy.

I reflect that it is nearly quarter of a century since I lived here, but I may well be back in Hawes sooner rather than later: when I call Hester, the printmaker from Horton, I discover that she's been commissioned to make new prints of Marie Hartley's sketches for an exhibition at the museum in summer 2020.[7] How curiously circular things can sometimes seem!

* * *

Fast forward to July 2020 and I board the train at Kirkby Stephen, having driven from my home in Durham on a Sunday morning. Railway travel in the COVID era is surreal: the platform is bedecked with anti-marketing messages, urging me and my ilk not to travel unless there's absolutely no alternative and to leave the train free for essential workers. I am unsure precisely which essential workers need to travel south from Kirkby Stephen late on a Sunday morning and I can count my fellow passengers on the fingers of one hand, with several to spare. None looks especially 'essential'. Indeed, to illustrate the farcical nature of this injunction, Northern Rail (aka 'the Government' at this time) has actually done away with half of all trains on the line, including those at commute-to-work times. After some lobbying, they have subsequently put on a bus replacement for these services.

Today's walk from Garsdale station to Kirkby Stephen is a re-run of the walk I made back in June 2009 with my long-standing pal, Rob, with whom I have enjoyed many walking adventures: besides Lakeland and Cheviot peaks, we made expeditions to Ben Nevis and Carrauntoohil, Ireland's highest mountain. I'd mentioned to Rob that I was minded to walk the Settle–Carlisle Way, with a view to updating the guidebook originally written by Colin Speakman and John Morrison. And so we'd booked rooms at the very comfortable Appleby Manor, with the idea of using the train to enable us to walk three one-day stages, from Garsdale to Kirkby Stephen, Kirkby Stephen to Appleby and, finally, on to Langwathby. It didn't work out quite that way in the event but, if nothing else, it did probably persuade me (as mentioned in the Introduction) that, back then at least, I had neither the time nor the application to write walking guides of the traditional 'watch out for the overgrown fingerpost on the left' kind.

From the perspective of our frailty as human beings, more than a little water has flowed beneath the bridge since that trip, beginning with a short visit I had to make to psychiatric hospital the following year, following an injury I suffered in a cycling accident. Then, I was diagnosed with stomach cancer in the autumn of 2013 and had chemo either side of Christmas and an operation in February 2014. While recovering in hospital in Newcastle I received a call from Rob. 'Guess where I am,' he said. I could have hazarded many guesses without hitting the nail on the head, for he too was in hospital, recovering from a major op after a routine outpatient procedure went suddenly and dramatically wrong. It's been a long haul for both of us since then. In my case, six months after my op I sustained what they call an incision hernia, caused by too much heavy lifting too soon. I had the hernia repaired in a big op in 2016, but then contracted an infection, which saw me back in hospital for three more weeks, with tubes in and out of everywhere, and slowly going crazy with frustration. After that little lot, my hip replacement, carried out under local anaesthetic 18 months ago, was a bit of walk in the park – I'd have been home the same afternoon if I hadn't had a slight dizzy turn. All these issues are, thankfully, behind us now (touch wood) and, yes, the pair of us do still walk together, though we've no plans to conquer any major peaks just at present.

Back to today, when I shall be pretty much sticking to the 'official' Settle–Carlisle Way route: not only does this offer fine views across the Upper Eden, from The Highway, beneath Mallerstang Edge, but it also follows, for much of the way, another 'unofficial' long-distance footpath – Lady Anne's Way, a 160km route devised by Sheila Gordon, from Saltaire, in memory of the redoubtable Lady Anne Clifford.

'Redoubtable' is one of those words that is sometimes applied too liberally. But Lady Anne Clifford proved beyond reasonable doubt that she was the wrong person with whom to pick a fight. She was effectively disinherited as a young woman when her father, Richard Sackville, Third Earl of Dorset, and (by marriage) also of Cumberland, died in 1605. Contrary to the family's own rules of succession, his vast estate – including, in the North, lands from Skipton to Brougham, near Penrith, and several grand houses and castles – went instead to her uncle and his heirs. Her mother, Margaret, survived her father and also felt aggrieved at this apparent injustice. It took Lady Anne until 1643 to regain her inheritance, whereupon, aged 60, she left her home in the South and moved north to set about making good all her castles, which had fallen into disrepair. She also repaired nearby churches and built almshouses for the poor and needy. She travelled much between the castles and eventually died at her favourite, Brougham Castle.

On an American website, *Amazing Women in History*, dedicated to 'all the kick-ass women the history books left out', Keri Engel writes:

Because her marriage to her first husband was reportedly difficult, contemporaries blamed Lady Anne's unyielding personality as a cause, even though the Earl's first marriage before Lady Anne was also a difficult one. Lady Anne's cousin Edward Russell, Third Earl of Bedford, compared her to the Rhône River, so we can guess that she had a wilful and unyielding personality, which was not viewed favourably in women at the time. Lady Anne was an important patron of authors and literature; and her many letters and diary, which she kept from 1603 through 1616, made her a literary personage in her own right. John Donne is reported to have said that she could 'discourse of all things from Predestination to Slea-silk [embroidery thread]'.

In the foreword of her guide to her walk, Sheila Gordon comments: 'I wished to strike a balance between sticking religiously to her routes (a great deal of which now lie under Tarmac[...]) while gaining a true flavour of the surrounding landscape. I had no desire to increase pressure on existing long distance paths, nor to stay totally in valleys, beautiful though they are, and so I have taken to the fellsides whenever possible.' So, it feels that the ethos of her walk chimes rather nicely with my own for the Settle–Carlisle Way.

Lady Anne's Way begins at Skipton Castle, her birthplace, in 1589, and ends at Brougham, where she died in 1676, but perhaps a highlight of the route is the so-called High Way, which runs at gentle gradients along the fellside, from Cotterdale, west of Hawes, to Pendragon Castle. Today I retrace my route with Rob, on field paths from Garsdale station, over the railway footbridge at Ais Gill Summit, and passing the tiny Lunds chapel, before joining the High Way next to the old youth hostel at Shaws, which was in a state of fervent renovation last time we passed.

So, disembarking at a deserted Garsdale station, and passing Ruswarp's memorial, I am caught short by the realisation of just how much the world has changed since I was last here, back in COVID-free November last year. I wonder with some anxiety how many of those changes may yet turn out to have an air of at least semi-permanence to them.

I have anticipated easy walking, but I am quite quickly disabused of such ambitions. I have forgotten just how much more rain has fallen on this side of the Pennines than in my native North East (I'm actually just a smidge west of the main watershed), and the moorland is a saturated sponge. Every step produces a squelch, some squelches being already higher than my walking shoes. Perhaps it was a day for the boots, after all... but too late now. And there is a second problem: thanks to the COVID lockdown, nobody has been walking these paths and they are disappearing as nature reasserts her supremacy. A single muddy sock has been placed, bizarrely, atop the post of a stile and I dub it 'the lone sock of doom', while failing to appreciate what impending misfortunes it may foretell.

But it is good to be on high moorland again: curlew, lapwing and snipe are all abundant. One of the former is enacting its broken-wing charade just a few metres in front of me as it seeks to lure me away from where its young may be.

As I near the well-tended south-facing house at Ais Gill Summit, a vole shoots through the grass in front of me. I turn to admire the broad view beyond the Dandy Mire Viaduct, past the Moorcock Inn, and on down Wensleydale. Dandy More Viaduct, unlike the one a little to the north, near Ais Gill, was not in the original Midland plans. It was built only when the workforce gave up trying to build an embankment, as the ballast they tipped just kept disappearing into the soft peat. The viaduct, presumably, sits upon limestone bedrock. I recall at school being told in geography that there were three gaps in the Pennines: the Aire, Stainmore and Tyne. But when I moved to Hawes I often wondered why the Wensleydale-Garsdale 'gap' fails to qualify as such: it is somewhat lower than Stainmore, which seems to me little more than a nick in the skyline. And the land at the head of the three rivers here at Garsdale Head – Ure, Eden and Clough – all rise in an expansive area of relatively flat land and broad vistas. Indeed, the headwaters of the Ure and the Eden are less than 400 metres from one another, before each turns respectively east and north. There is evidence too that this gap in the hills was exploited way back in Neolithic times, when axes from the important 'factory', in Langdale, at the heart of the Lake District, were taken via Mallerstang and Wensleydale to the Thornborough Henge complex, near Ripon.

The aforementioned van Cutsem lodge, a kilometre or more away, in the upper valley of the Ure, is, after the viaduct, the second largest object in this particular eastward vista.

I cross the tracks and descend to cross the Mallerstang road from the Moorcock, passing a flock of jet-black sheep on the way. I think they may be Hebridean, a guess later confirmed for me by Andrew, mentioned earlier, who keeps a small flock of Swaledales, near Hawes. I recall that Rob and I got a little lost crossing the expanse of moorland known as the Lunds 11 years ago, so I am at pains to follow the correct path this time. Using a larger scale map, this is not difficult as far as Blades Bridge. On crossing the bridge, however, the path vanishes, unceremoniously. I do my best to orientate myself in the direction shown on the map and find myself wishing that I had downloaded the map and GPS. I am crossing tufted marshland, dotted with thistles and, curiously, mint. I am clearly on a flood plain, and one that has been called into action in the fairly recent past. I pick my way through until a come across what may well be the correct route, just metres short of a stile. Suddenly, without warning, a pothole reaches up, grabs me round the ankles and pulls me knee-deep into its depths. I let loose a cry of anger and shock at just how cold the water is. Boots would not have helped.

Back on track, I approach the old 'village' at Lunds itself and am vaguely amused by the rather incongruous and superfluous finger post, which stands, bedecked with lichen, atop a drumlin, above the tiny collection of loosely assembled buildings, many of them in a state of disrepair. Scholars of Norse languages may wonder why the settlement is named after puffins, like Lundy (puffin island). However, it seems it comes from another Old Norse word, *lundr*, meaning a grove, presumably of trees. This is relevant hereabouts, because in the upper Dales and Cumbrian valleys, Old Norse words have long endured after Viking settlers migrated to the upper valleys, such as Langstrothdale, Ennerdale and Wasdale. When I lived in Hawes, I'd be asked sometimes: 'Ist thou laikin' t'neet?' It means: 'Are you playing football this evening?' The verb 'to laik' comes directly from the Old Norse *leika* and means 'to play'. It persists today in Iceland, the Faroe Islands and Scandinavia. I fear, however, I may have lived among the last generation of Dalesfolk to use the word, as our homogenised culture slowly extinguishes such local variations.

Back to my approach to Lunds: as I drop down from my drumlin I spot two chocolate brown birds, of medium size, flitting across the far side of a field gate. My latent subconscious bird knowledge tells me they may be woodcock. I peak through the windows of the tiny chapel, now an abandoned semi-wreck surrounded by toppling gravestones, some bearing eroded dates from the 18th century. It was a chapel of rest and is Grade II listed, notwithstanding its condition. A short distance beyond, a large old farmhouse is undergoing a complete renovation as I turn towards the steep path up to Shaws and I choose this as my lunch stop, removing my shoes and squeezing a cupful of rank water from each. In the gable end of the building, a few feet away, a starling zooms in to fill two gaping beaks that emerge from a gap in the mortar. I resolve to wait and get a picture next time. However, when the parent returns it is gone again almost immediately, passing the food to its offspring before I have even picked up my ready-primed camera.

I climb the neat stone steps beside the eponymous waterfall at Shaws, now a fine-looking dwelling, though I puzzle over access to it, which can only be via the roughest of tracks. Arriving on the High Way, I look down on the expansive home, which must enjoy superb sunset views across to Wild Boar Fell, as a woman comes out and hangs washing. It's an action she may soon come to regret, as a squally storm blows in. It feels more like sleet than rain. As the late Mr Spock might have said: 'It's July, captain, though not as we know it.'

Signs tell me that this is part of the 'High Abbotside moorland regeneration and black grouse recovery project'. Bracing myself against the wind, I spot a peregrine riding motionless on the ridge lift, before folding its wings and descending, like a depth charge, at astonishing speed. I see it crash into one of 'my woodcocks', which somehow, so far as I can make out, manages to escape. On matters more terrestrial, I have by now seen a further three voles. I have never previously seen four voles in one day, even dead ones brought in by the cats. However, there are more voles than people in the UK, so maybe I'm just making up for lost time.

The High Way descends gradually, as the crisp angles of Mallerstang Edge, to my right, and the high drama of Wild Boar Fell, to my left, begin to craft a narrower, more 'traditional' valley profile. On the other side of the valley, beneath Wild Boar Fell, the railway descends at a much more constant gradient, of precisely 1:100. The Edge divides the north–south valley of the Upper Eden from the east–west valley of the Swale and you could, if committed to a more upland walking experience, look for a suitable point at which to gain the southern end of the ridge and then follow it north all the way to Nateby Common. There's no formal right of way, but you'd be 'covered' by the Right to Roam rules. The rugged escarpments of Mallerstang Edge and Wild Boar Fell seemingly challenging each other from either side of the valley. But they flatter to deceive, for neither is the narrow ridge it appears to be. Rather, each shelves gently away out of sight beyond the skyline.

From Garsdale to Kirkby Stephen

I recall that Nine Standards Rigg, sitting just behind Mallerstang Edge, and a summit on Wainwright's Coast to Coast Walk, was the first 'mountain' I ever scaled with my elder daughter, Hannah. Or under her own steam, at least: I'm sure she hitched a ride up others in her 'backpack'. Nine Standards Rigg is well known for its curious stone cairns, which were an inspiration for the sculptor Andy Goldsworthy (of whom more later). No one seems to know precisely who built these, or why, and ditto the similar ones atop Wild Boar Fell, across the valley.

Now, however, I have an imminent rendezvous with my hosts for the evening and overnight – David Stewart, of Kirkby Stephen Mountain Rescue fame, and his wife and business partner, Chris. Together they run a very successful online walking routes resource called *Walking World*. Today they're heading south from where the High Way joins the valley road and the aim is to meet somewhere in the vicinity of Hell Gill.

We indeed meet up not far south of Hell Gill bridge and exchange the virtual hugs and handshakes that epitomise a society emerging from lockdown. David and Chris are accompanied by Theo, a labradoodle acquired shortly after lockdown began. They tell me the sad story of his former owner's terminal illness and their 'illegal' dash to Edinburgh to collect the dog. Their previous hound was an enthusiastic terrier, called Brough, who once forced our cat to seek refuge on the inch-wide crossbar of a sash window. Theo, however, is a proper softy of a dog and, as the day goes on, I shall learn that he is actually more like a cat than your typical dog.

As we approach Hell Gill bridge, to our left is a dramatic new super-home, probably a large barn conversion, with fabulous views to Wild Boar Fell. I reflect that, in 20 years, this back-of-beyond windswept Pennine landscape has become desirable real estate for those in search of solitude and a project – the old youth hostel, the large farmhouse at Lunds, and a smattering of smartly renovated buildings all bear testimony to a trend that may yet become a movement as the world adapts to the post-COVID 'new normal'.

Hell Gill is aptly named: you look down from the bridge parapet into a deep and murky chasm. When folk named it, they must have felt they were staring down into the murky underworld of Hades himself, for you can only just discern the water as it boils and bubbles over the boulders 25m below us. The gill is what's known as a 'slot canyon' – basically a narrow gorge carved out of the limestone by the fast torrent. The gorge terminates at Hell Gill Force, where the emerging waters tumble down the valley side, before turning north on their journey towards the Irish Sea. Those with a liking for gill scrambling, tipping towards canyoning, can enter from above the fall.

David recounts how his team once rescued a trapped sheep from Hell Gill. 'We like sheep – so much more realistic than using dummies on an exercise, because you never can tell if the dummy has died!' He also explains a little bit about the maths that underlies conducting a moorland search. It's all about achieving the precise correct interval between the searchers so as to optimise both the speed with which the terrain can be covered and the chances of finding the object of the search while still alive. Mr van Cutsem had been lucky, David says, as the chances of finding someone are still only 50:50, and that's if there's a scent for the dogs to follow. 'He was wearing dark clothes on a dark night,' adds David, with a shrug.

Before long we arrive at 'Water Cut', the first in a series of monumental artworks, called Benchmarks, which were created as part of the East Cumbria Countryside Project, in 1996.[8] Hewn by Mary Bourne, it is a large limestone carving, comprising two vertical 'blades' mounted on a plinth so that they face each other, with a slight gap between. The sides that face each other are serrated, as though perhaps representing gently lapping water. The sculpture stands on a vantage at the county boundary, beyond which the High Way descends more steeply, and it was intended by the artist to symbolise the power of the River Eden cutting through the rock on its journey to the sea, and our own human journeys through the rural landscape, and through life.

I guess it could specifically be a metaphor for my own journey and the life memories that it is stirring, although the more I look at it, the more I am seeing the blades of a pair of pinking shears, a giant clamshell or the claw of a killer crab. I suppose that's a fundamental of art, though – it's perhaps less about what the artist intends and more about what the viewer sees. And through its immensity (it stands maybe six feet or more tall) you can, by moving around, frame different views of the valley, or be reminded, as the artist suggests, of gateposts, or even, in its curved profile, the arches of viaducts on the railway. Dick Capel, who commissioned the works is, it turns out, a friend of David and Chris. (His book on the Eden Valley, *The Stream Invites Us* to Follow, discusses this and other public artworks.) We assemble for a socially distanced group photo: I mount my camera on its little spider tripod and set the timer. I fail to make it back to my posing position on time on my first attempt. On my second, I decapitate myself and give up...

The steady descent towards the valley road, where David and Chris have parked, brings blessed relief: Chris rifles through a few boxes in the van and proudly produces a pair of socks for me. Nothing can be done about my wet shoes, but the socks are one giant leap for footkind.

The walking is gentle and easy now, by the banks of the infant Eden, where swallows zoom back and forth in search of their insect prey, sheltered from the gale by the overhanging trees. I fancy that there are more swallows, swifts and martins than usual this year and, if true, this might be because there are more insects, because fewer have been blatted by cars during lockdown. Certainly my own car has lots of corpses on it now, but as it went almost nowhere for several weeks, it's been a far less potent killing machine overall. It's possible here to make a short detour from the riverside to visit the church at Outhgill, site of another recently erected memorial to the railway navvies. And, if you find the church open, a restored monument to another important figure in the life of the River Eden, of whom more later.

At Pendragon Castle, I have another important rendezvous. But first, some historical context... For, on arrival at the castle, on its mound above the river, I find myself cast back in time: not to the days when Lady Anne was marshalling teams of builders here, but to somewhat more recent days: to October 1989, to be precise. During my freelance days – before the publishing business took up more and more of my time – my partner in crime was the press photographer Barry Wilkinson. On one occasion he asked if I fancied writing the words for a story idea he had had about a team looking at cup and ring markings on Ilkley Moor. It was our first joint journalistic venture and we got ourselves a full-page spread in *The Times* and we rarely looked back after that. I'd spot quirky feature ideas in the Dales and we did a lot of work for *The Independent, Guardian, Observer, Telegraph* and others in the days when, if you were good, you could earn a decent living from freelance work. As we got more ambitious, we went further afield, once as far as Iceland. We were quite a formidable team in our day...

Back to the Upper Eden and the remains of a once fine castle, which, I reflect, looks in rather better shape than it did in 1989. When Barry and I visited then, it was the object of one man's quest to consolidate and restore it to a condition in which it might remain standing for the benefit of future generations. That man

Water Cut sculpture, Mallerstang.

All photographs are © Stan L Abbott unless otherwise noted.

Dentdale from Blea Moor, above; Arten Gill Viaduct, below.

Hebridean sheep, above, and fingerpost, below right, both at Lunds.
Navvy memorial at Cowgill churchyard, Dentdale, below left.

Pendragon Castle, above; Whernside Manor, below.

Staircase, above, and waterfall, below, at Shaws.

Lady Anne's almshouses (St Anne's Hospital), Appleby, above.
Terry's Farm, Little Ormside, below.

Roman Road north of Appleby, above.
Lacy's Caves, below *(caution – unstable paths in this area!)*

The banks of the Eden north of Armathwaite (*unstable paths*).

went by the hopelessly romantic name of Raven Frankland: he was a Cumbria county councillor, then aged 70, and a member of the Yorkshire Dales National Park Committee. His father had bought the castle ruins for the princely sum of £525 in 1963. My interview with him, and Barry's pictures, earned us a full-page feature in *The Independent*. Under the watchful eye of English Heritage, as it then was, Raven was painstakingly working his way through the ruins, with just the occasional assistance of farm workers and volunteers.

'We can't proceed too quickly or the walls will be exposed to the weather,' he told me. 'They have to be pointed as we remove the rubble, and we have to look at every teaspoonful of rubble as it comes out.' Barry took several pictures, of which one shows Raven, trowel in hand, in an arched window void, which beautifully frames Mallerstang Edge.

I recall Raven being particularly interested in the possibility that the Norman castle – unusual in that it was built without curtain walls – might have superseded an earlier Roman structure when it was built by Hugh de Morville in the 12th century. Those who know their history well will recall that de Morville was a co-conspirator in the murder of Thomas Becket.

But both Raven and his castle have many more romantic tales to tell. Let's begin with Raven's father, Edward, son of the famous chemist, Sir Edward Frankland, and a writer of historical fiction, among whose works is one in which the hero is thrown into crisis when he spends large sums of money to prevent the collapse of – you may have guessed it – one Pendragon Castle. 'My father had always wanted to have it but it never came on the market. Then, when it did come up for sale, it was a scheduled Ancient Monument, but nobody else seemed interested in having it,' Raven told me, in 1989.

Frankland Senior's other novels included one called *Arthur,*

Walking the Line

The Bear of Britain, whose hero is Arthur, the Celtic warrior, in a more down-to-earth version of the Arthurian legend. Again, it's not hard to discern the inspiration, as local legend has it that Uther Pendragon raised his son, Arthur, at this very spot. No, this is neither Tintagel nor Glastonbury Tor, but it should be remembered that the North of England and southern and central Scotland boast easily as many sites with Arthurian links as do Cornwall or Wales. Indeed, it seems that the castle is very much on the trail of both military and Arthurian buffs. The latter category even draws interest from across the pond, and I note that Edward Frankland's books remain widely available in the States. It was also, over the years, visited by would-be looters, lured by tales of treasure hidden in a vault, and the damage they caused had to be made good by Raven.

Back in the 1980s, Raven uncovered substantial vaulted chambers and twin spiral staircases either side of the main entrance. It must have made a fine site, before it was twice burned down by the Scots. But come 1660, and its redemption arrives in the shape of the determined Lady Anne Clifford, who, said Raven, would arrive from Skipton aboard a carriage with six horses, to be greeted by a crowd of 300. Her entourage would even transport a glazed window for the tiny bedchamber where she slept. Mary Queen of Scots passed by, en route to her incarceration at Bolton Castle, in Wensleydale, before Pendragon passed into the hands of the Earl of Thanet, who plundered buildings on his northern estates for their lead. 'Then it became a source of building materials for a lot of farms round about,' said Raven. I leave the last word on the Arthurian question to him: 'My father took the view that Arthur may well have been a general who fought in battles against the Saxons up and down the west of the country from Dumfries to Cornwall, and there is nowhere else I am aware of that claims to have been his birthplace.'

* * *

Raven Frankland died suddenly in 1997 and his widow, Juliet, one of the world's leading mycologists, asked her sister, Dame Gillian Brown, a former diplomat and the UK's ambassador to Norway, to help her to manage the Pendragon estate. Just two years later, Dame Gillian also died and Juliet went into decline, eventually dying in 2013. A couple of years later, the estate passed to one John Bucknall, who moved north to manage it, with his wife, Diana. I am meeting him today, at the castle.

I find him in a parked car, with Diana and a large dog. He jumps out and, almost immediately, launches into a gutsy rendition of the Pendragon verse at the start of this chapter. He may be only a cousin of Raven, but I can immediately see that he is every bit as eccentric, and every bit as enthused by being the owner of a medieval castle. However, where Raven was tall and spindly, John is somewhat shorter and just a little rotund. And where Raven was slightly measured in his words, John talks excitedly over the buffeting wind. Others, too, are enthused today, as a surprisingly steady stream of members of the public turn up (perhaps enjoying blessed release following the easing of lockdown rules), clamber over a few ramparts, and maybe ask the odd question of John. Some are just passing and have spotted the ruins, now clearly visible from the road in a way they were not 30-something years ago. Some may be Arthurian fans. At least two sound North American, though they are unlikely to have travelled here during the pandemic. John is well aware of Lady Anne's growing esteem in the USA, but what he wants me – and indeed other visitors – to do is to use our imagination to conjure up a picture of how the interior of the castle might have looked back in her day.

John invites me to imagine this as a place in which Lady Anne might have entertained her eminent guests, by inviting them to her hunting lodge. 'It was a country house for most of the time and a castle perhaps just once a year,' he says, as the howling wind now thwarts an attempt to record him on video. I briefly wonder if it might just possibly have been one of Lady Anne's pals who killed the last wild boar in England. But it was back in much earlier Norman times that this alleged slaughter led to the naming of the hill that overlooks the castle. That said, John believes, like Raven, that Pendragon was built on the site of a Norman motte and bailey castle. To the north of the castle, he suggests, there was once an extensive lake and those same guests of Lady Anne might have walked across a drawbridge down to the lake. There they might have rowed across the water and climbed a gentle indentation in the hillside to a belvedere, offering fine views back to the castle. Indeed, the existence of a drawbridge has quite recently been established by an American visitor with a drone, insists John.

Soon we are standing beneath the narrow window to Lady Anne's bedchamber, where John tells me: 'She was a most remark-able lady. She repaired her six castles between 1660 and her death in 1676. She must be one of the great repairers of historic buildings and indeed she quotes the Old Testament in "stepping into the breach" and repairing the wall.

'So it's a profound business, restating noble birth and its responsibilities, and it extended from castle walls to the farms, to looking after old people, with the creation of wonderful alms-houses at Beamsley, in Yorkshire, and in Appleby; the rebuilding of the churches – she did everything for her people. And her people, 400 years later, remember her with great warmth, but profound respect.

'Lady Anne was also extraordinary. She combined a passion for the ancient principle of nobility and the responsibilities of nobility, which go right back in England into Anglo-Saxon times.

But she is also a child of the Renaissance and one of the people that I have a great fascination for is the founder of English classical architecture, Inigo Jones, who did the drawings for dresses to wear at the Court Masques when Lady Anne was a teenage lass. And then, when she was the Countess of Pembroke, at Wilton [the family seat, in Wiltshire], it's quite possible and entirely reasonable to consider that Mr Jones would have come to Wilton House and sat at lunch, planning what became, in due course, the Double Cube room, the noblest room in England, at the beginning of our own Renaissance. So you have this curious blend at Pendragon of somebody who's reaching back into history but is part of and in the forefront of, the Renaissance in England, the new ideas, the classical world.'

John simply oozes not just enthusiasm for his subject, but also a deep and passionate knowledge: as a conservation architect, he has worked on some very significant projects across Europe and the world. His clients have included the Landmark Trust, for which he worked on the restoration of Palladio's Villa Saraceno, part of the Italian World Heritage Site.

Our conversation then swings tangentially to Lundy and the Landmark Trust and I realise that, if I don't manage things a little better, we'll still be here talking at dusk. I tell John I really have to resume my walk and I find Diana with David and Chris and the two dogs. 'Your husband could talk for England,' I venture to Diana.

'And some,' she replies. 'Though he is a creature of his imagination, whereas I am a scientist, a chemist by profession, and prefer proof to speculation.'

I can imagine how she must at times apply her analytical logic in an effort to ground her husband. But I have to confess no small amount of sympathy for John's ideas, which I find no less speculative than some of the ideas that may be presented as 'fact' by archaeologists.

John's parting gesture is to present me with a large, flat, well-wrapped gift, which I entrust to Chris's care as David and I prepare to resume our walk, while Chris heads for Kirkby Stephen in the van.

* * *

As we walk up the metalled lane, beyond the castle, David and I find ourselves face to face with a red squirrel. Upper Wensleydale and the Eden Valley are red squirrel strongholds and, crucially, not too many invasive American greys are seen hereabouts. Indeed, a few years ago, they administered contraceptives to greys in Wensleydale, though it's not clear how effective this was in suppressing the population, or if it just led to wild, uninhibited grey squirrel parties.

I stealthily remove my camera from its case and raise it to shoot. And then a van roars around the bend behind us and the squirrel disappears into the high branches.

David proves a knowledgeable companion as we continue our walk, skirting round the lower slopes of Birkett Fell. This craggy knoll is the site of one of the railway's accidental, or unintended, tunnels. It lies on a fault line and when the contractors tried to dig a cutting, it proved too unstable and they were obliged to tunnel instead. David points out where lead miners created a 'hush' on the opposite side of the valley, on Great Bell, where you can clearly see the continuation of the fault line. A hush was created by damming a narrow gill to create a body of water. The dam would then be broken and the water would rush down, exposing any workable mineral seams.

Lead workings here were never as extensive as those to be seen in Swaledale, Arkengarthdale, or in the North Pennines, around the Alston area.

A little further south, David points out a stone house, standing alone in a patch of woodland. Carr House was renovated as an off-grid dwelling, with its own small hydro plant, but owner Adam Hoyle had failed to apply for the correct planning permission and was ordered to demolish it. However, the demolition could not take place because of a bat colony. Eventually, in a highly unusual and groundbreaking move, the house was allowed to remain after a referendum of local people under the 2012 Localism Act.

As we head north, the landscape is rich with the evidence of previous populations: low mounds by the Eden suggest ancient roundhouses; a field full of 'pillow mounds' evidences a medieval rabbit warren; an old field system on the opposite valley side comes into view. The most significant visible relic, however, is Lammerside Castle, which sits on land belonging to nearby Wharton Hall. Technically, it is a tower house, rather than a castle – it's a Grade II listed building and on Historic England's 'at risk' register, because of the recent rapid deterioration of the remains. Historic England is talking to the national park to explore funding options for consolidation works.

So far as I can establish, a tower house differs from a pele tower inasmuch as it is a more generic term, which can be applied to a wide range of tall, fortified houses across Europe. Pele towers, and indeed the generally smaller bastles (reinforced farmhouses), are particular to the English and Scottish borderlands. Only about 100 free-standing tower houses remain in England, though there would, once upon a time, have been at least one in every parish. By contrast, the Mani peninsula, in southern Greece, boasts at least 800 tower houses in various states of repair and disrepair. Just for the record, Historic England says that Pendragon Castle is also a tower house, so there you go!

So, as our route veers away from a farmhouse and across a field to the castle remains, I judge it to be not unlike a smaller version of its cousin up the valley, so it's interesting to speculate upon the dynamic that must have existed between the two sets of occupants, the Warcop family (until its abandonment in the 17th century) and Lady Anne's family. And that's before adding the partially fortified Wharton Hall to the mix.

Historic England describes a two-storey, 14th century structure, with vaulted cellars. It once had two additional wings, to north and south. Its listing notes: 'The monument will add greatly to our knowledge and understanding of the wider medieval settlement and economy of this area.' Well, I guess it will – providing that it doesn't completely fall down before the remains can be further examined.

Now, David and I face a challenge: our onward route clearly crosses a field, before following the left bank of the Eden and climbing a little to Wharton Hall. That field, however, is of the freshly ploughed variety. We choose to assert our rights and use David's satnav to follow the correct line of the right of way across the middle of the ploughed land. Now, depending on precisely how you interpret the law, the farmer may have 14 days' grace to restore a footpath after ploughing it, so I could be generous and imagine that it was actually only ploughed yesterday and that, tomorrow, he will roll the route of the path flat and gravel it.

Moving on, we arrive at the third 'castle' in what we might call 'the Mallerstang trilogy'. We approach the aforementioned Wharton Hall, an imposing family home that is now the greater part of what remains of the original manor, which was built between the late 14th and 17th centuries and surrounds a medieval courtyard. Entry to this yard is via a gatehouse, now minus its roof and upper portions, adjoining the farmhouse to the right. This much you can just about discern by looking over the gate, which now firmly instructs walkers to take a detour to the west of this large working farm. Well, I say 'large working farm', but I think I should perhaps say 'rural factory', and I comment to David that I can really see little point in living in such beautiful surroundings if completely surrounded by noisy, smelly agricultural factory tack. I know that large dairy farms have to function, but do they have to completely dominate an adjacent medieval manor? And would it really be the worst thing in the world if farming were subject to a few more of the planning rules that rightly apply to the rest of us?

But now a little family history: the hall was built by Sir Thomas Wharton, whose family crest has adorned the gatehouse archway since the 16th century. Apparently, the Wharton name was originally 'de Querton' and thus, presumably, of Norman origin. Over time, *qu* became corrupted to *wh* in England, and so de Querton begat de Wherton, then de Wharton and, finally, Wharton. I have always been intrigued by Wharton Hall, as my mother's ancestral family name was Wharton, and she and my dad found an old Wharton grave from her family in the churchyard at Temple Sowerby, further down the Eden, when they became avid sleuths in pursuit of the family history.

I think they were always a little frustrated that the rest of us seemed to show no more than a passing interest in our more distant antecedents and, sadly, it was only after their death that the real stone-turning began. That was when my brother retired and his previous disdain turned, with the help of the Internet, into an almost obsessional pursuit of the family truth. Over the course of a couple of years he drove back the ancestral frontiers to the 17th century. He discovered hitherto lost branches in South Africa and, even more exotic, Burton-on-Trent (where he himself would sadly die in hospital a few years later of an undiagnosed cancer).

He found that the testimony of one ancestor had condemned the last man to hang on the celebrated gibbet in the Northumberland village of Elsdon; and he debunked fondly believed family myths, including the idea that we were the illegitimate descendants of Sir Walter Scott. Or that my father's father was the son of an itinerant knife-grinder in Swaledale, who had never registered his son's birth because he always got drunk on market day, in Darlington, and the registrar would be long gone by the time he sobered up. My dad went to his grave believing this tale, but it turned out the truth was more prosaic: my father's grandfather, a smallholder, had married his wife on licence after her release from Northallerton gaol, with hard labour, for stealing a purse, and the bizarre knife-grinder fiction had been woven to disguise the truth. And then there was the more recent revelation by my dad, in later life, that his father may well have sired a second family out of wedlock and that there might, therefore, be an entirely separate bloodline, in Newcastle.

And then my brother stumbled across the hitherto unknown Lancastrian branch of the family... Sarah Ellen Roberts, my great great grandad's first cousin, was born in Burnley, but moved to Blackburn where – in 1913, aged 41 – she was, apparently, accused of murder and practising witchcraft, having been witnessed slitting the throat of a child and drinking his blood with ice cream (as you would). At her trial, in Blackburn, she was found guilty and sentenced to death by being shackled and sealed alive in a lead-lined coffin.

The sentence was carried out on 9th June, but – just as the lid was closing on her coffin – she cursed and swore that she would return and seek vengeance in 80 years' time. When her husband, John, tried to inter her, he was unable to find a church that would permit her burial on consecrated ground. Having travelled the length and breadth of the country in search of a suitable resting place, he eventually set sail for Peru, where he purchased a grave for about five pounds, in the port of Pisco. There he placed a head-stone, which you can still find today. It reads:

From Garsdale to Kirkby Stephen

In memory of Sarah Ellen
Beloved wife
Of J P Roberts
Of Blackburn, England
Born March 6, 1872 and Died June 9, 1913

John, it seems, returned to England and was never heard of again in Peru. All of the foregoing must surely be true, because the story was published in several newspapers in the UK in 1993, including *The Sun* and *The Independent*. Indeed, by 1993, my most famous relative, and perhaps the most famous person in Peru since Paddington Bear, had become something of a tourist attraction in Pisco. After her story appeared on Peruvian TV in a 'documentary' about vampires, people began to flock to the town to buy hastily prepared 'vampire protection kits'. Her story had gained added momentum, it seems, when her tombstone spontaneously cracked shortly before the 80-year anniversary.

People began to say she was one of three 'brides of Dracula', the others being buried in Mexico and either Panama or Hungary. It seems, however, that she did not return to avenge her slayers in 1993 but, rather, found herself on the road to potential beatification as a saint. Why? Because her tomb was unusual in surviving an earthquake, which devastated Pisco in 2007.

Well, we all enjoy a good yarn – and far be it from me to permit the truth to intrude upon a tale as intriguing as this. However, Stephen Smith, from Cotton Town local history website, in Blackburn, assures me that Sarah Ellen was just a Lancashire cotton worker, with something of a yen for adventure. Her brother-in-law, Thomas, left Lancashire to run a cotton mill in Lima, in 1901, and Sarah Ellen's husband, John, would visit him in South America more than once, taking Sarah Ellen with him in 1913.

Sadly, whether through accident or illness, she died somewhere near Pisco and her death notice actually appeared in the
Northern Daily Telegraph four days later on Friday 13 June, of all
days. Her grieving husband carried her body into Pisco and then
the rumour mill took over. I guess we have to imagine how exotic
a Lancashire lass may have seemed in a small Peruvian town back
then, and so the collective imagination was fertilised – and then
further spiced in recent years by extreme journalistic licence.

Nor did John 'disappear without trace'. In fact, he returned
to Lancashire and ran a grocer's shop until his death in 1925, in
which métier he was succeeded by the couple's two sons for a further five years. The younger of the sons died in 1950 and that,
it seems, was the end of Lancashire Gargetts, although Stephen
Smith has located a branch of the family in Australia, descended
from John Roberts' sister, who emigrated in the 1920s.

Although disappointed to discover that the truth was so very
much more prosaic than the fiction, I guess I always knew they'd
stopped executing vampires and witches by the start of the 20th
century, even in Lancashire. It was, after all, all supposed to have
happened 300 years after the execution of the Pendle Witches. But
the story lives on in Peru, having been turned into a stage play and
a much viewed Youtube hit, called *Sarah Ellen: ¿Santa o Vampira?*
I had aspirations to pay family homage at her tomb one day and
maybe sooner rather than later. Then COVID came along…

Oh, I should probably add that my brother was unable to
substantiate any link between our Wharton ancestors and the
former occupants of the eponymous hall.

* * *

Almost imperceptibly, the wind and rain have both died away
as, leaving the farm behind us, we meet fell ponies with young

foals and pass an ancient oak, before dropping down and crossing the Eden into Nateby, one of perhaps half a dozen satellite villages round Kirkby Stephen. Rather than take the less interesting route straight to the station, we return to the banks of the Eden, where we encounter another Dick Capel commission: the Poetry Path, a series of 12 poems by Meg Peacocke, etched into stone by local artist, Pip Hall. David is a little unsure about some of the poetry, he tells me: I find it hard to judge, as erosion and lichen have been busily doing their bit to integrate the artworks into the landscape. However, both these and the Benchmarks, it could be said, extend a fine tradition of landscape sculptures begun by Andy Goldsworthy, whose beautifully crafted Sheepfolds series, stone-built in the traditional manner and installed at locations throughout the country, drew inspiration from his time living at Brough in the early 1980s. I recall how radical his work was back then and remember writing about it for *National Parks Today*.

We enter Kirkby Stephen by the 'back door', crossing the old North Eastern Railway in its surprisingly deep cutting, before bridging the river to reach the market place. The rain arrives again shortly after us.

Chapter 4

Red Kites, Red Squirrels
and Tea and Biscuits

From Kirkby Stephen to Appleby

Now clean, now hideous, mellow, now, now gruff
She swept, she hiss'd, she ripen'd and grew rough,
At Brougham, Pendragon, Appleby and Brough.

> Thomas Grey's parody of an inscription on the Countess
> of Cumberland's tomb, after having visited the grave of
> Lady Anne Clifford, at Appleby

Once again I can count my fellow passengers comfortably on
the fingers of one hand, as the train returns me efficiently from
Appleby to Kirkby Stephen. I have driven here from my overnight
stop chez David and Chris, high on the flanks of the Pennines,
from where it enjoys surely among the best views from any house
in the North of England. It sits not far above the former Belah
Viaduct on the old North Eastern Railway (NER). A picture on
their wall reminds us of what a magnificent sight it must once
have been, with its cast-iron lattice construction. It once carried
two tracks 60m above a deep ravine and was close to half a kilometre long. The line climbed at a challenging 1:60 to reach the
summit, which was just over of 425m – somewhat higher than
Ais Gill, on the S&C. Its structures were designed by Sir Thomas
Bouch, whose name was irrevocably tarnished by the collapse of

the badly built Tay Bridge. The iron viaducts were unceremoniously demolished with great haste after the NER line closed in 1963, a century after it was built. Had it survived, it would today rival the S&C for the title of England's most scenic line, even if the S&C trumped it for its overall engineering quality.

In Kirkby Stephen yesterday evening, we shared a birthday curry with David and Chris's son, landlord designate of the soon-to-be Old Forge micro-pub. When it does open, it will be Kirkby Stephen's second micro-pub – there might even be three, but I'm told that the Taggy Man is technically a 'small pub' rather than a micro-pub. So the second one is L'al Nook, which sits down a lane at the other end of the high street. David and Chris know the owners and feel the two establishments will complement each other, rather than compete. David explains that The Old Forge will feature keg beers from the family's own micro-brewery, in Brighton, while L'al Nook, he says, focuses on cask beers that have to be consumed over a weekend. Once the casks are empty, that's it for the week. I do think micro-pubs have brought so much more diversity to the whole concept of the pub, which is now steadily evolving away from outmoded pub estate models, with their Byzantine leasing rules, which seem carefully devised to penalise enterprising publicans.

Up at David and Chris's place, I'm finally able to open my present from John Bucknall: it is a set of beautiful historic etchings of Pendragon Castle. I feel deeply honoured. Talk turns to peregrines and their dietary habits, as Theo clambers cat-like onto Chris's lap. He need only learn to purr to finesse the deceit. I am pleased when the authoritative bird book on the living room shelf confirms my diagnosis of woodcock and also suggests peregrines like nothing better than a bit of game bird for lunch.

* * *

Walking the Line

I am walking today in boots, as my shoes remain too wet, despite a night by the dehumidifier. It is a sad fact of life that our feet get bigger as we age... if you think of walking as being like hammering a steak, you'll appreciate that the process is both inevitable and irreversible. It can manifest itself in painful conditions, like plantar fasciitis, which happens when your flatter feet are able to absorb less shock from the impact of walking. It used to trouble me when I was overweight, but I find that having most of your stomach removed as a remedy for cancer can also be quite useful for weight management, and it rarely troubles me any more.

My boots, which used to fit perfectly with a pair of hiking socks and a thinner pair beneath, are now snug with only a thinnish pair of sports socks. And I have a long day's walk ahead of me. It will begin on limestone and so should be dry underfoot. When Rob and I did this stretch (or most of it) some 11 years ago now, it began with a significant detour, as our route took in more of the Westmorland limestone by skirting the Smardale gorge to the west and entering Crosby Garrett beneath the impressive viaduct that defines the western end of what I remember as one of the most attractive villages in the Eden Valley.

I want to return to Crosby Garrett today, as the vicar there has recently installed not one but two memorials to navvies and their families who were buried in unmarked graves near the church-yard. Although the most dramatic way to approach the village is from Crosby Garrett Fell, with the viaduct framing the village in front of you, it represents a detour of probably three kilometres and I know that this is already a long day's walk. My route is fairly direct: a short distance down the busy road from the station, towards Kirkby Stephen, then via a walled lane that ascends the fell, from close by the old Iron Age hill fort of Croglam Castle.

The initial bit of A-road walking is inevitable: there's a good path now from the station 1.5km or so to the town, but my track up the fells can't easily be reached from it. Although the forecast hints at the possibility of rain later, the morning now features enough blue sky to clothe the legs of a shipful of sailors, in response to which I choose to discard the zippy bottoms of my walking trousers.

The lane up the fell is pretty overgrown in places, and lined with blackthorn, which promises a good sloe harvest in autumn. I emerge onto a high intake meadow, which, once crested, opens up a fine railway vista, with the line defining the edge of the open limestone landscape. All it needs is the arrival of a charter train, its loco in full steam as it begins its ascent of the upper valley.

A short stretch of road brings me to an architectural fault line, as I arrive at Smardale Hall, a grand 15th-century construction, seemingly in Scottish baronial style. Apparently it sits on the site of another tower house, like those I saw yesterday. Although mostly of limestone, I can see rather incongruous red sandstone intrusions here and there. All in all it's an impressive building in an attractive location, marred only by another industrial-scale untidy complex of farm buildings around it.

By the time I arrive at Smardale station, on the old NER, from Kirkby Stephen (East) to Tebay, I am emphatically in red sandstone country: the red sandstone that is the epitome of so much of Cumbria, and especially the part that used to be Westmorland.

Look on the map and the words that spring immediately to mind are 'Smardale? A station?!' There is really nothing at Smardale besides the hall – and nor was there ever, though you might generously say that the station is conveniently situated midway between the two 'significant' settlements of Waitby and Crosby Garrett. And the station itself is not just a token country halt, but comprises substantial buildings. It is now an attractive home, in the sturdy style found on the NER, although more likely built by the original owner of the line, the South Durham and Lancashire Union. The road here crosses a bridge above the station, and clearly signposted to either side are access points to the nature reserve in the gorge carved through the limestone by Scandal Beck.

You can walk along the old railway through the nature reserve, all the way to the NER's Smardale Gill Viaduct, and beyond, to Newbiggin-on-Lune. It is a delightful walk, as the railway is notched halfway up the steep-sided gorge amid mixed woodland, rich in wildlife. It occurs to me that, if walking the Settle–Carlisle Way, you could still, if you wished, make that detour, so as to arrive in Crosby Garrett from the fell, and beneath its viaduct. Once again, it would add more than three kilometres to your route but this would, arguably, make for an even more attractive walk than the one I mentioned earlier, via the limestone fell. There's just one slight problem at the moment…

The story behind this problem begins in the 1980s, when British Rail (BR), then owner of Smardale Gill Viaduct, wanted to demolish it because it had fallen into disrepair in much the same way as threatened the Ribblehead Viaduct: water ingress from a leaky deck, combined with freeze-thaw action had caused the outer part of one pier to collapse. It was saved by the specially created Northern Viaduct Trust after BR was refused permission to knock it down by a planning inquiry, following which the structure was listed by English Heritage. BR donated the viaduct and the £230,000 cost of demolition towards the £350,000 cost of restoration. It was a good solution all round – BR no longer had the liability for the magnificent 14-arch viaduct and Cumbria Wildlife Trust was able to link two sections of its nature reserve by means of a high-level footpath. All well and good, but in 2018 the handrails installed at the time of the restoration were deemed inadequate to meet more modern safety rules and the viaduct was closed, pending £50,000 being raised to replace them, most likely with something uglier.

Pending this being done, you can still do this walk, but will have to descend to Scandal Beck and climb back up 30m on the other side. At least that would afford you a different perspective on the structure, as it strides obliquely across the valley.

* * *

In my head, Scandal Beck flows south and west to join the River Lune, but descending to the footbridge that crosses it, near Chapel Well, I'm reminded that it actually flows north-east, to join the Eden, north of Kirkby Stephen. Without geological evidence to support this theory, it feels reasonable to infer that the gorge was cut during the Ice Age, perhaps draining a glacial or interglacial lake to the west of the limestone. Checking on the map, I see that the beck actually swings back eastward beyond the gorge and its source is on the western flanks of Wild Boar Fell, less than two kilometres from the Upper Eden.

From the beck, I climb a narrow hedge-lined road to its crest and eventually come to Crosby Garrett. The first memorial to the 30 S&C navvy casualties from the unmarked graves at the village's St Andrew's Church is to be found beneath the viaduct itself. It comprises three granite gate stoops of different sizes, representing a man, woman and child. The navvies' settlement here, in the tradition of the time, was called Balaclava, again after the Crimea. It bears a simple marble plaque, as does a similar single stone pillar in the churchyard itself.

St Andrew's sits atop a prominent hill, dubbed 'Crosby Fell'. I cannot determine whether the hill is a big lump of glacial debris or a protrusion of harder rock, but its dominance of the surrounding landscape is such that an Anglo-Saxon settlement predates the Norman church. Setting aside earlier prehistoric remains scattered across Crosby Garrett Fell for the moment, the village owes such fame as it may possess to the finding of a Roman helmet. This event occurred on the fell, on the way from the village to the Roman road, which runs south from near Penrith to a substantial Roman fort, near Tebay. The Crosby Garrett Helmet was found on the site of a Romano-British settlement and is thought to have possibly belonged to a local man who served with the Roman cavalry. It may have been more ceremonial than practical and was actually found by a detectorist, carefully hidden inside a stone structure.

The helmet sold at Christie's in 2010 for a cool £2.3 million to a private buyer, after Tullie House Museum, Carlisle, and the British Museum's joint bid fell short of the mark. It has nonetheless returned a couple of times to Carlisle for special exhibitions. It crosses my mind that a little bit of interpretation on the Roman past, pre-history and the railway here in Crosby Garrett wouldn't go amiss. It might include an explanation as to why the viaduct, now listed, comprises brick arches built at a skew above stone base pillars. Ian and Andrew Gordon, in their Dalesman Settle–Carlisle walk, also passed this way and were a little alarmed to find no pub. Now I do regard Crosby Garrett as among the most perfect of my Cumbrian villages to date, but a nice wee micro-pub and self-service museum would surely be just the ticket. There is also very occasional talk of bringing the station back to life, but it was among the first on the line to close, in 1952, and I am not really persuaded of the wisdom of reopening all the old halts, as there has to be a balance between getting there quickly and getting there at all, even on the slowest of stopping trains. Should I open a micro-pub in Crosby Garrett, my views on this subject may yet change.

The churchyard is my chosen venue for lunch, with the hefty tomb of one George Greenwood as my backrest: he died exactly 100 years before I was born. From my vantage I can see across the plain to the Pennines. Workmen in the house below me are playing loud music, which ought to detract from the serenity of the village, but somehow brings it to life instead.

As I wander round the church to the unmarked graves, a cheeky red squirrel appears in front of me: two in two days is good!

* * *

My plan for Crosby Garrett onwards is to head more or less east out of the village to rejoin the 'official' Settle–Carlisle Way (and indeed the Speakman-Morrison version) at Soulby. Convinced I know the correct road to take, I march briskly out of the village without checking the map again. After ten or 15 minutes, I see a tall railway bridge hove in to view – well, inasmuch as anything can 'hove' when you're travelling at walking pace. I'm puzzled as the only railway around here is the S&C, and that's behind me… isn't it? It is definitely a working railway, which narrows the options down to just one, so it's time to get the map out and check. Yes, I have left the village on a slightly west-of-north heading, instead of north-east.

Loath to backtrack and acknowledge having wasted precious time and the best part of two kilometres, I identify a route to Little Ormside, from where it is a tad below three kilometres of pleasant riverside walking into Appleby. I shall, in the process, trim about two kilometres off my originally intended course. All good, then!

Buoyed by a sense of relief that my failure to check the map has not cost me too dear (on the contrary), I stride forth with renewed purpose. Although there are no more than a few houses dotted around, a lot of these minor roads, which make for easy walking, bear names. I reach the end of Gallansay Lane and the eponymous Gallansay, where I make a right down Newlands Road. At the junction is a huge wild gooseberry bush and I make a mental note either to return to pick them in August or tip off friends in the valley. I take a track left along the top of a cutting after I recross the railway. As the track bears right, there's a warning that the footpath is closed during flooding. No such misfortune today, I reassure myself, as I enter a walled route alongside pasture, with horses.

The way is okay at first, if a little overgrown. Soon, however, nettles and thistles replace the more benign grasses and flowers, only in turn to be trumped by self-sown hazel and birch trees. Now it's not just scratched and stung legs, but arm scrapes and the risk of an eye-poke. At one point I have no choice but to scale the fence and its accompanying ditch until the overgrown apology for a footpath emerges into the pasture via something that may once have resembled a stile. I exchange pleasantries with the curious horses, eventually to emerge into Grassgill Bottom farm and its stables, where a young woman exercising some horses gives me a friendly wave. I wonder if she knows what a state the right of way is in. Or if she even cares.

I'm soon on the B-road that links Soulby with Appleby, but traffic remains very sparse. Appropriately enough for the time of COVID, it's called Mask Lane. A couple of council road repair lorries, parked up by the road, are the only sign that life does indeed go on. A couple of kilometres along the road and I take a track to the right, which should then take me left along woodland at the edge of Little Ormside Moor and into the village. I note from the map that the 'official' Settle–Carlisle Way at Little Ormside also duplicates Alfred Wainwright's 1938 Pennine Journey. If anyone were ever in any doubt as to the influence on our walking culture of the curmudgeonly Mr W, it is worth remembering that only he has ever succeeded in getting his routes named on maps, whether they be on rights of way or not, without any prior formal official endorsement.

I refer, of course, to his fine Coast to Coast Walk, generally preferred these days to 'official' long-distance routes like the Pennine Way. I doubt whether his Pennine Journey will ever share that special status, as it is a very long route, but you never know. *A Pennine Journey* is an interesting book, in that it allows the late A's prose, normally confined to little asides to illuminate his route illustrations, freer rein. Wainwright completed this journey – from Settle, up the Pennine flanks to the east, along the Roman Wall, and back down the western side of the hills – in September 1938.

He and his compatriots at this time felt 'sick, upset, nervous', little realising that they were standing at a crossroads in history, with a long, hard, terrible war ahead. Halfway through Wainwright's walk, Chamberlain went to Munich and returned with his famous, if useless, piece of paper and, back home, Wainwright 'found solace in memories of my escape to the hills.' And, to help his imagination return to such happier times, he wrote it all down. Somewhat remarkably, it was very nearly a full half-century later that he mentioned the existence of the manuscript to his publisher. It duly then appeared in 1986. 'Narrative non-fiction' may be the rather clumsy descriptor of such work in the publishing industry these days (the 'new journalism' of Truman Capote or Tom Wolfe being just so passé), but if you think it's a new, or even newish term, read *A Pennine Journey*. It offers an extraordinary contemporary perspective on life: from societal norms, such as male attitudes to women, to the everyday and mundane, like habitual and inevitable cigarettes. Looking again at the book I think how interesting it would be to follow in Wainwright's footsteps; stay in the inns he stayed in; meet the modern contemporaries of those he met more than 80 years ago.

But, unsurprisingly, I would not be the first: indeed, there is a Pennine Journey Supporters' Club, among whose aims is to achieve National Trail status for its 400 or so kilometres in time for its centenary. A guide to the route, illustrated in the Wainwright style, was published in 2010.

But back to the matter in hand: navigation. I am about to make another significant navigational error. Or, I am about to encounter my worst route obstructions yet. At the conclusion of today's walk, I shall be firmly in the camp of the latter belief. However, when I later seek to turn the day's events into prose, I am tempted to contemplate the unthinkable – that I was not precisely where I thought I was. The answer will become apparent only when I return to the location a few weeks later to make further checks.[9]

Anyway… as I was saying, I take a track on the right and look out for a sharp turn to the left, called New Road, after no more than half a kilometre. I look carefully at the shape of the land and of the plantation my left. I'm sure that I am where I think I am and conclude that the track has been planted over with barley. I follow the edge of the field, alongside the plantation, close to the stream marked on the map. I am confronted by a barbed wire fence. A farmer on his tractor shuttles the loom that is the next field, driving back and forth to turn the fresh mown hay, ready for baling. If am in the wrong place, surely he will jump from his tractor and shout 'Get orff of my land!' That he does not fills me with renewed confidence as to where I am, so I scale the fence and continue.

Thinking I must have turned left too soon, I then follow another track, over the beck and up the hill, which I'm still confident is Little Ormside Moor. I do this as I now believe the 'correct track', despite all cartographical evidence to the contrary, is ahead of me on the skyline. I reach said track but it peters out to my left, before entering woodland. Instead of heading for near certainly impregnable forest, I descend the grassy slope. A couple of hundred metres in front of me, a roe deer is grazing. I take a picture then pause to switch to a longer lens, but she's gone in a flash, taking the fence into the plantation while hardly breaking step.

I head for the corner of the field, but my way is blocked by a fence topped with barbed wire. I scale the fence with the help of a substantial oak tree and reward myself with a refreshment stop. Slightly remarkably, I have a 4G signal and so I see if I can confirm my location on Google Maps. It says that the inconsequential watercourse next to me is Greenber Syke – a trickle that idles back the way I have come, to eventually, after about two kilometres, end its short life in Bleatarn. I am at the watershed between the Bleatarn catchment and the somewhat more significant one of the River Eden. More importantly, I am just one field and one gate away from the correct route. As I gather my bits and bobs to continue I'm treated to the fine sight of a red kite and a buzzard sharing a thermal. What a magnificent addition the red kite is to our skies. This is the second I have ever seen in the Eden Valley, the previous one being perhaps as many as ten years previously.

It is not clear from precisely which reintroduced population Eden Valley red kites may have come. These fine birds are quite gregarious and so do not colonise new locations quite as quickly as might be expected, especially as some gamekeepers persecute them in an effort to protect grouse chicks, even though red kites feed mainly on carrion and are not thought to threaten grouse. Their prevalent live prey is earthworms, though they may take rodents so I guess, by extension, grouse chicks are possible, if unlikely. But that does not excuse illegal shooting and poisoning. So, given the number of grouse moors on the Pennines, it seems not all that likely that the Eden Valley birds have made it here from the east of the country. Which means that they have more likely come either from Dumfries and Galloway, or from Grizedale Forest, in the South Lakes.

Walking the Line

The website *Raptor Politics* reveals that the phased release of birds in Grizedale led, in 2014, to the first red kite chicks to hatch in Cumbria since 1860. That was near Coniston, when three chicks were successfully raised. Back in 1860, a pair of red kites successfully raised chicks, here in the Eden Valley, near Armathwaite. How wonderful to see them back in the valley, just a few kilometres from that last breeding success. Or, maybe they've just been lying low here for the past 180 years…

Of course, because red kites feed on carrion, it's very easy to tempt them into your garden with meat and other scraps and, just as with urban foxes, such feeding may breed its own problems. Feeding wild animals that don't really need it can only encourage population growth beyond the level that the local environment can naturally sustain, and there are reports that human intervention in the Chilterns may yet push the current 600 breeding pairs there to, or beyond, a sustainable level.

* * *

Through the gate and back on the 'official' route, I'm quickly up through the gears and passing the end of the track that I should have been on. However, even at this stage, I'm still thinking 'blocked footpaths' rather than 'bad navigation'. I enter Little Ormside by the prosaically named Terrys Farm [sic]. It is fronted by a quite magnificent cedar of Lebanon. This kind of tree may enjoy hot summers in its natural home, but it can withstand cold winter temperatures and this one appears to thrive in the Eden Valley, even though, back in Lebanon, it is on the International Union for the Conservation of Nature's Red List, meaning it is 'vulnerable' and likely to become endangered, because of deforestation at the higher altitudes at which it thrives.

The cedar of Lebanon is important in many ancient stories and belief systems, not least the Jewish and Christian traditions. Moses told Hebrew priests to use its bark in the treatment of leprosy and the tree features in Psalm 92: 'The righteous will flourish like a palm tree, and grow like a cedar in Lebanon.' It is also the tree that sits at the very centre of the Lebanese flag, which one might hope would afford it some additional protection at such difficult times for it.

Great Ormside, once a stop on the S&C, proves another improbably attractive little village, as my route meanders round the back of the settlement and along the rim of and across a busy little gorge, called Jeremy Gill, before following the Eden – now broad and tranquil – through woodland then pasture and, finally, parkland, to enter Appleby at the top of the hill by the castle. Or, as I choose to do, by sticking closer to the river and crossing on the footbridge beside the ford, famous as the location at which Gypsies and Travellers wash their horses during the annual fair for which the town is famed. This year, however, for the first time in recent memory, there is no Appleby Horse Fair, thanks to COVID. But of Gypsy and Traveller life and culture, more later. (*Note*: from here on, I mostly use 'Gypsy', as this remains the term most favoured by this community at the time of writing.)

I return to the station by the elevated road, from which vantage I recall watching some of the bareback horsey antics at the Fair a few years ago.

* * *

My day is not yet done: I have a meeting with a surviving descendant of Lady Anne herself: Anthony Charles Sackville Tufton, Sixth Baron Hothfield. It's a pleasant, windless, sunny summer's evening as I drive the few kilometres to the speck on the map that is the village of Drybeck. My destination is Drybeck Hall, which is shown on the map with that wiggly script that denotes a historic building. As 'halls' go, Drybeck is actually fairly unprepossessing – it's a long, two-storey, 17th century house of the customary red sandstone, with mullioned windows.

Anthony, casually dressed in checked shirt, blue jumper and beige chinos, ushers me beneath an arch to sit me on a reclining chair by a garden table, while he goes to fetch tea and biscuits. We are going to have a socially distanced outdoor chat, as pre-agreed. I wonder briefly if, having permitted my heavily taxed body to subside into the chair, I will ever be able to get up out of it again. I'm being served by a baron in a truly lovely spot: Drybeck Hall's beautifully tended garden sits proud, quite high above the road below. The view across the valley of Dry Beck is calming, attractive and tranquil. When my tea and lovely dippy biscuits arrive, I feel the glue attaching my bottom to my seat begin to set even more firmly.

Anthony is a delightful host, with a friendly and relaxed demeanour and a sprightly look that defies his four score years. I can't help but like him as he begins to unfold the story of his Cifford ancestry, in regard to which he exudes real pride, not to mention immense respect for Lady Anne and the principles she established, which have passed down through generations of subsequent Cliffords. Indeed, Anthony is the current chair of the trustees of the almshouses that Lady Anne built in Appleby to provide a roof for the poor widows of the town. Her legacy lives on, albeit with a tweak: 'We do take divorcees now as well!' Anthony says.

Lady Anne was his eighth great grandmother, meaning he is a tenth generation Clifford. Of course, Appleby Castle was among Lady Anne's prized possessions: she rebuilt it in the 1650s after it was partly demolished after being besieged by the Roundheads in the second English Civil War. The castle has been in private ownership for some decades now and is currently the private home of the Nightingale family, so the family seat is now the rather more modest Drybeck Hall.

From Kirkby Stephen to Appleby

'We didn't inherit the castle,' Anthony says. 'We bought back a bit of the family estate here: my father and my uncle put their heads together and they were allowed to put in a bid to buy some of it.' Today the estate still includes high land at North Stainmore, just a stone's throw from David and Chris's place, where I stayed last night, and David says that the Tufton name features prominently in the deeds to their home. Indeed, the Tufton Arms in Appleby is a reminder that this branch of Lady Anne's descendancy is alive and well and living near Appleby today.

My main reason for meeting up with Anthony today is to see the bronze maquette of Lady Anne, created by a local sculptor, Diane Lawrenson. Diane, who lives in the village of Winton, just outside Kirkby Stephen, likes iconic female figures, and wants to realise a statue of Lady Anne for public display in Kirkby Stephen. The idea of creating and selling the maquettes is to raise sufficient funds to achieve the overarching objective, of which more shortly.

'I am very, very pleased to be involved with this statue, which is being put into the market square,' Anthony tells me. 'It will be the only existing statue of Lady Anne Clifford, who is a very important lady in this neighbourhood. She is still talked about as if she was here only yesterday.' He asserts that she was 'a very early feminist' because of her determination to fight her disinheritance, and her refusal to give up 'her Westmorland'.

Anthony is also the heir to a proportion of Lady Anne's extensive collection of writings, the most significant part of the others being in the county archive at Kendal.

I could happily spend more time in Anthony's lovely company, but food and rest are banging at my door, and so I wave farewell as I head back towards Appleby and onward to Langwathby. I pause as I pass through Appleby to take a look at Lady Anne's almshouses. They are sturdy little cottages, which one might call 'highly desirable' by today's standards. They must have been quite luxurious back in the 17th century.

* * *

Given that Lady Anne wrote so much, you'd be forgiven for asking where, precisely, her work sits within the great body of English literature. Well, let's begin by saying that her legacy is no stranger to academic examination. For starters, there's the extensive collection of her work, with commentary, assembled by the now late D.J.H. Clifford in a book called, simply, *The Diaries of Lady Anne Clifford*.

'It's quite heavy going,' says a smiling Anthony Hothfield of the collection, and I'm pleased, as I have struggled with some of it. If Lady Anne were alive today, I fear she might be a truly maddening member of the Twitterati, recording the minutiae of each day and sharing them with the world at large. Though, to be fair, I think that much of what she wrote in her diaries was never intended for broader public consumption.

D.J.H. Clifford presents Lady Anne's diaries in four sections, from 1603 through to her death in 1676, reflecting the fact that her diaries comprised several separate manuscripts, each now residing in four or five different places. He calls these respectively *The Knole Diary, The Years Between, The Kendal Diary* and *The Last Months*.

The Knole Diary chronicles some of Lady Anne's time when married to her first husband, Richard Sackville, whose country seat was at Knole, near Sevenoaks. It now forms part of the Sackville Collection, in the Kent County Record Office, at Maidstone. In it she alludes to her ongoing battles with her uncle and the flighty, spendthrift Sackville, third Earl of Dorset, as she sought to lay hands on her inheritance. *The Years Between* comprises the manuscripts now held by Anthony Hothfield, as well as a modest volume at the British Library. *The Kendal Diary* provides the most complete and extensive section and is in the Cumbria County Records Office, at Kendal. The original diary relating to her final months is in the care of the Hasell-McCosh family, whose stately home, at Dalemain, near Ullswater, is perhaps best known as the venue for the annual World Marmalade Awards, at which – I have to tell you – two of my own preserves have had the honour of being highly commended. These were my Last Days Of The Raj very spicy marmalade, and my Thor's Breakfast, featuring hedgerow fruit and nuts that the Viking settlers might have put in their jam.

I can imagine it was no mean task for D.J.H. Clifford to assemble all these diverse pieces of the Clifford jigsaw but he has done so in such a way as to create, if not an autobiography, then at least a near complete record of Lady Anne's life in her own words. He adds his own occasional commentary, so as to provide context. Thus, he opens *The Years Between* section with Lady Anne's motto: 'Preserve your Loyalties, Defend your Rights', which seems a suitably apt summary of her application.

He writes thus in his introduction to *The Years Between*: 'No notes of Lady Anne's have survived covering the years 1620, 1621 and 1622, so other sources will have to be relied upon to continue the story.'

With a degree of understatement, D.J.H. notes that Lady Anne 'became very depressed at the successive deaths of her three little boys'. Not only was her melancholy 'for the obvious maternal reasons', but these deaths brought into sharp relief the fact that her brother-in-law, Sir Edward Sackville, the Earl of Dorset, whom she disliked with some gusto, still remained her husband's heir.

Thanks to his extravagant living, Sackville faced a decline in health that belied his tender 34 years, observes D.J.H., but supporting such largesse meant he was also heavily in debt, to the point that he was obliged to sell or lease most of the Sackville properties. D.J.H. quotes Edward Hyde, Earl of Clarendon (1609–74) thus: '[Sackville's] excess of expenditure in all the ways to which money could be applied was such, that he so entirely consumed almost the whole of the great fortune descended to him, that when he was forced to leave the title to his younger brother, he left, in a manner, nothing to support him.'

Lady Anne found greater cause for optimism on the female side of her legacy, as D.J.H. records: 'Her fifth child, Isabella, was born in 1622, and both she and her sister Margaret, referred to as 'The Child' in *The Knole Diary*, grew up, married well, and were a constant source of pride to their mother.'

Of *The Kendal Diary* – a continuous record right up to within three months of Lady Anne's death – D.J.H. writes: 'Here we have the private thoughts of an ageing, stubborn and "Proud Northern Lady", as Martin Holmes [a biographer of Lady Anne] has so aptly called her.'

He perceives an Anne who is, by this stage of her life, largely at peace with the world, her daughters having happily married and produced many grandchildren, of whom she is obviously very fond. 'They visit her regularly,' D.J.H. writes, 'and she is often in touch with them by letter. Their births, marriages and deaths are all minutely recorded. Anne hardly makes any mention of the world outside her own domain. There is scant mention of international or even national events, in contrast to the records made by her contemporaries Pepys and Evelyn.'

Such 'peace' in those days, however, seems to have been relative, as Lady Anne herself records:

And by a Letter I received this morning from my Daughter Thanet dated the 30th of December I came to know that she is much troubled with Paine in the head, but all that her Posterity are well, and that Lord Hatton was married to his second wife Mrs Yelverton the 21st day of that month, being St Thomas' Day; his first wife being my Grandchilde who was blown up with Gunpowder in ye Isle of Guernsey.

The greater tragedy here is that it appears the death of said grandchild was the result not of illness or hostilities, but of a lightning strike on the gunpowder store at Castle Cornet on the island, on December 30, 1672. This caused a mighty explosion and fire and Lady Cecilia Hatton (née Tufton) was killed by falling masonry after she ran to the nursery to pray. Among the six others who perished in the carnage was her mother-in-law, the Lady Dowager, though her husband, Lord Hatton, survived, as witnessed by Lady Anne's note of his subsequent remarriage.

D.J.H. is even bold enough to quote Lady Anne in the same sentence as Pepys and Evelyn. The latter, for those who don't know (myself included, until recently), was an English writer, gardener and diarist, whose writings covered a remarkable 66 years of his life up to his death in 1706. His family had become wealthy through the production of gunpowder and, who knows, they may have been indirectly involved in the death of Lady Anne's granddaughter.

While Lady Anne tended to steer clear, to some extent, of politics, Evelyn wrote in depth about major events of the time, including the Fire of London, the Plague, the rise of Oliver Cromwell and the execution of Charles I. That Pepys remains more widely recognised today is attributed to his greater depth and focus on a specific period of time – the decade beginning 1660.

I suspect that even Lady Anne herself might be flattered to find herself mentioned in such company, not least because – as I have said previously – she was writing for different, less public, reasons.

I do think that the title of a student thesis, written by Jenisha Sabaratnam, an undergraduate at the University of Berkeley, rather nicely casts a different light on the achievements of Lady Anne – 'Lady Anne Clifford: From Idealized Gender Warrior to Exceptional Literary Bureaucrat'.[10]

We have already noted that Lady Anne has proved to be of much interest among American feminists, and this student seeks to interpret the truth in a slightly different context. She writes:

> This essay proposes that Lady Anne Clifford was exceptional in a distinctive way. She was a literary bureaucrat, a woman who chose to compile and publish a large number of personal and official documents in an attempt to record the events and struggles of her life. In fact, it is principally for this reason that feminist and gender historians and scholars have been able to learn so much about Anne in the first place, and iron-ically, to justify the arguments they have created in regards to her. It is only unfortunate that in Anne's attempts to leave behind her own sources for the future, she has been subjected to a narrowed assessment of understanding, the value of her accomplishments misinterpreted, and the truth of her story inaccurately studied for decades.

Scholars in this country are also very interested in Lady Anne and her legacy, nowhere more so than at the University of Huddersfield. Indeed – copious though Lady Anne's writings are – academics have been steadily pushing up the word count in the 'about Lady Anne' column, perhaps in subconscious pursuit of the giddy total in the 'by Lady Anne' column. All this tends only to confirm that, whether through what she did or what she wrote, Lady Anne remains a source of fascination nearly 350 years after her death. Professor Jessica May, at Huddersfield, has written extensively on Lady Anne's 'marriage strategies', her family politics and 'female alliances', among other subjects, these papers being published in learned journals from here to Nebraska. In 2018, Manchester University Press published her book, *Anne Clifford's Autobiographical Writing*, with the aim of bringing together *all* her known autobiographical texts, suitably annotated. She notes that the late Vita Sackville-West – herself a descendant of Lady Anne's first brother-in-law, Edward Sackville – was ahead of D.J.H. in assembling some of Lady Anne's diaries for publication, back in 1923. All of which academic tittle-tattle leads neatly to Virginia Woolf. Where else?

A poet, novelist and gardener, Sackville-West was also Woolf's lover. Woolf's *Orlando: A Biography*, in which the hero changes sex to become the heroine, and goes on to immortality (or thereabouts), is generally presumed to be based upon Vita Sackville-West's character. Sackville-West was actually born at Knole House, and so the familial and geographical connections make it perhaps inevitable that some scholars might speculate that the true inspiration for Orlando was not, or at least was not only, Vita Sackville-West, but (also) Lady Anne herself. Nicky Hallett, down the road from Huddersfield at the University of Sheffield, cites also the connection that both women were 'dispossessed of their estates by patriarchal legal process' (primogeniture).

In the abstract to her paper, *Anne Clifford as Orlando: Virginia Woolf's Feminist Historiology and Women's Biography*, she writes: 'This article makes a new and specific identification for a source of the young Orlando's persona in Anne Clifford (1590–1676), a Sackville Elizabethan ancestor. For this connection there is ample, but until now largely ignored, evidence in the text and manuscript of *Orlando* and in other work by Virginia Woolf, and by Anne Clifford and Vita Sackville-West themselves.' She evidences this by citing pre-publication drafts of *Orlando*, in which Lady Anne is actually named. In the final version, the Lady Anne character has, however, been transposed into Orlando's mother.

Nicky Hallett's paper appeared in *Women's History Review*, in 1995. I do find academic study of historic characters in literature and elsewhere fascinating – indeed, we are back here to the Brontë/Heathcliff question. But unlike journalism, which deals with contemporary subjects and living people, neither Lady Anne nor Emily Brontë (nor Virginia Woolf, nor Rita Sackville-West) is in a position to respond. Were Lady Anne able to comment on her new androgynous persona from beyond the grave, she might perhaps pronounce: 'I am most grievously perplexed to learn today that I am charged with having commenced my life, not as woman born of woman, but as a man. Let no person hereby attest to the supposed truth of this manifest falsehood.'

* * *

A couple of weeks after my visit to Drybeck Hall, I am keen to meet the creative mind behind Anthony Hothfield's maquette, so I take a little trip to the village of Winton, just outside Kirkby Stephen. I recall Winton, which is one of several 'satellite' villages around Kirkby, from my time living at Hawes – they used to do a grand Sunday lunch at The Bay Horse back in the 1990s, and I'm pleased to note that it continues to enjoy five-star reviews more than a quarter of a century later.

Winton is also on the route of the 'official' Settle–Carlisle Way, which heads roughly east out of town, before turning north. The passage of time has created in my mind a false picture of Winton: quite simply, I don't recall at all the pretty village green, where The Bay Horse stands. I now have to reappraise the entire place as it is actually another super-lovely Eden Valley village, which I had quite forgotten. And, amid that super-loveliness, is the garden of Diane Lawrenson.

We are meeting Diane in her green enclave as her husband, Kevin Howley, who makes the moulds for her bronze castings, is having to shield during the pandemic. It is a beautiful little cottage garden, full of birds and birdsong and there is a little gazebo overlooking a small pond, lined with reeds and rushes. At this time, there is a lot of talk about the impact on mental health of protecting people's physical health, through measures like shielding, or indeed, keeping children at home. I reflect that, if nothing else, Kevin can at least enjoy this beautiful space.

Diane is shy, if quite intense, and I quickly recognise that her relationship with place is very powerful. In a previous life she lived at Haworth, and learned her craft at nearby Keighley College of Art, and she was steeped in and fascinated by the lives of the Brontës. 'Being in Haworth, it was all Brontë, Brontë, Brontë, and Lady Anne was on the periphery.' Despite not being in 'Brontë country', what Winton offered was the opportunity to create ample studio space – in large outbuildings, just off the garden.

It also provided the opportunity to engage with a prominent literary woman from 200 years before the Brontë sisters. 'I looked at trying to encapsulate a woman who was intelligent and had a great duty to her family, and I imagined a woman then becoming her husband's "property".

'Her husband was bit of a wastrel, a bit of a gambler,' she continues, with some understatement. 'She determined to do right by her family, her mother and her offspring, and she seemed to have a sense of humour. I thought: "This is a tall order!" I just thought that the subject was too vast to capture – an aristocratic woman who was determined and yet she was a fair and caring person, who built almshouses, little churches and Sunday schools.

'All the fight was going on before she arrived here: it was after the English Civil War and a lot of land had been confiscated.'

But it was a 'confiscation' of a different kind that really stirred Diane to action. That was when the Yorkshire Dales National Park moved to add much of the old county of Westmorland to the area under its protection. 'I remember someone saying to me: "They think we are Yorkshire but we are not!" They had lost their Westmorland identity. People who come here imagine that they are still in Yorkshire – all of a sudden we are just the "bit between the Dales and the Lake District" and we have no identity.' To be fair to the national park, it was government in London back in 1974 that did away with Westmorland, just as it facilitated the annexation by Cumbria of so much of Yorkshire. And the new signage for the extended national park here does at least bear the title of 'Westmorland Dales' as its most prominent feature.

Diane continues: 'I think that the people reflect the area: they are curious and very supportive, lovely people. So, when everything was going to go, including the Tourist Information Centre, I thought: everyone's doing their bit in this place to keep it going… what can *I* do? And so I looked back at Lady Anne and I did a little figure and said: "What do you think about that?"'

And so was born the idea of remembering the great lady by means of a statue in the market place, not far from the Tourist Information Centre (which did not close, and continues in business, thanks to the town council). The completed Lady Anne will look similar to, but not identical to Anthony's maquette, which is, of course, a reflection of the artist's developing interpretation of her subject at the time.

'She was a very, very tiny lady – she was about 4ft 10ins, but everyone was quite small then. But she has got to actually stand out, so I made her so she would not get lost in the crowd – she'll be just short of 7ft on her plinth.'

From Kirkby Stephen to Appleby

I am talking to Diane beside a bust of a woman, which sits on a modest plinth in the middle of the lawn and I'm curious to know who she is. Diane does not tell me the precise identity of the model, but says: 'I borrowed a little bit of her feet, hands, toes for Lady Anne and I was a bit bossy at times and she [the bust] is a little thank you to her.'

And so we move on to a different part of Diane's little estate: the summerhouse and adjoining workshop. In the former is one of those suspended, shell-shaped chairs; the room is full of light and inspiration and a few lines from a verse of Wordsworth's collection of five poems that feature the imagined romantic persona of Lucy are on a plaque on the wall:

I travell'd among unknown men
In lands beyond the sea;
Nor England did I know till then
What love I bore to thee.

And then we enter the workshop and I suddenly see another side to Diane: a big display on the wall is entitled 'Creation of a Bronze'. Except that it isn't – for the English here is subordinate to Welsh: *Creun Cerfluniaeth Efydd*. It turns out she is a member of the Royal Cambrian Academy, a centre of excellence for artists, based in Conwy. 'I lived in North Wales as a child and you must have a Welsh connection,' explains Diane.

There are a few pieces of Diane's work in different parts of the room and I'm immediately drawn to a statue of an old lady, peering into her bag, at the bottom of which can be found a hand mirror. I believe it's called 'Mortal Coil' and it seems to positively scream out for empathy. 'That's her whole life in the bag,' Diane says.

Then, in another corner, are statues of three women. I don't really need to ask: they are Anne, Charlotte and Emily, and Emily is the one with a slightly aloof posture. I ask Diane what she thinks of the idea that Emily's Heathcliff was modelled on Richard Sutton. She chuckles and says: 'There's only one person that Emily modelled Heathcliff on and that's herself!'

I think this might be a nice note on which to sally forth, but there is another treat in store: Diane has a kind of invitation-only little room, in which she hangs some of her own pictures, which are a combination of pastels and oils. I feel privileged for the invitation as her work carries with it a lot of her own personality and emotions. And quite a lot more of the Brontës! I wonder if Lady Anne may one day find quite as much space in Diane's heart.

Chapter 5

Return of the Pied Piper, the Underworld and Whirly Birds

From Appleby to Langwathby

Skidding wildly down the slippery ramp
young Gypsy lads and lasses ride bareback
on their glistening feral mounts
into the baptismal waters of the River Eden
these aspiring Romany guardians of the genus equus
these water gods and nymphs of this tribal gathering
these natural spiritual acolytes in this ancient ritual
arrogantly parade their pride and expertise
before an admiring audience of onlookers
all deeply envious of their youth their lifestyle
and the sheer wild hedonism of their existence
Appleby Horse Fair by Mick Yates

As is the norm in the time of COVID, I entered the pub yesterday via one door and left this morning by another... Don't take that the wrong way – I certainly haven't been drinking for twenty-four hours – but I have spent a very comfortable night at the Shepherds Inn, on the village green at Langwathby. Last night I drank a good pint and a glass of sauvignon blanc, which turned out to be from Romania. It was excellent, with none of the slightly sulphurous taste that can sometimes come through. But then mine host, Stephen Wilcock, ought to know a thing or two about wine – he was once the sommelier at Sharrow Bay, the celebrated Lake District country house hotel on the shore of Ullswater.

Today my walk will start from Appleby, and the display board at Langwathby station duly tells me that the year is 2014 and the time is, recurrently, 0805. My train pulls in at the correct time of 0852 and arrives, without fuss, at Appleby, as scheduled, at 0905, thus once again proving that the real problem with rail punctuality is passengers. Take them away and life is just so, so much easier.

My plan is to diverge from both the Morrison-Speakman route and from the 'official' Settle–Carlisle Way. I mentioned in the Introduction to this book how, when walking this section of the route back in 2009, I became hopelessly lost in a recently planted forest. However, it wasn't just the getting lost that had been my problem that day. For the privilege of taking in the admirable village of Dufton and its excellent pub, you have to add close to two kilometres to the route. What really took the biscuit for me 11 years ago, however, was finding myself heading due south to arrive in the village of Long Marton, which is only just north of Appleby. When I look at the map now I do struggle to understand why I did it this way, as there is a perfectly good footpath direct from Dufton to Long Marton. My recollection is that I particularly wanted to route the walk via Dufton so as to meet the Pennine Way there, as we were trying to create such commonalities so as to assist in another project, which was to create a collection of suitable accommodation providers along the major long distance footpaths in the North.

Anyway, today I have chosen to take a route via the old Roman road because I know this to be both good walking and direct. But I shan't leave Dufton without mention of the remarkable Ron and Angela Barker, who, until quite recently, ran High Cup Winery, at Keisley, just a smidge beyond Dufton. I got to know them shortly before I heard a story on the radio in 2010 about people making wine out of grapes growing in their London gardens. With a couple of vines on the south-facing front wall of our home in Durham, I thought I could do the same to produce Northumbrian Wine from grapes grown across the North East.

I approached Ron to see if he might be our winemaker as, having tried his fruit wines, I knew his abilities. A couple of newspaper appeals later and I had pledges from enough growers to amass plenty of grapes and so, come autumn, headed over the Pennines with 25kg of fruit. We made wine from Northumbrian grapes for five or six years – it was a very drinkable blush wine, great on summer evenings. Ron then followed up by launching his own Eden Valley wine, similarly the produce of home growers in the valley, though, unlike our east of Pennines variety, all the Cumbrian grapes were grown under glass, whereas ours were a mixture of indoor and outdoor.

Remarkably, the winery did, at various times, even grow its own grapes, fully 250m above sea level, on the spring line of the Pennines. Ron said he would get a decent harvest one year in three. His and Angela's venture was in the outbuildings of a beautiful farmhouse, with some of the finest views in the valley, across to the mountains of the Lake District. They bought the farm at the height of the foot and mouth disease in 2001, and not only did they create the winery there, but they also installed an art gallery and tourist information point.

Then, in 2017, I think, after Ron had suffered a minor stroke, they decided to give up winemaking, sell off their stock and sell the house, so as to be able to live nearer their growing tribe of grandchildren. We had endured a couple of poor grape harvests and it felt like the right time to bring down the curtain on Northumbrian Wine too. Ron and Angela's departure formally brings to a close what was a fun episode in my own life but, somewhat more importantly, marks the loss of what was, in the shape of their lovely fruit wines, a wonderful asset to both tourism and to the breadth of Cumbria's renowned local food produce. I reflect that Ron and Angela came to Cumbria at the height of an animal plague, then left during a human one.

*　*　*

As I cross the busy A66 on the way out of Appleby, I reflect on the fact that, for the first time in many years, the town has not hosted its famous Horse Fair this year. The fair has no parallel in the UK (there is a much smaller event twice yearly at Stow-on-the-Wold) and attracts thousands of Gypsies and Travellers each June. Its influence is felt a long way from Appleby as traditional horse-drawn caravans make their way to the town. You'll see them processing over the Pennines on the A66; you'll see them camped on verges all over the North. This year, in the absence of the fair, a couple of caravans even camped by a roundabout on the edge of the estate where I live, in Durham City.

County Durham, like many parts of the country, has a large Gypsy population. Indeed, I often think that Gypsies live invisible lives in full sight of the population at large. A House of Commons paper in 2019 said that about 63,000 people in the UK self-identified as Gypsy in the most recent census, but it concedes that this is likely to be an underestimate. I would suggest it is likely to be a hugely significant underestimate, as Traveller lifestyles and formal state activity like data collection are not easy bedfellows.

The Romani are an ethnically distinct people who spoke their own language until the 19th century. They migrated west from India hundreds of years ago, but the travelling community does also include travelling people of non-Romani heritage. So, the Appleby Horse Fair attracts a wider spectrum of travelling people than just 'true Romani', and this is especially the case since the growth of social media.

These days it is not just Appleby that 'enjoys' a love-hate relationship with the Horse Fair, but communities the length of the Eden Valley and beyond. As the likes of Billy Welch, self-styled 'King of the Gypsies', is always at pains to point out, anti-social hangers-on who cause trouble in Kirkby Stephen or sleepy Eden villages are unwelcome among those who value the true Gypsy tradition.

It is remarkable the extent to which people at large are ignorant of the ways of this community, and it is questionable whether the likes of Channel 4's *My Big Fat Gypsy Wedding* has done anything at all to address such ignorance. Even 'serious' TV documentaries, such as a recent one that used flawed statistical analysis to look at criminality on a Travellers' site, add little to the collective knowledge.

My own induction into some aspects of the lives of Gypsies and the world of travelling showmen came when I was a young reporter, in Darlington. One of my first big jobs on arriving at the old *Evening Despatch* was to cover the trial for murder of Lawrence Wood, a Gypsy horse dealer from East Durham. It was also one of those cases that inevitably captured the more salacious side of the public imagination: attractive young woman marries wealthy travelling showman 40 years her senior; has an affair with a dashing Gypsy man, 11 years her junior; husband takes out life insurance on his young wife shortly before her incinerated body is found in the back of a burnt-out gold coloured car...

It was July 1979 when Lawrence Wood found himself in the dock accused of murdering his (by then) ex-lover, Miriam Culene, young wife of elderly showman Fred Culene. The trial took a great many twists and turns and the Crown's case was that the accused had got tired of Miriam and murdered her.

It all seemed a bit too easy for the prosecution, and so it turned out… In the course of researching background for publication after the trial, one of our reporters learned that a prosecution witness had been pressured into providing an alibi for Fred Culene's sons at the time of his wife's murder. This bombshell revelation led to the trial being halted and, in the end, the jury found Lawrence Wood not guilty.

I caught up with Lawrence Wood and his lurchers in the shabby East Durham pit village he called home, after the trial, and once again asked myself whether he might have been capable of murder. Our meeting served only to reinforce my view that, as a semi-literate boy from a disadvantaged background, he'd been an easy fall guy and there were others with stronger motives.

In the course of my own background research, while Wood was still in the dock, I did learn a little of the way travelling people lived then: I have an abiding memory of the dingy squalor of a vast caravan encampment on the north side of Doncaster. In those days such locations were as near to shanty towns as you'd find in this country – local authorities were obliged to provide adequate sites for travellers, but not all did and there were not enough sites to meet demand. Not much appears to have changed… a report by the Equality and Human Rights Commission in 2019 stated that despite some instances of good practice by local authorities, they have often failed to provide sufficient sites, 'and the lack of suitable and secure accommodation underpins many of the other inequalities that Gypsies and Travellers encounter'.

As I say, leading invisible lives in full view of a population that prefers not to see. I think the trouble is that some people find it too easy to distrust those whose heritage is different, or who choose to live a different lifestyle. At the root of the problem is the simple fact that an itinerant lifestyle does not fit neatly with most aspects of a society built around the concept that a fixed address is an intrinsic part of who we are as individuals. That fixed address is crucial to everything from paying your taxes and receiving your benefits, to ensuring that your children get an education. By not having a permanent address you may struggle to gain access to society's broader benefits but, perhaps worse, a section of the population will conclude that you're not 'paying your way'; in short, that you're not part of society. From there, it's but a small step to the kind of demonisation of Romani and Travellers as a community, of which we are all too familiar.

But back to Appleby: somehow, every June (except 2020), hundreds of ornate traditional horse-drawn caravans emerge as if by magic and make their way to Appleby. I never cease to marvel at their sheer number and I still have no satisfactory answer to where these caravans, and the families they contain, are hidden for the other months of the year. I wish I could speak with absolute authority on the subject, but my Romani research has been perhaps the biggest casualty with regards to my investigations in the time of COVID. But, for the record, the Gypsy caravan comes in many different varieties but has only been the preferred means of transport for the past 150 years or so. Called a vardo (from the original Persian, *vardon*), it can travel about 25km or so in a day, so this can, of course, add to the impression of caravans everywhere: they are simply on the road somewhat longer than the cars that flash past them on the Pennines.

Few of the original models from early last century or earlier have survived the triple tests of time, woodworm and weather, but there's at least one company building them, in Norfolk. However, when I speak to Laurence Ward, the owner of the Gypsy Caravan Company, he tells me that as near as damnit 100% of his business is for people who are neither Romani nor Travellers. 'We're not really selling to Travellers and, to be honest, they probably wouldn't buy from us. My guess is that it's the same old caravans circulating within that community. In the last five to seven years, with *glamping'* – his rather weary emphasis – 'a lot of people have hit on Gypsy caravans, yurts and so on as an interesting way of offering accommodation.' So, I'm none the wiser as to finding out how the current, seemingly significant, 'population' of vardos is actually sustained or even expanded.

Most of the vardos you'll see on the road are of the 'bender' variety, comprising a cart chassis, with a part-oval, canvas-covered, bowed upper living area. I see them as a crucial accessory for those visiting the Appleby Horse Fair as a means of reasserting their cultural identity. The other traditional Gypsy vehicle, of course, is the sulky, or horse-drawn carriage. In my reporter days there'd often be tales of unofficial sulky races on the A66 at Appleby, usually in the early hours of the morning before the traffic built. When I lived at Hawes, the annual (though now defunct) Hawes Sports was the biggest thing in town after the sheep sales and the gala. It was an evening of harness racing, or trotting, and there'd be bookies on the course and all the paraphernalia of a mainstream racing event, though I was frequently told that the insiders knew all the likely winners, so I was wasting my cash.

When I visited the Fair once in the 1980s, the Gypsies were camped behind a tall wire fence on the wrong side of the A66. It looked like an internment camp. Over the years, various approaches to policing the fair have been tried, ranging from the light touch to the hopelessly heavy-handed, the latter exemplified by the idea of penning everybody into a compound. It didn't work and didn't last, and we are, today, in a period of relatively laid-back policing. The primary emphasis is on protecting public safety. I recall seeing a TV documentary in which the female officer in charge was working with the community to ensure that the river level was safe, before giving the green light for horses to be washed in the ford by the bridge at Appleby, in the traditional manner.

That documentary also featured a rather grumpy older gentleman who had, if I recall, retired to Appleby and said that he was utterly miserable during Horse Fair week. My response to that is: if you can't put up with it for a week or two, then go on holiday at that time, or don't choose to live in Appleby in the first place. It's like moving to the Isle of Man and complaining about motorbikes in TT week. By and large, the two communities rub along okay in Appleby during the fair, and there are those who are happy also to see opportunities. I've heard that, in better times, the Mason's Arms, at Long Marton, serves a popular Gypsy breakfast.

The aforementioned Billy Welch, 'King of the Gypsies' and the 'main man' at the Horse Fair, is a determined defender of the traditional Romani and is always frustrated by those who give the community a bad name. In an interview with *The Northern Echo* he has described how his community faces what he calls 'the last acceptable form of racism', citing Gypsies being denied entry to pubs, clubs and restaurants, even though they make as much contribution to society as anyone else.

Certain sections of the media are also prone to jumping on opportunities to bash the Gypsy and Traveller communities. A more considered position comes from Janette McCormick, Deputy Chief Constable at the College of Policing, who says inequality and poor job prospects facing Travellers need to be tackled: 'There seems to be a deep-seated and accepted prejudice that demonises people from the community. You wouldn't call any other ethnicity inherently criminal. There is no evidence to suggest we have a disproportionately high crime rate around Traveller sites.'

Not all right-wing media are rabidly anti-Gypsy. A piece in *The Spectator* not too long ago took a look at how the community was evolving to take on new and impressive roles in business, and quoted Billy Welch thus: 'I could take you to mansions, people who have houses worth millions, who drive Rolls-Royces and Bentleys, who have tennis courts, wine cellars and swimming pools.'

Like many in the community, Welch is an enthusiastic Freemason, which may also surprise some. 'But they hide their roots because if they don't, people stop trading with them,' he continues. 'I lost a lot of business when I started to organise Appleby. There are Gypsies and Travellers living in expensive apartments near Harrods, who spend half the year in Dubai. Then there are the 500, as we call them, who own skyscrapers in New York, who are all originally English Gypsies. They turn up at our big weddings in limos, and they still pull on at Appleby, at least once in their lives.'

In the absence of the 2020 Horse Fair, *The Travellers' Times* collected some reminiscences of past fairs on its website. Sherrie Smith, a Romani activist from Hertfordshire, recalls visiting Appleby in 2019 with a colleague and her daughter, and spending a week up to her ankles in mud. But that failed to dampen spirits and she says: 'It's a complete celebration of everything that we are about.' She speaks of 'feeling so safe with all of my own people'. But perhaps the most poignant comment she makes is this: 'On the last day, Raymond Gurême, the French Roma Holocaust survivor, was there and he gave a speech and I felt truly honoured to be there.'

* * *

Leaving Appleby on the north-east side of town today, there's a little over a kilometre of road walking until I reach the roundabout that marks the start of 'unreconstructed' Roman road. The buzz of the A66 is never far away and I reflect that it may well be for this reason that the 'official' route chooses to head much further out of town to the north-east, before heading north-west to Long Marton and Kirkby Thore. For me, however, treading in the footsteps of those who came and so changed Britain trumps all that. Sometimes I feel the Roman legacy is a little enigmatic, in part because the collapse of the Roman Empire in Britain seems to have echoes in the fall of the Soviet Union in its suddenness and in the obliteration of much of its physical legacy. Even Hadrian's great Wall itself was mostly plundered for building stone, which is one reason why Northumbrian farmhouses are so sturdy and well built (of neatly quarried rectangular stone). The extent to which citizens of the Empire, many of whom came from far-off lands to work on building the Wall and for its subsequent defence, remains largely the subject of conjecture, although advances in DNA analysis do hint at a lasting legacy. Even my own and my wife's DNA analyses reveal traces of DNA from the Near East and Middle East, so maybe, just maybe...

Today, even the Roman road proves to be more than a little overgrown: it is a hawthorn-lined avenue, which is its own linear landscape amid the pastures. Shortly after I cross the S&C, below me in a deep cutting, I look for the remains of a Roman fortlet, to my right, but can discern no trace. A tall beech tree boasts a succession of bracket fungi, like a staircase to its loftier branches. My feet are already wet again from long undergrowth, and I can feel something sharp between my toes, and so I pause to investigate... only to find that the little toenail of my left foot, pinched by my too-small boots yesterday, has been incising a groove in its neighbour, which I now address by wrapping it in a sticking plaster.

As I resume my steady progress, the way becomes easier and the reason for this is soon apparent: I am sharing the track with a flock of sheep, some black, some white. My official adviser on matters sheep later confirms that the females, with their jet-black coats and sharp white facial features, are Zwartbles, while the tups are Texels. Zwartbles became critically endangered in the Netherlands before their introduction to the UK in the 1990s. They're popular with smallholders and also cross well with other breeds for butcher's lambs. Texels have become increasingly common in the UK since they were also introduced from the Netherlands (Texel is one of the Wadden Islands, off the Dutch north coast) 30 or so years ago. They are prized for their lean meat, and a good stud tup will fetch a fine price at auction. Indeed, just six weeks after my walk, a six-month-old Texel tup fetches a staggering £368,000 at the Scottish Texel sales, in Lanark – that's a cool 30-odd per cent up on the previous world record. I see no pound signs in my little followers today, but they're a friendly bunch and they keep me close company for perhaps a kilometre until we reach a gate and stile. They stare at me in disbelief as I have failed to pour large bags of 'nuts' into their troughs.

I cross a minor road, beyond which a concrete driveway serves a farm, Powis House. However, the embankment of the old NER, from Appleby to Penrith, runs parallel, a few metres to the left, and so I choose this elevated course instead. It is perforated by rabbit burrows like a Gorgonzola. It is also, once again, populated by sheep, who clearly recognise in me some kind of Pied Piper figure and demand a pat on the head and a neck tickle. Flute in hand, I defer once again to my sheep adviser, who tells me that these are a cross between a Texel tup and Swaledale ewe. The result is delicious, chocolate brown beasts and cream ones, all with thick curly wool. As there's no feeding trough in sight, I begin to wonder if I'm somehow scent-marked from my earlier encounter.

Before long, I leave my four-legged companions behind and drop off the old railway embankment, which, ahead of me, consumes the route of its Roman predecessor only, in turn, to be obliterated by the A66. I cross the latter, bound for the banks of the River Eden, en route to which I pass the site of Redlands Bank Roman camp. Once again, there is no hint of what once was. My plan is to walk the riverside as far as Kirkby Thore and then take a back road to Temple Sowerby, where I shall join the 'official' route for most of the remainder of the way to Carlisle. By contrast, before that, the 'official' route crosses my own at Kirkby Thore to join the riverside as far as Temple Sowerby.

My own riverside walk begins at Bolton Bridge, the approach to which is adorned by an even bigger and better gooseberry bush than the one I saw yesterday. I locate the route between the field edge and riverbank and descend to the water, to sit on a rock and eat my elevenses. It looks an ideal spot to catch sight of a dipper or perhaps even a kingfisher, but I see neither. A lone female walker waves from the opposite bank.

There are two choices confronting me as I set off along the river: the 'correct' line of the right of way is just to the left of field, which is planted with barley. In places, however, the story is a familiar one: lack of use during lockdown has permitted free rein to giant coltsfoot, thistle and cow parsley. Where it is passable, it is at the cost of scratches and wet shorts, so I opt instead for the alternative, which is to walk in the final furrow of the planted land. I am by no means the first to do so. The barley mono-culture has pushed colourful intrusions to its margins, but here and there, along its edge, traditional floral incursions hold their own: the delicate purple petals of meadow cranesbill shine amid the uniform green, like amethysts scattered across a baize table.

The Eden now has entered a lazy phase, meandering across an increasingly broad flood-plain. As I veer away from its banks towards Kirkby Thore, I skirt the scarcely visible remaining evidence of an oxbow lake, where the river has abandoned an old meander to cut a more direct course. I am headed for another large, industrial-scale farm, this time mixed dairy and arable. It's one with which I am familiar at a distance, passing it regularly on its other side as the A66, here a single carriageway, squeezes through Kirkby Thore.

As I approach the farm itself, a pair of oystercatchers is mobbing a lone crow and I admire the pair's brazen tenacity. I reflect, as I so often do, that there can be very few oysters so far from the sea. As ever, of course, the moniker is a misnomer and, even on the coast, they're more likely to eat more accessible prey, like cockles or muscles. Here, they'll be scoffing earthworms and insect larvae, which I dare say will give their sharp bills time to recover before they return to the sea for winter. I am surprised to learn that some species of this bird are not doing well and one even became extinct in the 20th century. I've always thought of them as abundant, and they're a fond sight for me as the national bird of the Faroe Islands, where I have spent more of my overseas time in the last couple of decades than anywhere else. By tradition, the oystercatcher returns to these remote wind and rain-lashed shores on March 12 each year and its return is shared with the Feast of St Gregory. Its status as the islanders' national bird means that, unlike some other seabirds, the oystercatcher is never eaten by humans.

I study the map closely to determine by which route I should pass through this mega-farm. Gates and large numbers of penned cows lie between me and my egress to the main road. As I open the second of these, a man on a tractor calls out and tells me that I am not on the right of way. I tell him that's not what the map says. 'It's been moved,' he replies, and permits me to cross the farmyard to the other side, to reach the correct route.

To be fair, however big and smelly, this is a well-kept farming enterprise, and one with more than touch of humour and self-mockery, as its tidy front lawns are grazed by life-size models of cows (Milton Keynes-style) and deer. As I reach the road, a new fingerpost indicates the repositioned public footpath.

I cross the road bridge into Kirkby Thore and then cross the A66 to the Bridge Bistro: it is closed, but only because it is Tuesday and I am truly delighted to discover this wonderful place is still in business, despite the pandemic. The reason for this joy is that Linda and I must have passed it a hundred times without stopping, as the Kirkby Thore bottleneck is usually something that you just want to get through without delay. Then, with lockdown looming (albeit unbeknown to us), we thought we'd take a look.

We were pleasantly surprised to find that the Bridge Bistro is so much more than a wayside refreshment stop – it is a high quality little restaurant. The woman behind it is Louise Reay, who, with her husband, Matthew, bought the former pub, renovated and transformed it, brought in a quality chef and opened in 2013. We enjoyed hearing about the project from her over the best meal you're ever likely to enjoy within 20m of an A-road anywhere in the UK. I recall our conversation taking place over my salt squid starter. Louise had, some time before lockdown, already brought in additional hygiene precautions, including hand sanitiser on entry, but her chief worry was one of the kitchen team going down with COVID. 'We'd have to close,' she said. But now, some three and half months on, they are still here, albeit with reduced hours, social distancing and a new focus on takeaway menus.

For the first time in my life I venture towards the heart of Kirkby Thore itself, via the road that connects Town End, by the bridge, with the little village green, no more than a kilometre further on. What a lovely road it is, its red sandstone cottages and well-tended gardens, with their gladioli and red hot pokers, face each other across the street as if to say 'my side of the road is so much prettier than yours'. It is not a wide street and there are parked cars, yet, somehow, huge wagons from the British Gypsum plant pick their way through the obstructions to reach the A66.

I am no big fan of bypasses – they are bigger and noisier than the roads they replace and tend, paradoxically, to increase, rather than decrease traffic overall. This is because new roads satisfy pent-up demand from motorists who can now make more and longer journeys with greater ease. It's a subject I could go on about. I helped publish at least two quite learned tomes on the subject back in the 1990s when the Department for Transport, as it then was, was just coming round to accept what the academics had known for long enough: that the biggest single driver of more road traffic is the building of more roads. All that said, Kirkby Thore badly needs alleviation from the heavy traffic that afflicts its charming idyll. The government has pledged (for, I think, the 999th time) to complete the dualling of the A66 and it appears that (after some debate) the new line of the road will run between Kirkby Thore and the gypsum plant, to the east and north-west of the village, and thereby take the industrial traffic away.

* * *

In their book *Open Fell, Hidden Dale*, recalling late 20th-century ways in Dentdale, John and Eliza Forder looked not just at the lives of those eking a living from the rough uplands, but also about what lay beneath that landscape: the hidden world of stalactites and stalagmites; of subterranean lakes and creatures that never see the light of day. For every landscape, however intricately woven or charismatic in its colours, is no more than the two-dimensional surface of millions of years of history that lie hidden beneath what is exposed to our eyes today.

It was a major geological event, many millions of years ago, that created the Eden Valley we know and love, dominated to the east by the great, sheer ridge of the Pennines, and extending west all the way to granite massifs of the Lakeland fells. But that huge event – in which the land to the west of the Pennines broke away and subsided – also laid the foundations for the creation, over eons, of a quite beauteous underworld. For, sitting close to the equator, this low-lying land became an inlet of a tropical sea, whose shallow waters evaporated to leave layers of salty deposits, which eventually became submerged beneath new layers of rock.

These one-time tropical paradises are buried all over the UK. Their legacy is the rich and varied deposits of salty minerals – plain sodium chloride (table salt) beneath the Cheshire Plain, polyhalite and potash beneath the North York Moors. Here in the Eden Valley it is gypsum – a mineral, which, if you look at a geological map of the country, is normally found roughly along the line that divides ancient 'highland' Britain from the younger, 'lowland' rocks to the south-east. The Tees-Exe Line, you may recall from school geography lessons, runs, as you might expect, from the mouth of the River Exe, in Devon, to the mouth of the Tees, interrupted to the north-west of its line only by the intrusion of the 'much younger' Cheshire Plain.

If it helps, you can imagine the solid, granitic, old northern and western rocks standing firm as the slowly rising Alps came along later to ripple the landscape all the way across France and southern England, creating the Downs, the Chilterns and the Wolds, before hitting the buffers formed by the older 'highland' rocks to the north and west. You might imagine the salts that would come to form the gypsum deposits south-east of that line being created by waters washing down into depressions from the higher land to the north. These deposits comprise some of the oldest gypsum workings in the country, which would have sustained the demand for ornamental alabaster to decorate the cornices of fine Victorian homes.

In the Eden Valley, the deposits would have collected in the basin formed by the collapse of the Eden fault and they comprised alternate layers of mudstone and gypsum, all now compacted beneath 300m of rock accumulated above them.

We are, of course, a nation built upon coal, which is, I would guess, the most prevalent useful material dug out of the ground. But that may tend to blind us to all the other products mined and quarried across the country. Cumbria has seen its share of mineral extraction, with both coal and iron ores once being important, as well as lead, copper and even gold, not to mention the quarrying of slate and all the various stones that make up the county's architectural vernacular. But, besides tiny quantities of coal for domestic use, gypsum is the only mineral that is deep-mined here today and I desperately want to take a look at the process.

My initial requests for a visit to the county's only remaining working gypsum mine drew a blank: we were in the middle of a pandemic, after all. But, harnessing the freely given support of *The Cumberland and Westmorland Herald*, I was able to get in touch with the right people so as to access the keys to this wonderful underworld. And, in thanking *The Herald* for its support, a word of thanks too to its new owner, Appleby-based businessman, Andy Barr, whose Barrnon company is a 'boutique engineering services provider'. At a time when even quite large regional print media are struggling, how refreshing that Mr Barr chose to rescue *The Herald* from administration earlier this year. Not only that, but he then returned to print *The Keswick Reminder* – a local title much loved by local residents – after it had ceased publication during the pandemic. Both papers have enjoyed a rebrand and now feature both colour pictures and more modern design. *The Herald* is reported to have quickly returned to profit and the tale is a useful reminder that there remains a viable niche for truly local print media.

And so it was that I found myself turning off the road near

Long Marton on an August day, into what looks like a misplaced collection of office buildings in the middle of the countryside. Blink and you might miss it: in fact, I do, and have to back-track.

Here, at Saint-Gobain's Birkshead mine I meet first with Derek Main, the manager, and Jim Davies, Chief Mining Engineer. In total there are 28 people working at the site, of whom 15 are 'mine operatives'; eight are engineers of one sort or another, and the remainder are administrators of one sort or another. Although it all feels about as different from a coal mine as you might imagine, a significant proportion of the workforce is made up of ex-coal miners, some of them from the old private Blenkinsopp mine, near Haltwhistle, and some from the anthracite drift mines, near Alston.

Together they bring about 125,000 tonnes of gypsum out of the ground each year at Birkshead, but the target is to raise this to 170,000 tonnes in 2021, through greater efficiency. The extra tonnage is required in part to make up for the loss of most of the 'ready-made' gypsum that used to come in by rail to the Kirkby Thore plant as a by-product of desulphurisation processes at Drax power station, in the Vale of York, and Fiddler's Ferry, near Warrington.

Derek explains to me how this will be achieved – essentially, most of the gypsum at the moment is extracted by blasting and then digging out. Going forward, the miners will use a tunnel-boring machine, attached to a conveyor. This will excavate a fair depth of the available gypsum seam and then the rest will be mined using explosives, as is currently the case. I learn that the mine is actually the deepest gypsum working in the country, and quite possibly the world, at some 300m below the surface. This means that the mineral deposits support quite a lot of rock above them, and so large supporting 'pillars' need to be left in place – so, at this depth, only about 55% of the total available mineral can be extracted.

I see in Derek Main not just a man who clearly enjoys his job, but one who has been offered a second career chance and seized it with both hands – the same hands he found himself sitting on for just the space of a few months in between the end of deep coal mining in the UK and getting his post at Birkshead. Born to a modest family in West Lothian, at the age of 16 he applied to the National Coal Board and found himself down the pit at Polkemmet – which was the biggest producing mine in Scotland over its lifetime – as an apprentice. He stayed at Polkemmet until the Scottish coalfield 'imploded' in 1989, then moved south, to Doncaster, the following year. There, he worked in half a dozen different mines, rising through the ranks until he found himself responsible for closing down the final underground mine, at Thoresby.

'One of the biggest achievements in my career was closing the business,' he tells me with candour. Energy prices had slumped and there was simply no future for deep-mined coal: an orderly closure was the best that could be accomplished. That was in 2013 and Derek presumed that was the end of his underground career – until the opportunity with Saint-Gobain arose a year or so later.

Jim is another whose blood might well run black if you cut him: 'Coal mining goes back quite a way in the family, quite extensively, in Nottinghamshire and Yorkshire.'

Both men feel a deep lure to the underground. As Derek puts it: 'It's about people, so in terms of leadership it's a case of being present and being supportive. There is absolutely no reason not to go underground, when we can be at the production face in 20 minutes.'

I learn that the deep mining of gypsum is relatively rare, with most being quarried: 'Cumbrian gypsum is not particularly good quality in the scheme of things, with a purity of 68–72%.' Plasterboard production requires a purity of closer to 90%, and so locally sourced gypsum is mixed with imported mineral, quarried in central Spain and Almería. Part of the aim of increasing production at Birkshead is to reduce the costs incurred through shipping from Spain, and so work is ongoing to overcome issues around lower levels of purity.

Before heading to the mine itself, I undertake my safety induction, learning how to use my potentially life-saving equipment and where to seek safe shelter should there be a collapse while I'm underground. In reality, though, this is an extremely safe working environment and I have no apprehension whatsoever as we climb aboard a Land Rover for the trip below ground.

We follow the road down through a pair of wide doors, rather as though we were entering an underground bunker. Once through the doors, the road descends both steeply and roughly, as we bounce over the uneven debris of the mine's floor, towards the gypsum-face.

My immediate impression is that the sight that meets my eyes as we head for the deep does not match up with whatever preconceptions I may have had. In the absence of any real knowledge, I think I had imagined the gypsum coming out of the ground in powder form, rather like plaster of Paris. Of course, had I paused to think about it for a moment, I would have realised that half a kilometre of earth above, and millennia of compression, would have turned it into solid rock. And so it is: it glints like unlustred silver in narrow bands along the walls, ceiling and floor, alternating – like Liquorice Allsorts – with browner strips, in which the compressed clay, or mudstone, content is higher.

There may be fewer than 20 people working down here, but I soon have the impression of a subterranean city, with workshops, store rooms, garages, places to eat and repair facilities. Furthermore, the mine's roadways – divided by the extensive supporting pillars of gypsum – are arranged on a grid pattern, so we might be in some bizarre cross between Hades and Manhattan or, more prosaically, Middlesbrough. The roadways are neatly carved, their high stripy ceilings rising like some Gothic revivalist approximation to ecclesiastical architecture.

Closer inspection of the walls of the mine reveals more subtle touches of beauty: like the 'daisy burst', in which colourful crystals of metallic minerals form clusters within the off-white crystals of gypsum.

After bouncing along for 20 minutes or so, we arrive at the working face, only to find the new Roadheader tunnelling machine languishing idle: it is broken and won't be back in action until a replacement part arrives. It's a disappointment, as I would have loved to have seen its grinding circular jaws gnawing at the walls and roof; and the product of such energetic nibbling scuttling off along the conveyer towards the huge tipper trucks, which can climb slopes as steep as one-in-four to convey the rock to the surface. When in good health, it can carve a six metre roadway to a height of five metres (a little under half the total height of the seam), and it is fitted with huge 'vacuum cleaners' to minimise the creation of dust.

We turn our attention to inspecting the safety chamber, which offers a safe haven for miners in the event of their being trapped by a catastrophic accident. It may not be all that big, once you've negotiated the airlock, but it is not uncomfortable, equipped as it is with generous oxygen supply, first aid equipment and even games.

From the mine, the 'raw' gypsum makes the short journey to the Kirkby Thore plant across the fields by way of covered conveyors. With a selection of gypsum rocks of varying hues as my keepsake, and with one daisy burst among them, I make my own way two kilometres or so to the plant by car, to meet Production Manager Philip Sant.

I want to complete my understanding of the entire production process from start to finish, and we begin by visiting the dedicated rail sidings, where the Spanish quarried product arrives. I'm invited to get a bird's-eye view of the complex by following Philip to the summit of the open aluminium grid walkways, which run alongside the conveyor belts that deliver the raw material around the plant. He tells me how a previous visitor, who didn't have a head for heights, froze near the top of the climb. This, inevitably, immediately puts me on edge, to the extent that I make it perhaps only ten metres or so up into the air before suggesting that we might now return to terra firma.

If there is one overarching impression that I shall take away from the plant it is its cleanliness: Philip tells me of the immense strides taken over the years to reduce dust content in the factory atmosphere. At least I'm pretty sure that's what he was telling me, but it can be quite hard to catch the words when wearing earplugs.

These are at their most useful where the gypsum rock is ground down in huge vessels, like giant American-style washing machines until it becomes, effectively, plaster of Paris. Now, anyone who has ever mixed plaster of Paris will know that adding water to the ground crystals creates an exothermic reaction – that's to say, it gets hot as it sets. Philip reminds me that this is a wholly reversible operation so, when the rock is ground down and its water content is released, it will absorb heat energy.

This plant produces both bagged plaster and plasterboard. Some of the latter can actually benefit from the relatively high clay content in the locally sourced mineral, as this helps in the manufacture of a soundproof board. I am mesmerised by the process of reintroducing water to the gypsum, and encasing it in a seemingly eternal sandwich of thick paper, to create the standard plasterboards that are pretty much ubiquitous in house construction these days. The machine that chops the continuous sheets into the correct-sized boards at the end of it all is even more fun to watch!

* * *

Returning to my walk, and passing through Kirkby Thore in early July, I make a modest detour to the north-west, to the rear of the houses, so as to skip a little stretch of road walking – and, hopefully, to catch a glimpse of the Roman fort of Bravoniacum. Now, if you look at the 'accepted' map of Roman roads in the North of England, you'll see one called the Maiden Way, which descends from Carvoran, on Stanegate, near the Roman Wall, via the high fort of Epiacum, or Whitley Castle, near the old lead and silver mines, just north of Alston. It scaled the western Pennine escapement via Melmerby Fell and was, for some time, a drovers' road. Its legacy is not a right of way in all places, but people do trace its inexorably focussed route across the high moors and it is on my 'list' of walks that I really should try.

The Maiden Way was always thought to end at Kirkby Thore, at its junction with the High Street, now the A66. However, when the Department for Environment was using LIDAR (ground-penetrating radar) to improve flood management and environmental mapping in 2016, its work revealed unexpected Roman remains, including the course of a road. This would constitute a logical extension of the Maiden Way southwards, to the fort at Borrowbridge, close to the M6, just to the north of Tebay. As with today's other 'Roman remains', Bravaniacum turns out to be invisible to the naked eye at ground level.

I exit Kirkby Thore via a single-track byroad, with tall hedges, which takes me uneventfully to Temple Sowerby. As I enter the village by what was, in pre-bypass days, the A66, I see the homes that line the road through eyes that were blinkered when passing through at speed. To cut to the chase, these are among the smartest houses you'll see anywhere in the county: great piles of places, with glass-walled balconies gazing across to the morning sun as it rises above the Pennines.

Opposite them, on the village green, is the tallest maypole you might ever expect to see, topped with a cockerel on a weather vane, which confirms what I already knew: today's wind is from the west. I walk a little further and enter the churchyard, where I begin an inspection of every single gravestone and tomb. I am looking for the Wharton grave, discovered so many years ago by my parents. Thirty-odd years of Cumbrian weather since their discovery have perhaps taken their toll: many of the stones are quite bereft of inscription and I fear that this once-tangible evidence of my mother's branch of the family tree may now be lost.

Temple Sowerby has a very neat, tree-adorned village green, just beyond the church, and I select a wooden bench on which to enjoy my lunch, checking Viv Crow's Rucksack Reader guide to the 'official' Settle–Carlisle Way ahead. I know Viv and she's a conscientious, prize-winning writer of guidebooks, so I have every confidence that she will get me safely to Culgaith and back to Langwathby in good time this evening.

As I leave Temple Sowerby, I cast my mind back to the days when my pal Ronnie Faux lived in the village. I first met Ronnie at the World Hang Gliding Championships, in the Yorkshire Dales, in 1983, when I was editor of the national hang gliding magazine *Wings!* and he had the grandiose title of, I think, Adventure Sports Correspondent at *The Times*. A kind, gentle and very funny man, Ronnie enjoyed a range of titles in his latter years at the newspaper, and his final assignment was as Yachting Correspondent. Indeed, I recall that when he lived at Temple Sowerby, a large boat on his drive pretty much dwarfed the house and there was talk of adventures in the Inner Hebrides.

Ever modest, but with no good reason to be so, Ronnie counts more than one ascent of the Old Many of Hoy and two Cresta Runs among his feats. He also had a private pilot's licence and a share in a Piper Cherokee at Carlisle Airport before acquiring a microlight. I recall a jaunt in the Cherokee to the Isle of Man one day for a book launch, and many other aerial adventures, but it's the stories he tells that get me in stitches, like following the first Irish ascent of the Old Man, only for the leader's trousers to fall down; or the day his wife, Frances, drove a borrowed cruiser aground on Loch Ness (most embarrassing for *The Times*'s official naval man!) while he was 'using the facilities' below deck; or when, as a very junior reporter on *The Telegraph and Argus*, in Bradford, he interviewed a striptease artiste with a pet python, which emptied its bowels on his head as he and the paper's photographer followed her up to her attic.

As I put distance between myself and Temple Sowerby and such happy memories, Cross Fell looms large before me. The Pennine wall that fills the horizon is the legacy of geological events that took place back in the days when the super-continent Pangea was breaking apart. At that time, the land that is now the Eden Valley slipped down as the Earth's crust stretched. Over time, the basin thus created, which was then a desert zone quite close to the equator, filled with sand (and mineral salts, of course). This is the red sandstone of Cumbrian villages and it owes its colour to iron and other mineral deposits from 'the desert years'.

The other obvious legacy of the Pangea split is the ridge itself: the Pennines here are, essentially, a large block of sandstone – the Alston Block, and its underlying granite, and the Great Whin Sill's intrusions of volcanic dolerite, to be precise. If you imagine this entire block tilted gently towards the North Sea, then the Pennine escarpment before me today is the exposed western edge of this block. It stretches from Stainmore in the south to the Tyne Gap, to the north. The continuity of the ridge is interrupted only by such features as the dramatic whin sill intrusion at High Cup Nick and outliers, like Dufton Pike. To the south are the limestone and gritstone of the Yorkshire Dales.

Now imagine a big lump of cold, stable continental air drifting across from the North Sea and slowly sliding up the sloping Durham plateau to the top of Cross Fell and the other summits that comprise the Pennine ridge overlooking the Eden. This cold air, squeezed between the rising land and a stable layer of air above, here meets unstable moist air blowing in from the Atlantic. The resultant meeting of these contrasting air masses can, in the right conditions, create what's called a rotor, with the dense and 'heavy' eastern air tumbling down the face of the range and 'bouncing' back up in a circular motion a few kilometres out into the valley. As this air gathers moisture, a cloud is then formed above and in front of the Pennine ridge.

This cloud is not a stationary piece of sky: it comprises the constantly condensing water vapour as the air cools before tumbling back down the face of the hills. It can take the shape of a long cigar and is called the Helm Wind, the only named wind in these isles. If you ever visit Lake Geneva, you may chance upon a large illustrative board by the lakeshore, featuring lots of named arrows. Each of these names is a different wind that ruffles the water of the lake and knowledge of these is a must for mariners. On the eastern side of the Rockies, the Chinook can bring unseasonal pulses of warm Pacific air to the Great Plains. The North Pennines are not the Alps or the Rockies but they should be proud to possess our only named wind, the derivation of which is most likely the similar Anglo-Saxon word meaning a helmet, after its tell-tale cloud marker. That said, I do note that there is also a Helm Beck, a limestone stream that's a habitat for freshwater crayfish, over by Great Ormside, leading me to wonder if the name may have another, more local, origin.

Walking the Line

It doesn't pay to underestimate the Helm Wind, as it too is capable of wreaking havoc. Back in 1863, a writer in *The Border Magazine* reported: 'I have known it strike like a chain-shot into a plantation of Scotch fir and larch, at Flakebridge, near Appleby, and for a space of about 150 yards in width, have seen nearly every tree torn up by the roots, and those trees which happened to have better hold of the ground, and refused at once to yield, had their tops snapped off, as if they were so many dried twigs or windlestraws.' More recently, Ron, at High Cup Winery, has seen his vines lashed by the Helm and anyone living in the valley will have their own tales of its force. It has reportedly blown the coal from a fireman's shovel on the S&C, though an objective analysis of such claims might observe that the draught from a fast-moving locomotive can be pretty fierce too.

There is no Helm Wind today; we shall need to wait for a cold north-easterly across the Pennines for that. But, as I cross the broad lawns that front Acorn Bank, I must speculate that its popular gardens are far enough from the Pennines to escape the wrath of the Helm.

The fine National Trust country house at Acorn Bank remains COVID-closed, as does its walled herb garden, but its wider grounds are open. I make a wrong choice here and add a significant meander through the grounds of Acorn Bank or, more specifically, the wooded valley of Crowdundle Beck, below the house. I waste a certain amount of time retracing my steps and going in a circle before I find myself back below the house itself and can reorientate myself.

Although the current house dates from the 17th century, the origins of Acorn Bank are much earlier: lying within the manor of Sowerby, the site was gifted to the Knights Templar in the 13th century, very possibly reflecting a pre-existing presence in the area, and hence the addition of the word 'Temple' to the name of the village. In the 14th century, the Knights Templar began to be seen as a threat to the then status quo and their lands were gradually confiscated. The land in Temple Sowerby passed to a name that will have a familiar ring to readers: the fifth Baron Clifford, Earl of Westmorland. Acorn Bank itself may or may not have been included in this confiscation, or it may have passed to the Knights Hospitalier, who, like the Knights Templar, were dedicated to waging bloody crusades against Islam.

In the late 19th century, the house was in the possession of the Boazman family, from Aycliffe, in County Durham, who pioneered the mining of gypsum in Cumbria. The remains of their drift mine, which yielded 12,500 tonnes of the mineral a year and employed more than 20 people for around 50 years, can still be seen.

Fast forward to the 20th century, when the dilapidated manor house was bought by the author, and heiress Dorothy Una Ratcliffe and her second husband, Noel Mcgregor-Phillips. Dorothy (or D.U.R., as she was known in literary circles) appears to have suffered serial marital misfortune. Born in Sussex, her barrister father was originally from Scarborough and she returned to Yorkshire – to Leeds – with her philandering first husband, Charles Ratcliffe, nephew and heir to the wealthy Edward Brotherton, later Lord Brotherton of Wakefield. She was Mayoress when Edward was Lord Mayor of Leeds, but all that Brotherton's nephew could offer her was venereal disease, the treatment for which left her unable to bear children.

She and second husband Noel travelled widely between the wars, but he died suddenly in 1943. Four years later she married a photographer and journalist, Alfred Vowles, a long-term friend, and the couple gifted Acorn Bank to the National Trust in 1950. The interesting thing about D.U.R. is that much of her copious opus was written in Yorkshire dialect. She was passionate about the life and lore of the Yorkshire Dales, as well as Romani culture, both of which she wrote about extensively, while campaigning actively for the Yorkshire Dialect and Gypsy Lore societies. She became a prolific collector of books and documents, and alumni of Leeds University (of whom I am one) will be familiar with the name Brotherton, as the Brotherton Library and its vast collections are housed in a domed redbrick building, which sits behind the neo-classical (Greek revivalist, if you prefer) Parkinson Building, whose once soot-stained, but now gleaming white, Portland stone tower rises above Woodhouse Lane and can be seen from across the city. Within the Brotherton's learned walls can be found the late D.U.R.'s literary collection. Other mementos, including fans, miniatures and, poignantly, baby bonnets, are in Leeds Museum.

The Thoresby Society is a body dedicated to the history of Leeds and the wider area and I rather like a verse of D.U.R.'s, found by society member and author Eveleigh Bradford, who suggests it would make a fitting epitaph for her.

Here lies a lover of rain and sun,
Loving, and loved by everyone;
left these beautiful dales to find
The dales where the heavenly rivers wind.

I track down a copy of one of D.U.R.'s books, published in 1961 by Dalesman, from a secondhand seller in Otley, and am very pleasantly surprised to discover what elegant prose she writes. *The Cranesbill Caravan* is a gentle and idyllic tale about a family travelling by horse-drawn caravan through the Yorkshire Dales. But it is a chapter about an encounter with gypsies encamped at Bainbridge that catches my eye:

Matt smiled: 'We shall be very obliged to take tea in your living wagon if we may coom tomorrow afternoon. Soon we mun be on the road for t'new Fair.' And so it was arranged that Mr and Mrs Matt would find their way at about four o'clock to our pitch at 'Hope Alone'.

'Thank goodness only two of them are coming!' said AC as we drove away.

'Is it a New Fair?' enquired Rosemary.

'Oh, no!' I replied. 'It is generally believed that this horse fair at Appleby, sometimes called Brampton Fair, was chartered by James II in 1685, and that there was an even older fair on the same site.'

Doy said gravely, 'They must not come to our caravan for my grannie in Richmond says gypsies are "good-for-nowts", who never go to kirk and that in the olden days they used to steal children.'

* * *

Returning to Crowdundle Beck, it is with a sense of relief that I finally exit the woodland to follow the banks of the beck across open meadowland, thence to pass beneath the four-arch, 17m tall Crowdundle Viaduct. A short stretch on the road, crossing the old country boundary into Cumberland as it crosses the beck, brings me to a nice, clear fingerpost announcing my route on to Culgaith. As I cross vast fields of clover, Viv's directions are clear and precise but I nonetheless run into trouble at the point at which the route is supposed to strike diagonally across two fields. I check and recheck the instructions and compare these with the right of way marked on the map. There appears to be nothing for it: I make a detour through a gate and then, having crossed the field on diagonal, as instructed, am obliged to scale a double barbed wire-topped fence at a gap in the hedge, my route guide providing necessary protection from the spikes. My irritation is all the greater because, for once, I am quite sure that any error is not mine, and I suspect illegal obstruction.

In the village I find myself in conversation with a couple of other walkers who live in the village and are keen supporters of the railway, they say. I mention what I'm doing and where I've come from today, including my difficulties with the right of way. They frown and look puzzled and say they weren't aware of any obstruction to the path. I may be obliged to return to Culgaith and check it out again.[11]

I have entered the village through a small estate of new houses and there's clearly been a lot of building work going on recently. This is a village on the rise. Consequently, Eden District Council puts Culgaith at the top of its wish list of station reopenings and, to be fair, the population figures are not dissimilar to those of Langwathby or Lazonby, if you ignore nearby Kirkoswald in the latter. However, my previous caveats about adding more stations endure. Culgaith is actually a slightly curious station as it is out of keeping with others on the line, having been built in the so-called Derby Gothic Midland style four years after all the others, after the local vicar lobbied for the village to have its own halt.

To leave the village, Viv describes a 'narrow, twisting path between the houses'. The only snag is that the start of said path is now all but invisible, as whatever once divided it from the neighbouring garden is now gone and all that remain to indicate a right of way are the low remains of a small stile. So, that's another unnecessary kilometre logged...

I now have perhaps 1.5km of road walking to reach a long, pretty much straight stretch of old drove road. I think I am walking briskly in the afternoon sun until a young woman with a labradoodle on a lead powers past me, only for the dog to immediately slow to my own pace. We laugh and I quicken pace as much as my wearying legs permit, so as not to disadvantage her too much. I comment that there do seem to be a lot of new homes in the village. She tells me how she and her partner settled on Culgaith as lying roughly between their workplaces, though in these days of home-working, such 'musts' may acquire the status of mere 'desirables'.

She adds that the big new houses at the bottom of the village are mostly lived in by older people and are beyond the reach of a young couple's budget. I reflect once again that, while not sharing Lake District property prices, there's no shortage of fine homes, old and new, in the Valley... for those who can afford them. My temporary companion tells me that her mother has been able to come up from the Midlands, having been locked-down at home since March. The dog is Mum's and is clearly enjoying his holiday, as the pair eventually speed off ahead of me beneath the warm early evening sun.

The drove road taking me the final stretch to Langwathby is great walking but, uninterrupted as it is by such unnecessary things as bends, it does seem rather to go on forever. Now I begin to pass the occasional car parked in a way that suggests secret lovers at play: I must be getting somewhere near the end of the road. And then I am greeted by a large complex of huge sheds, to the left of the road. A sign on the gate tells me to 'KEEP OUT' in large black capitals on yellow. Smaller letters refer to 'HACCP Disease Precautions Critical Control Point' and the sign bears Dupont (The Miracles of Science) and Virkon (The Science To Kill Pathogens) logos. In these times of plague and disease, it all looks decidedly ominous. A second sign provides emergency contact numbers and an Environment Agency Permit number. Curiouser and curiouser... I'm almost disappointed to learn later that it is no more than a poultry-rearing site.

Not a great deal of research is required to learn that HACCP stands for Hazard Analysis and Critical Control Point, so there's a tautology for you. And only a tiny bit more investigation yields the information that this is a factory rearing 140,000 chickens at a time and the permit relates to the regulation of its emissions – 140,000 chickens do produce a lot of poo and, one way or another, it finds its way from here back onto the land. There's also a bio-mass boiler but it burns 'virgin' timber pellets, which will surely not come from the timber plantation I pass a little further on.

Eventually, having turned onto a side road, I see the road from Melmerby to Penrith on my horizon, tantalisingly close, yet irritatingly far away. Barley and pasture have given way to maize, though doubtless for animal rather than human consumption.

At last I reach the road and soon begin the gentle descent into the village. As I pass beneath the railway there's still a brown sign to the Brief Encounter Restaurant, on the station platform, although it is now, more prosaically, Langwathby Station Café and appears to be up for sale again. I rather mourn the passing of the Brief Encounter moniker, with its unsubtle reference to that forbidden affair-that-never-was in the 1945 David Lean film of that name, for which Noël Coward wrote the screenplay. Some rank it among the ten best British films ever and it certainly evokes much of the conflicting social pressures immediately after the war, as people returned to a more constrained moral climate. Now, if you want to enjoy an illicit encounter *à deux* with a veneer of post-war romance, you'll have to go to the Brief Encounter tea room at Carnforth station, near Lancaster, which is, after all, where the movie was actually shot. Back in Langwathby, however, the station café is currently offering a rotating menu of semi-exotic takeaway dishes on evenings only.

On the other side of the station drive, there's another sign beneath the brown one, pointing to Frank Bird Poultry. I guess Frank must have sensed a certain inevitability in his career choice.

And if Frank's turkeys fly no more than the ostriches that once lived in Langwathby, there is a machine at Frank's place that certainly does fly: and to very good effect. For this little Cumbrian village is, a little unexpectedly, the second home of the Great North Air Ambulance Service, of which more shortly.

Finally, back at the Shepherds Inn, a pint of Wainwright seems a fitting choice as the evening sun treats the tables overlooking the green to a share of its pleasantly warming rays, as children and adults play ball in a way I had almost forgotten these past weeks. I slip across to the village shop, hopeful of finding a large-scale OS map to avoid further navigational faux pas on my remaining days, but to no avail. Finally, back with my pint, I ease my feet from my shoes and await the arrival of Linda, who will join me for dinner.

Chapter 6

Flightless Birds, Geese and Mushrooms

From Langwathby to Armathwaite

THE floods are roused, and will not soon be weary;
Down from the Pennine Alps how fiercely sweeps
Croglin, the stately Eden's tributary!
He raves, or through some moody passage creeps
Plotting new mischief – out again he leaps
Into broad light, and sends, through regions airy,
That voice which soothed the Nuns while on the steeps
They knelt in prayer, or sang to blissful Mary.
That union ceased: then, cleaving easy walks
Through crags, and smoothing paths beset with danger,
Came studious Taste; and many a pensive stranger
Dreams on the banks, and to the river talks.
What change shall happen next to Nunnery Dell?
Canal, and Viaduct, and Railway, tell!
'Nunnery', by William Wordsworth

In around March 2020, a new word entered the English lexicon. Or at least, a word that had been around for quite a while acquired a new meaning, when endowed with an initial capital. As the home became the office, and the idea of travelling or meeting others turned from everyday reality to distant aspiration, a race began to find new ways to meet each other online in as 'realistic' a manner as possible. You might have thought that the likes of existing business networking tools, like Skype or LinkedIn, would have been in pole position to fill this rich new niche. But both of these are, these days, part of the dead hand of Microsoft, whose days of swift and nimble innovation are long past, if they ever existed at all. And the failure of Skype and its ilk to offer a stable, user-friendly, affordable meeting 'interface' left the door open to new nimble-footed tech upstarts, like Zoom.

And so it is that I find myself in a meeting with Andy Dalton, Assistant Director of Clinical Services at the Great North Air Ambulance, not at his office at Langwathby's heliport, but he at his home in Carlisle, and me at mine, in Durham, after my return from the Eden Valley. The helicopter ambulances are run by a charity and Andy's role is in clinical governance – 'ensuring how we treat our patients is safe'. He joined the service 14 years ago, having been a paramedic with the Cumbria ambulance service for ten years before that. In normal times his job is split between Langwathby and the service's new headquarters, at Eaglescliffe, on Teesside (it also has a forward base at Newcastle Airport).

'The Great North Air Ambulance has been in existence for close to 20 years and, in some form since the 1990s,' he tells me, though in the early days it was little more than a 'flying ambu-lance'. In the early 2000s, the process of bringing doctors on board the aircraft began. 'That was a model that wasn't really prevalent in the UK, other than in London – a model in which clinicians at the hospital come out to treat the patient at the roadside.' The HEMS (Helicopter Emergency Medical Services) model is now prevalent, though not universal, across the country.

There's an ongoing debate in the air ambulance community between the respective merits of 'scoot and run' and 'stay and play' tactics, or whether it is best to treat the patient at the scene or get them to hospital. 'There is some evidence that staying at the scene is not good for the patient,' Andy says. 'But you have to get to hospital and get there alive.' Which is where the on-board doctors come in. 'It's gone from a single air ambulance team with two helicopters and the odd doctor when one had a free shift, to a seven-days-a-week, eight till eight operation, with a doctor and paramedic team.'

When I speak with Andy, the service has just taken delivery of a brand spanking new helicopter to replace one of the older machines in the three-strong fleet and enabling faster operation in more marginal weather conditions. 'The Cumbria aircraft is one of the older machines and we are looking to replace that with the next generation type of aircraft.' To do so, of course, demands money and, as Andy says, 'We have entered interesting times for fundraising, with COVID. We are down, but not as much as we predicted, which is very good, and the fundraising team is working very hard to replace that.'

Andy describes the rather special nature of the Langwathby operation, combining challenging physical terrain to the west of the Pennines, while the major network of trauma hospitals lies outside Cumbria, in Newcastle, Middlesbrough and Preston. 'As a result, the Cumbria helicopter spends a lot of time criss-crossing the country.' When attending incidents in the mountains, the team works closely with colleagues in both airborne search and rescue (SAR) and the local mountain rescue teams. 'We aren't a search and rescue service: we are a specialist medical intervention aircraft. Search and rescue get people in and out from difficult places. They have paramedics, but we come in with blood, surgical interventions and so on. We are limited by the weather – their aircraft is bigger, more powerful and can fly in difficult weather conditions.'

I wonder if the Cumbria aircraft, based in sleepy Langwathby, is kept as busy as the two machines in the North East, but Andy tells me: 'Call-out wise, they are roughly equal but the aircraft on the west needs to transport patients greater distances.' Indeed, as the crow (or helicopter) flies, parts of the North East – from about Alnwick, north to the Scottish border – are actually closer to Langwathby than to Eaglescliffe. And the Langwathby helicopter will, from time to time, also cross the border into Scotland.

The Langwathby base was chosen because a centre nearer the coast would have been less efficient (only sea on two sides) and because Frank Bird was able to provide a suitable base on favourable terms. It is the ambulance control centre that is responsible for deciding when the helicopter should be despatched, and, Andy says, it gets about 400 call-outs a year, with a strong bias towards summer. 'Though we can sometimes go two or three days with nothing.'

I wonder how difficult it is to work with seriously injured patients, to which Andy gives a candid reply: 'I block out a lot of nasty stuff, so I sometimes struggle to remember some of the jobs we have done. One of the benefits of what I do here now is that, because of the way the charity works, we get to meet quite a lot of people who have recovered and come back to see us.' That's real job satisfaction, he says.

Not long after our conversation, the Great North Air Ambulance hits the national headlines as it reveals it is trialling a jet pack that will enable a paramedic to zoom (original meaning) up the fells to an injured patient, James Bond-style. A truly cutting-edge operation!

* * *

So, back to Lamgwathby's Shepherds Inn, in July 2020, and I rise ahead of Linda, in line with the complex logistics demanded by today's walk. Over breakfast, I chat with Jim, from Sussex, who's been staying here all week, as it's a central location from which to visit his clients in the North of England and southern Scotland. He sells mining engineering equipment and this is his first stay in the area. He says he very much likes what he's seen and casually mentions that, while driving up, he stopped in the Dales and quickly ran up Whernside. 'As you do!' I think to myself.

So, today, I drive to Armathwaite, park the car at the station and get the train back. Meanwhile, Linda will drive to Lazonby, whence she'll return with her friend Carol and we'll all walk together back to Lazonby, from where I shall continue to Armathwaite in the company of my sister June, who lives atop the Pennines, near Alston.

Inevitably, such arrangements all take a bit longer than planned and so I nudge back the intended meeting time for lunch and meanwhile reflect on the days when no visit to Langwathby was complete without calling in to see the ostriches. Some may remember the 'ostrich boom' that never happened, back in the 1990s, when investing in 'ostrich futures' proved one of the fastest ways to lose money, after owning an airline, restaurant or football club. Twenty years and many lost fortunes later, *Farming Weekly* summarised it thus:

Ostriches were primarily imported from South Africa. But while there was a modicum of consideration given to actually farming the birds for their meat, the focus was largely on building up numbers and selling eggs and chicks.

There was inadequate research into the management, slaughter and effective marketing of the end product and, once the sector emerged from the establishment phase, those who had made hefty financial commitments suddenly found themselves with a commodity that was hard to shift.

The result was a gradual collapse and commercial ostrich farming was left in the hands of a few die-hards. The British

Domesticated Ostrich Association still operates to support the handful of ostrich farmers in the UK, but the expected expansion of ostrich meat production never happened.

One of the reasons for that was price: at £26 a kilo back then (now £45 for a prime 1kg steak) it was – and is – far from cheap, even if it does offer a super-healthy low-fat alternative to beef. *Farming Today* laments its failure to catch on more and, given the number of other products from the bird – from eggs, to feathers to hides, to treatments for haemophilia and cataracts (I kid you not) – perhaps it deserves a second chance.

Eden Ostrich World closed its doors for the last time in 2012, citing a run of poor summers. Well, this is the Pennine foothills of Cumbria, so it was never going to be the Kalahari, was it? I suspect that Ostrich World enjoyed its best season when it acquired a Shetland pony that had shared a field with a zebra. Shortly after arriving at her new home, she gave birth to a zorse, or horse-zebra cross. I remember the wee one was a pale chocolate colour, with dark chocolate stripes and zebra-style tale, rather than the tassled horse variety. I don't know what ultimately became of it, but he or she seemed a sprightly thing. Because of the different number of chromosomes in horse and zebra DNA, the animal would not have been fertile.

* * *

I am stirred from my equine reverie by the eventual arrival of Linda and Carol, and we strike off through the upper part of the village (the opposite side to where Ostrich World used to be), heading through the feed mill for open country. Our route today follows the Morrison-Speakman original and the Settle–Carlisle Way, which are coincident. The advance forecast hinted at today being the best of the week and it is beneath a blue sky, punctuated by fluffy white cumulus, that we reach open countryside. I am now permanently 'beshorted' for the rest of the walk and have renewed energy after yesterday's killer distance. Thank the Lord I didn't do the 'Dufton extension'.

It has indeed been the strangest of summers and it's good to meet up with friends again, even while keeping a cautious distance, and hearing about the daughter who joined us as a pre-teen on a holiday in Spain what seems like only a few months ago but who will, amazingly, now graduate later this summer. What worries me most about the passage of time is the clear evidence that it simply is not a linear process. Who remembers how the summer days stretched before us, seemingly to some invisible time horizon, when the school holidays started? Or how we emerged from life's complex maze to one day arrive at a 40th birthday party, only for 50 to come five years later and 60 just a couple of years after that? Now I am at that moment in life when, to be realistic, I have to work out carefully just what I can still squeeze in while still fully ambulant, cognitive and wakeful. And another COVID blow: the nagging doubt as to whether I will actually get to some of the great unvisited places that have awaited my arrival for so long.

But enough doom and gloom! The best approach is surely to enjoy as much as we can when and while we can, and today is no exception, as it genuinely is a day when it feels good to be alive. We leave behind us the field of tall corn and cross the intriguingly titled Briggle Beck. The dictionary tells me the name may come from American regional English via a Scots word, meaning 'to fuss about ineffectively', which seems rather apt for a small beck in its upper reaches.

The route takes us through the adjacent villages of Winskill and Hunsonby. It is a mark of the universal prettiness of Eden Valley settlements that, though either could surely grace a calendar of 'best Cotswold' or 'best Sussex' village views, they can't make an Eden Valley top ten. The villages butt end-to-end at an acute angle and we take the third side of the triangle, via a field path, before joining a very pleasant country lane out of Hunsonby. The lane opens out eventually to offer two options, one taking us in the direction of Long Meg and Her Daughters and the other to the village of Little Salkeld. It's a genuinely difficult choice, for I rarely tire of visiting any stone circle. However, I have a future date with Long Meg as part of a planned expedition around most or all of Cumbria's stone circles.

As this journey will feature in a book to be published by Saraband in 2022 I shall pause for long enough now only to say that this is one of the largest and finest stone circles in the whole country and, like so many others, it comes with its own particular legend: that the stones in the circle are a coven of witches turned to stone by a Scottish wizard. It is said that it's not possible to count the stones (there may be 59) and reach the same number twice. If you do, the wizard's spell may be broken. Watching over the circle from a slight distance is Long Meg herself, a menhir of red sandstone, decorated with cup and ring and other marks. But enough, for I do not wish to spoil the story for you.

Our route today, however, will take us via Lacy's Caves – a series of open-windowed chambers carved out of a red sandstone cliff above a picturesque stretch of the River Eden. Before locating the riverside path, however, we have to reach the village of Little Salkeld. And to do so requires the crossing of a field with a small herd of cows. The cows are a little frisky and Linda and Carol opt to stick close to the fence at the edge of their field, while I face down the herd in the centre of the pasture. It is a fact that many more people die beneath the horns and hooves of cows and bulls than are mauled by sharks. Five times as many are killed by cattle as by dogs. What the stats don't provide is an accurate split between death by cow and death by bull, but there are far more of the former grazing on our rights of way than the latter. And, until a few quite well publicised cases in recent years, it was generally presumed that cows were mild-mannered beasts. Indeed, even as I complete this work, an inquest is taking place into the 'unprovoked' killing of a grandmother by stampeding cows in Northumberland.

You are at most danger from cows when you have a dog and/or the cow or cows have calves. Today, neither of these is the case and so, while they are making me feel uneasy, I don't feel I am in danger. Soon the herd loses interest in me and I continue to the field gate. However, on turning round, I see that the cows have discovered Carol and Linda, the latter of whom is now climbing the barbed wire fence: I implore her not to, but she will have none of it and – when she eventually finds an exit from the adjacent field to which she has fled – cites numerous cases of death by cow. Well, although I have been a bit rude about some farmers and, specifically, their at times cavalier attitude to rights of way, any walker should expect to encounter cows from time to time. In that eventuality my strong advice is firstly to give them a decent wide berth so as not to appear threatening, and in no circumstances come between a cow and her calf. And don't take dog into a field of cows if you can possibly help it.

This may be somewhat easier said than done if your dog is your best friend and constant companion. Certainly keep it on the lead and remember that, if push comes to shove and you're in real danger, the only option may be to let the dog go, while bearing in mind you will be wholly responsible for any damage the animal then does. Then again, if you're the kind of dog-owner who thinks it is actually okay to hang plastic bags of dog poo from trees, then go fill your boots, for all I care. Further checking tells me you shouldn't make eye contact with threatening cows. Given that this is precisely what I have just been doing, it's useful info, if coming a little late.

And so, with the partial exception of one person's now perforated leggings, we arrive in Little Salkeld in one piece. I recall that, on a previous visit to Little Salkeld, you could still work out which of the pretty cottages was once the village pub, but it seems now to have cast history aside and changed its name. Then again, I may have looked in the wrong row. Punnets of juicy redcurrants and an honesty box sit outside one gate, but we have currants aplenty back home.

A curious fact about Little Salkeld is that it is pretty much unconnected to Great Salkeld, which does have a pub, and a pretty fine one at that. Not long after the pub died in Little Salkeld, the Highland Drove, in Great Salkeld, appeared to face a similar fate, until rescued by a villager, Donald Newton. He has turned it into an acclaimed village boozer, with real ales, open fires and awards that include Les Routiers' Northern Dining Pub of the Year. It is a truth that ought to be universally acknowledged that a pub in possession of a half decent location must be in want of a good landlord or landlady. Which, in my tortured perversion of Jane Austen, means that – even at a time when pubs are generally struggling and closing at alarming rate – the right team, with the right effort can cleave success from the jaws of historic failure. It will always help if they have ownership on their side for, to me, it is the greed of the pub leasing estates that has sown the seeds of decline in many cases. In what other industry would investment and innovation by the lessee be rewarded by higher lease charges to reflect the consequent increased trade?

But to get to the point, if Little Salkeldians wish to visit the hostelry that once provided refreshment and succour to those driving cattle from north of the border, they will have to own or borrow a dinghy, or go all the way back to Langwathby to traverse the Eden. If you look at the map, you can see the stubs of lanes either side of the river and it appears that there was indeed once a bridge, but it may have disappeared early in the 19th century. The drovers continued to ford the river, just downstream from Nunwick Hall, and may well have found their way ultimately to the long drove road I took yesterday. It was a way of life that died with the coming of the railway.

At Salkeld, the station on said railway was in Little Salkeld and, though it remains in reasonable nick and is occasionally cited as a case for reopening, the simple fact is that it would be not much more than 2km from Langwathby and barely three from Lazonby. I note that the parish council over the river in Great Salkeld has consulted the public and produced a well-written, quite comprehensive Village Plan. Yet the document mentions neither the station nor a bridge across the river in its section on communications, despite exploring ways of better connecting the community with Penrith to help older residents. So, the only amenity that remains in Little Salkeld is its water mill. I know its little café won't be open, as maintaining any kind of social distancing would be close to impossible, but I also know that the mill has worked flat-out these last weeks to mitigate the disappearance of flour from supermarket shelves. We walk down towards the mill, but a lady in a garden tells us it's closed. So we abandon the short detour.

* * *

Back home after my walk, I telephone Little Salkeld Mill and speak to Cheryl Harrison, who took over the working mill from Nick and Ana Jones, in 2014. The Joneses had run the place for four decades, so it has a long history of turning out high quality, stone-ground grains. It is not a very happy Cheryl who tells me that she and her husband, whom she calls simply 'the miller', are approaching the end of their tether. Frustrated city folk with no flour have, she says, scaled the gates of the mill during lockdown, been abusive when told there's a waiting time for flour, and generally behaved badly.

'I'm not sure what the miller's thoughts are but I am a retired teacher by trade and I think that the behaviour of the human race is changing, and not very nicely,' she says. 'We feel a little rundown and disappointed.'

Running the mill, she reminds me, depends on the water level in Robbery Water, which turns the water wheel. This is a fact that some members of the public are not prepared to accept, so Cheryl is, in turn, minded to draw her own lines – to cut a long story short, the Harrisons may be selling up. While I dare say another enthusiastic couple may buy the mill and extend its tradition, it is a sad commentary on varying standards of behaviour during the difficult weeks and months of lockdown.

Even as she speaks, news bulletins report on wild campers in the Lake District chopping down trees for barbecues, camping on the dry beds of a reservoir and leaving behind them veritable truckloads of rubbish, and even equipment in good condition. I have struggled to get my head around this latter observation until my daughter observes that some festival-goers at Glastonbury abandon all their gear when they leave.

* * *

Returning to today: as we retrace our steps from the mill road to the centre of the village, a car draws up and the driver winds down his window to ask us if we are headed for Lacy's Caves and warns us that there's a large sign on the gate advising that the path is closed. 'But it's okay, you can get through,' he adds.

On reaching said gate, we see that there is indeed a very large sign telling us to go no further. It's made of metal and painted red, with large block capital letters and it clearly means business.[12]

I can't say for certain what we might have done without the advice we received. We would, very possibly, have carried on anyway. Or perhaps we would have backtracked and gone via Long Meg.

As it is, we are now headed for another location that goes by the name of Long Meg: the former Long Meg gypsum and anhydrite drift mine. Once it had its own railway sidings and it actually closed as recently as 1976, nearly a century after it began work. As part of my team effort with *The Cumberland and Westmorland Herald* to get myself underground at Birkshead Mine, I acquired, following a reader's tip-off, a book called *The History of BPB Industries*, where BPB stands for British Plaster Board, and dates back to 1917. A little sticker inside its front cover reminds me rather sternly that the volume is 'for internal circulation only to employees and pensioners of BPB Industries Ltd and its subsidiary companies'.

The book tells me that, in 1916, 'what now [1973] substantially constitutes the northern regional division of British Gypsum [...] was, in 1916, an ailing company [...] operating under the aegis of the Carlisle Plaster and Cement Company'. This company had been formed in 1911 by the merger of three local businesses, including the Long Meg Plaster Company. Quarrying for gypsum at Long Meg began as early as 1879, with mining following in 1895. The latter, it seems, was not hugely successful in those early days as the gypsum seams were squeezed by layers of anhydrite to just two feet thick. Only later was it realised that mining the anhydrite was profitable in its own right. Nor was the merger, which combined the mine with interests in the production of cement, plaster of Paris and alabaster, entirely successful, as the combined concern merely brought into sharp relief the lack of capital that typified all three contributing companies.

Inevitably, the business went into receivership and was ultimately acquired by a concern called the Gotham Company. So, perhaps it was a case of Batman to the rescue, or – more probably – the intervention of the First World War, which brought a predictable spike in demand for some of the company's products, and the eventual conclusion of the takeover in 1918. However, the mine lease had lapsed and it only reopened in 1922, when A.V. Bramall began mining gypsum for the ICI plant at Billingham, on Teesside. A few years later, this production ceased, upon the discovery of easily accessible seams of gypsum. The newly formed Long Meg Plaster & Mineral Company built up a plaster trade of about 200 tonnes a week and this continued until 1940, when the business was acquired by BPB.

By all accounts, conditions for the 20 or so miners at Long Meg were fairly primitive, with illumination provided by par-affin lamps comprising quart milk tins with a string 'wick' inserted through the lid. 'Smoke so filled the air that it became ingrained into the skin,' the book says. 'Many a worker was highly embarrassed to find that when slightly sweating at a dance, his face would be streaked with black marks.'

This wasn't quite the end of the road for Long Meg mine: in 1954, anhydrite mining resumed for the production of sulphuric acid at a plant at Widnes, and output climbed to 300,000 tonnes a year – a figure which even today exceeds that of gypsum produc-tion at Birkshead. The mine only finally closed in 1976, by when it had yielded in excess of five million tonnes of mineral. The dedicated signal box, controlling the Long Meg sidings complex, on the S&C, closed a few years later and it fell into disrepair.

The way to Lacy's Caves weaves through the old industrial site and past a large electricity substation, before passing close to the relatively low viaduct that takes the S&C across the Eden. It's a popular photographic variation for those seeking to capture the passage of steam trains on the line, affording a pastoral rather than a rugged moorland setting. We pass a large and elaborate mosaic made from old bits of brick and depicting the journey of the Eden through the valley. The associated information is hard to find these days but my recollection is that it was produced by local schoolchildren. It would be nice to see it brought back to life.

Beyond the viaduct, our route follows an old tramway that would have served the anhydrite drift. You can still see the remains of the odd rail and sleeper. Apparently one of the old saddle tank locos now resides on the Bowes Incline preserved railway, on the edge of Gateshead.

Beyond the tram track, the path is less well constructed and features stretches of boardwalk and other reinforcements. As it descends towards the riverbank it is in quite poor condition, though probably not poor enough to mandate its closure. Before long we reach Lacy's Caves. Last time I visited, I was in a bad vertigo phase. As a teenager I could happily bound across Striding Edge and, in my 20s, clawed my way up Lord's Rake. Aged 15, I even walked across the Pont du Gard, which stands nearly 50m tall, is only about a metre wide, and has no parapet – for no better reason than that my sister did it. Latterly, however, I simply don't like heights. To be more accurate, I dislike exposed positions from which I might fall. I have a fear of falling (and of other people falling), rather than of heights. If heights were the problem, I would be unable to fly in either a small aeroplane or an autogyro, or in an Airbus A380. I took up hang gliding partly to try and overcome my irrational fear and thus discovered I was unafraid of heights, though I was (quite rationally) scared of one day getting into an awkward spot that it was beyond my ability to get out of.

My vertigo was not helped by my worsening hip, as this affected my balance, though I didn't really understand this at the time. Anyway, last time I was here I simply couldn't bring myself to walk along the ledge to the caves, but today I have no such problems. So, another important and not wholly expected tick for the new hip.

Views down the river towards Lacy's Caves, suggest that they are almost like houses, with a roof, but the 'roof' is actually the natural slope of the hillside above. Beneath the caves, there's a vertical drop of perhaps ten metres. But who was Lacy and why did he carve the caves? Well, he was the third child and eldest son of the Sheriff of Newcastle, Richard Lacy, and born in 1766. On his mother's side, he was descended from the Cumbrian Dacre family. On his father's early death, Samuel Lacy inherited extensive lands in Newcastle and enough ready cash to buy Salkeld Hall and its surrounding estate, which ran all the way from the Eden to beyond Long Meg and Her Daughters. He renamed it Eden Lacy, and the title endures two centuries on.

Lacy would have been able to see the caves hewn from the sandstone of the riverbank a few kilometres downstream, at Corby Castle, which still belonged to the Salkeld family, from whom Lacy had bought his new estate. Equally, he may have visited the much older St Constantine's caves on the opposite, Wetheral, bank of the river. Such curious structures, with their languid river views, would surely have chimed with the sentimentality of the early days of the Romantic age. In any event, Lacy decided he would like his own, if you please, and charged an employee with carving them. He planted the riverbanks with rhododendron and laburnum and would entertain guests in the five chambers. Supposedly, he even employed a 'hermit' to add authenticity to his folly.

Also supposedly, he tasked workmen with dynamiting Long Meg and her daughters so that the fields could be ploughed. But the monument was saved when a clap of thunder sounded, just as work was about to start and the labourers, aware of the folklore surrounding the circle, were so spooked that they downed tools and fled. However, all this seems to be no more than hearsay and it may even have been the Salkeld family who had this idea, years before Lacy came onto the scene. In any event, it didn't happen, and, with the caves, Little Salkeld can boast two proud stone edifices (three if you also count Little Meg, the smaller stone circle 600m from Long Meg). Little Salkeld, Great Salkeld; Long Meg, Little Meg: this is a land where size clearly matters!

Leaving the caves behind, we climb the bluff that forms their 'roof' and exchange words with a lone walker. She warns us of sticky conditions ahead, but we have suitable footwear, which she does not. We continue along the top of the river gorge and, although boardwalks have been installed at some point, these are in poor condition and there's a huge amount of surplus groundwater, which means the way has to be carefully selected. That said, neither is this succession of obstructions sufficient to command the closure of the path. Progress remains slow over some distance, until, eventually, we emerge into open pasture and a welcome stretch of dry conditions under foot. To our left it is clear that the cliff is slowly sliding down into the river and I do wonder if this is why the path is supposedly closed. It is most likely a legacy of Storm Desmond, which forced hitherto unknown quantities of water down the Eden Gorge in December 2015. That said, unless you were standing on the edge of the cliff as it fell, it's hard to imagine any real danger.

When we eventually meet the road at Daleraven Bridge, there is no closure notice, so it all seems more than a little silly. After following the road for a short distance, we take a path through meadows to Eden Bridge, where my sister June awaits, as too does lunch. A man with a drone is just a few feet from us. But he has nothing to say, so absorbed is he in finessing his flying, ultimately landing the craft on a level stretch of sand by his feet. He packs it all away and departs, still without uttering a word. A flock of Canada geese nearby remains undisturbed.

* * *

This is, I think, the third time I have seen my sister June since lockdown started and we shall walk together to my night stop, at Armathwaite. As Linda and Carol cross the bridge to Lazonby, June and I head up the hill towards Kirkoswald. A permissive footpath has been created so you can walk inside the field boundary, rather than on or by the road. This development reflects the fact that the correct name of the station is Lazonby and Kirkoswald. A curious fact about the former is that the railway here runs through a short tunnel. It is the railway's second 'accidental tunnel', but whereas the first such unplanned structure, Birkett Tunnel, was built to counter unfavourable ground conditions for a cutting, Lazonby Tunnel's raison d'être is rather more prosaic – it was installed at the request of the local vicar, who didn't want the view from the vicarage spoiled. It is less than 100m long.

Given that the name of the village on top of the hill in front of us is, literally, 'St Oswald's Church', it is slightly surprising that said church sits at the edge of the village and somewhat below it, almost as though it were an afterthought. And yet, as parts of it date from the 12th century, this can hardly have been the case. As we walk the permissive path at the edge of the meadow, the church is set back, at the foot of the hill, and is surrounded by a walled cemetery. We speculate that, during Storm Desmond, the waters may just about have lapped at this wall.

But having the church so far below the village was not without its problems: it may have been impossible to hear its bells. Indeed, in recognition of this fact, no one ever bothered fitting bells and, instead, erected the bell tower on top of the adjacent hill. The present tower was built in the 19th century: it sits within a small walled quad on a bluff above Raven Beck, but it is generally presumed that other similar structures preceded it.

Across the beck are the ruins of Kirkoswald Castle, built in the 13th century on land belonging to Hugh de Morville, Lord of Westmorland and, as previously noted in respect of Pendragon Castle, one of the Thomas Becket assassins. After being destroyed in a Scottish raid, it was rebuilt by a branch of the Dacre family, which went from rags to riches to become one of the most powerful in the Borders. Internal features of the castle, including ceiling beams and stained glass, found their way to Naworth Castle, east of Brampton. This latter is today occupied by the Hon Philip Howard, heir to the Earl of Carlisle, who has opened some of his finest rooms for weddings and other events.

In the 16th century, the Dacre family would convert the nearby pele tower into a seminary but this role was short-lived, as the Dissolution of the Monasteries followed just 25 years later.

Returning to the church, both ends of the building have interesting features. Outside its west wall, a sandstone plaque reads:

To the greater glory of God and the honour of Oswald King of Northumbria 634–642 AD Patron of this Church. This tablet was placed over St Oswald's Well. For with Thee is the well of life and in Thy light shall we see light. Psalm XXVI 9.

You can lift the adjacent lid and lower the metal cup provided, on its chain, to draw water from the spring below, which flows on beneath the nave. The water is still used for baptisms.

The reference to King Oswald is a reminder that the Anglo-Saxon Kingdom of Northumbria ultimately reached all the way from the Humber, across the entire breadth of the country and right up to the Firth of Forth. It was the greatest and most learned kingdom in these islands. Oswald is said to have visited while touring 'the pagan North' with St Aidan. It is unfortunate that the term Northumbria has become so abused, so that these days its use can refer to almost any geographical area, providing it includes the post-1974 county of Northumberland plus something else. The somewhat lamented regional member body, Northumbria Tourism, covered all the counties of the North East, but only as far south as the Teesside conurbation. Northumbrian Water still covers a similar area. But Northumbria Police covers only Northumberland, plus what used to be Tyne & Wear – that is, Newcastle, Sunderland and the three boroughs on the banks of the Tyne. Northumbria Euro-constituency no longer exists, but it covered only Northumberland plus North Tyneside. Call me sentimental, but I feel that we, as northerners, lose much by not properly recognising the rich legacy of Northumbria.

To extend the theme of Northumbria and its influence, the east window depicts St Oswald with St Cuthbert, Christ and the four Evangelists. St Cuthbert was, of course, a leading figure in the early Christian Church, 'graduating' as a monk, at Melrose, before moving to Lindisfarne and ending his days as a hermit on Inner Farne. His reputation as a healer on his various journeys earned him the epithet, the Fire of the North. After his death, and under the ongoing threat of Viking raids, his monk followers carried his remains on a long journey. This took them to the Cumbrian coast, at Workington, perhaps with the intention of crossing to Ireland. Legend has it that a violent storm blew up and the waves that engulfed the ship turned to blood. Sensing their 'master' didn't want to go to Ireland, the monks looped back into Dumfries and Galloway, before heading south, down the Eden Valley and on into Yorkshire. A final flourish was a concentric loop northward, culminating at his final resting place, where Durham Cathedral now sits atop its tall promontory in a loop in the River Wear.[13]

The 'cult of St Cuthbert' grew up centuries later and there is, for example, a St Cuthbert's altar in Furness Abbey. This cult most likely inspired the exceptional number of churches dedicated to St Cuthbert, most especially along the route taken by the monks up the Eden Valley. There are at least 17 St Cuthbert's across Cumbria. Just some of those in the Eden Valley are at Cliburn, Clifton, Dufton, Edenhall, Milburn, Great Salkeld and a couple in Carlisle itself.

But to Kirkoswald: well, in my unofficial prettiness stakes, this village might just edge into the lead. I can't believe I have never visited it before, nor heard from anyone just how pretty it is (it's a deserved past winner of Britain in Bloom). The steep main street is lined by attractive rose and wisteria-adorned cottages, while the centre of the village is graced with Georgian architecture. Two pubs, the Crown and the Fetherston Arms, sit on opposite sides of the hill, near the cobbled old market square, the latter taking its name from the former occupants of the pele tower. Variations of the Fetherston name include Featherstone, Fetherstonhaugh and Featherstonehaugh, this latter being pronounced, I believe 'Fanshawe'. The late-Victorian novelist, Maria Fetherstonhaugh, was married at St Oswald's.

The coming of the railway brought mixed results for Kirkoswald: yes, it was now better connected, but the downside was that the market left the village for a new location beside the station in Lazonby.

Our idyllic appraisal of the village is tarnished rather, as we climb the hill to its edge: a too large lorry has caused a jam at the road junction and is creating a stink of diesel and burning clutch.

Quite soon, we leave the road for a pleasant path across fields and into the faintly manicured parkland below Staffield Hall. We speculate that that it has the feel of early Capability Brown about it, but he doubtless had his disciples. Built for the marriage of Lady Jane Aglionby into the Fetherstonhaugh family in the mid-19th century, the hall is today a rather luxurious ten-bedroom 'holiday cottage'.

The short-cropped pasture we are crossing is being enjoyed by more Canada geese and is studded with freshly surfacing mushrooms. Now, I generally consider the season for our favourite edible fungus as August to October, so these appear to be a bit early. However, *The Wild Food Guide* says May to November, so what do I know? I do love fresh mushrooms but there's little point in my picking them. No such restraint from June, who stuffs her rucksack, even though she professes not to be all that fond of them. My niece, however, is, and she'll be on her way down from Scotland soon.

Back on Tarmac, we cross Croglin Water, on its tumbling journey down from the flanks of the Pennines. Until a few years ago you could here join the Nunnery Walks, which used to be open for the public to enjoy the successive cascades and views across the river, at a point at which it sheds its languid cloak to don instead a riotous mantle of spume, as it enters a rocky gorge. Given that Wordsworth himself found space in his opus to praise the waters of Croglin – in the prescient verse, hinting at the coming of the railway, at the start of this chapter – it seems a crying shame that this mixed woodland is now out of bounds, and for reasons that remain unclear. My suspicion is that the answer lies in the fact that visitors used to pay a nominal sum for entry and, in levying such sum, the owners may have assumed a more significant degree of liability than would ever be the case if the paths were simply established public rights of way. An over-enthusiastic land agent may have advised that the cost of assuring the safety of guests on sometimes narrow ledges above rushing water simply could not be justified.

At the gates to the 'Nunnery' itself, another red squirrel scampers up a beech tree. The large hall through the wrought iron gates is built on the site of a one-time Benedictine nunnery. It was once also a guesthouse but appears now to be a generous private residence.

A short stretch of off-road walking, and we enter the rather curious hilltop ribbon settlement of Ruckcroft. Given the level of competition, this village will never make it to my top table, but it deserves mention for the quality of its views across to the Lakeland Fells, where the distinctive saddleback contour of Blencathra and the greater, more distant bulk of Skiddaw define the northern massif, to the north of Keswick. And, far beyond, you can make out the unmistakable form of Criffel, like a Scottish cousin of Whernside.

On his Pennine Journey, Wainwright, by now south of Appleby on the return leg of his circumnavigation, catches a glimpse of 'a long line of hills rising dimly along the far edge of the plain'. He goes on: 'I had forsaken them; made other plans. Now, having seen them, I wanted dearly to go. They were calling me; their voice was the moving of the wind amid the rocks of chasm and precipice, the rush of cataract and murmur of the mountain stream[…] There are no hills like the hills of Lakeland.'

I do sometimes wonder about Wainwright, who was nothing if not perverse, whether he only ever walked other than in the Lakes solely to remind himself of his spiritual home. Of the 34 books that he wrote or drew, 16-and-a-half are non-Lakeland titles, so it's not as if he didn't get about a bit. But I do feel his sheer adoration of the Lake District mountains may have left him blind to some extent to the alternative qualities possessed by other places, not least in other parts of the North. Fair enough, in the same volume, he speaks highly of Blanchland and of Hexham and falls in love with the Roman Wall and his imagined version of how it would have appeared when in its full former glory, but you sense this is a qualified admiration. Fair enough, perhaps the Eden Valley was simply less lovely between the wars, but I don't feel he ever appreciated its undersung charm, sitting neatly as it does between the superlative Lakeland Fells and the sturdy wall that is Cross Fell and its siblings. We can only guess how he might have written of Switzerland, the Lake District on steroids and more, had not the outbreak of war stifled an ambition to go walking there.

I too love the Lake District and spend much time there. I have climbed Blencathra many times, though never via the nerve-shredding stickleback of Sharp Edge. It was easily ascending Skiddaw and two subsidiary peaks for (surprisingly) the first time in the summer of 2018, but then taking more than four hours to limp down again, that finally persuaded me to get something done about my hip. Oft repeated ascents by various routes of other peaks – the Old Man of Coniston, Helvellyn, Scafell, Scafell Pike, Great Gable and many, many more – are mileposts along the road of my walking life. Scrambling up Catbells, Causey Pike or Barrow, near our cottage, in Newlands, are a joy as I more frequently shy away these days from grander challenges.

But I hold in similar affection precious moments atop peaks in the Dales, the Cheviots, Scotland, Wales, Ireland, or further afield in the Faroe Islands, Norway, Guadeloupe, Antigua... So, as I gaze across today, I am drawn back to other times and the sense of achievement attached to reaching each summit. But allowing my memory and imagination to drift does not make me wish to be there right now nor, more importantly, to not be where I am at this moment. My journey from Settle has been a special one and it shall remain special until the moment I round the Crescent, in Carlisle, and see Citadel station before me. So, right now, I am content to gaze upon Blencathra from afar and then enjoy a Lakeland return in its own due time.

Viv's book invites us to go left through a wooden gate, but this has been inconsiderately replaced with a steel one – perhaps the single most frequent confusion visited by farmers upon guide-book writers. Fortunately the fingerpost remains in place and we descend through a lush, as yet unmown meadow, then cross a succession of fields and stiles until we reach a collection of large cages, each housing rescued waterfowl. A crow has somehow managed to sneak into one of the cages and is flying dementedly back and forth, crashing repeatedly into the invisible mesh. We find a woman outside her house in the little settlement of Longdales. It is she who owns the rescue centre and her next rescue will be of a blue-black scavenger, rather than a multi-coloured fowl. The well-manicured lane though the village is getting a closer trim as we pass a man with mower and a job to do.

The final stage of our journey today is through Coombs Wood, planted by the Earl of Carlisle back in the 18th century, but now in the hands of the Forestry Commission. We descend steadily by a long, straight timber road, passing a few local people out strolling as we go. Most of the trees are conifers – Scots pine, larch and Douglas fir – though the Forestry Commission aims to introduce more native broadleaves to diversify the habitat. There is little birdsong, but the track margins are illuminated by the mauves and purples of betony, common spotted orchid and common centaury.

A single constant chirping and clicking catches my ear but, when I pause to ask June if she has noticed it, the creature immediately falls silent, only to restart when I set off walking again. It proves to be nothing more exciting than the lesser spotted rucksack strap, in mating ritual with the tawny camera case.

After what feels like an eternity of unchanging forest

scenery, we reach Graeme Mitcheson's 'Vista' – a red sandstone sculpture that is another in the Eden Benchmarks series. It features shoes and other items of clothing, discarded by their owner, who chooses to go for a swim. There's also a map, serving as a sundial and a little face on the sculpted cap references five enigmatic faces carved into the cliffs above the Eden, down below us. We are, of course, on the wrong side of the river to see these. I would like to see them, but there's no right of way on the other bank so to do them justice may necessitate a kayak.

The carvings may or may not have been the work of one William Mounsey, who was born in Carlisle around 1808 but became an amateur, and somewhat eccentric, archaeologist in 1850. His various exploits included walking the Eden from mouth to source. At the latter, he carved a large piece of Dent marble with a Star of David and words in Greek, Latin and Hebrew. Whether in an act of anti-Semitism or simple ignorance, the work was smashed by railway workers in 1870. However, a limestone replica was created as recently as 1989 by Shalom Herman, a Jewish traveller, and placed in the church at Outhgill, in Mallerstang. The inscription on it reads: 'William Mounsey, a lone traveller, commenced his journey at the mouth and finished at the source, fulfilled his vow to the genius and nymphs of the Eden on 15 March 1850.'

Mitcheson's sculpture is the signal for us to descend to the edge of the shelf above the Eden and commence the final short stretch to Armathwaite. The woodland becomes 'more native' and there's open land beyond the fence, where, suddenly, I catch sight of another red squirrel scampering along beside us. We reach the bridge at Armathwaite and cross to the Duke's head and a welcome drink, bidding farewell as my sister heads off to catch the 'last train', or bus replacement service as it is more correctly known.

Chapter 7

Paradise Left Behind

From Armathwaite to Carlisle

There Eden's lofty banks
Now nearer crown with their inclosures green,
As with a rural mound, the champaign head
Of a steep wilderness; whose hairy sides
With thickets overgrown, grotesque and wild...
From Paradise Lost (Book IV), by John Milton

Armathwaite is by no means a large village, but it is probably the largest of the three Eden Valley halts on the S&C. So, it boasts two pubs, rather than just one – the Fox and Pheasant, just across the river at the north end of the main street, and the Duke's Head, my digs for the night. A third, the Red Lion, is no more.

Tom Coward, landlord at the Duke's Head, has been very helpful to me in the run-up to the reopening of pubs after the spring 2020 lockdown. He – along with Stephen, at the Shepherds Inn in Langwathby – gave me the confidence to go ahead with the five outstanding stages of my journey.

Given my previous remarks about pub estates, I'm delighted to learn that Tom, with other family members, acquired the Duke's Head from Punch Taverns in 2019. Prior to the deal, the pub was listed as a 'community asset' by Eden District Council, with the aim of ensuring its continued use as a pub, should the owner wish to sell. Tom was previously landlord at the Bluebell, in Dalston, on the edge of Carlisle, so him taking the reins ticked everybody's boxes: Punch got its sale, Tom and Co got their own pub and the village retained one its pubs, along with new local management.

Once again, the organisation to comply with COVID rules is impressive and reassuring, as is the décor of my smart room. In fact, Tom and the team have not hung around and watched the grass grow during lockdown: they have completed a refurb of all the letting rooms, and remodelled the garden to maximise the opportunity for guests to mingle at distance out of doors.

I should say that this is my second visit to the Duke's Head. My first was in unhappy, if rather different, circumstances in the mid-1990s, and was to the wake for the funeral of Hilda Pickles. She was a lifelong friend of my mother and an author – in 1993, my company published *Crooked Sixpences Among the Chalk*, her memoir about teaching during the Depression and the Second World War. She wrote beautifully about her classroom experiences in the East End of Newcastle, Teesdale and Cumbria. She was also a prominent local councillor in the Eden Valley.

Having almost accidentally become engrossed in Wainwright's 1938 Pennine Journey and fascinated by its place in the popular history of the pre-war years, I now (back home) find myself rereading passages from Hilda's book. To mirror the Wainwright experience, I look at Hilda's account of taking very poor children on a summer camp, up the Tyne Valley, shortly before the Second World War put a stop to such things. She wrote:

Many of the children only had plimsolls for their feet: none had both an overcoat and mac. The four-year-old coughed all night and dirtied his pants all day. The poor little fellow was completely bewildered and his eyes were seldom without a tear and his nose was never without a drop. At night, Dorothy and I kept up a perpetual perambulation of the tents to see where water was leaking in or children rolling out. The kitchen 'shelter' fell down one midnight, and a cow ate our teacloths off the hedge. Every scrap of wood was soaking, and Dorothy and I were perpetually red-eyed through coaxing wayward fires.

I wonder if 'Dorothy' might have been my mother. She continues:

Strangely enough, the children loved their 'holiday', and were loathe to leave, even the two little boys. I can still picture them with six girls, tousled and triumphant, gathering wood in the rain. War, not weather, put a stop to these holidays.

When Hilda became an Eden District Councillor, she was, as many were, an 'Independent', which tended then to mean 'Tory'. Not in the case of Hilda, who, like my mum, was always of a Left-leaning persuasion. Hilda was a founder member of Northern Arts, which was a pioneering pan-regional body, funded by all the local authorities in the North East and Cumbria for the purpose of developing the arts in the region. It was way, way ahead of its time but eventually became subsumed into the Arts Council, chopped in two and divided east and west.

The Arts Council began a process of 'levelling up' regions, like the Midlands, to Northern standards, which in practice meant a further dilution of the Northern Arts foundation work. Ultimately the Arts Council, facing reduced central funding, rationalised its regional presence and the pioneering ethos of Northern Arts became just so much ancient history.

* * *

From Armathwaite to Carlisle

Well breakfasted, I drive up Station Hill and, Viv's guide in hand, set off on the short distance along the road: today shall be a bit of a Morse code waltz of path-path-road-road-path, slow-slow-quick-quick-slow. But it is a beautiful morning and the sun soon starts to burn off the moisture forgotten in the verges by the heavy dew.

It has been perhaps the most pleasant revelation of my walk that, however weary my legs are at bedtime – however much my feet throb – come morning I am truly refreshed. I have followed Linda's injunction to cold bathe my feet to reduce the inevitable swelling, then warm bathe them to restore the circulation. It seems to have helped. I have not once woken in the middle of the night with hellish cramp, which would once have been inevitable after such exertion. I put this also down to magnesium, which can be sprayed on weary muscles. It is also one of the regular supplements I take. There is sound scientific reason behind this: as a nation, and indeed beyond our shores, our soil has been so depleted by over-cultivation that it is now lacking in essential minerals. Ergo, so too are our fruit and veg. Calcium is not an issue – our bones should get enough of that from our diet and, anyway, too much calcium supplement and you'll end up with kidney stones. Most medical opinion warns against potassium, the third in this triumvirate of trace metallic elements: it can damage your kidneys. I do try not to take too many supplements as this is of benefit only to Holland & Barrett *et al*, but I also usually take glucosamine, for joint lubrication, and psyllium husks, a soluble fibre that really seems to keep my cholesterol levels in check and save me from GP pressure to take steroids for the general benefit of the drugs industry and broad-brush statistical outcomes.

I feel a sense of joy at embarking on my final leg, while still possessing working legs, and, if I don't check myself, just a tiny sense of pride that I am indeed now close to my goal. A brisk walk down a gently sloping field below the railway embankment, a brief 'no, after you!' with a woman and a wayward dog at a gate, and beneath the line to rejoin another road, a little busier than the standard country lane.

I pass the majestic Drybeck Viaduct (no relation to Drybeck, the Hothfield seat, near Appleby) as it skips across the broad tributary valley, to my left. The valley conveys only a modest stream, as the name implies, and I suspect another glacial melt-water overflow as the Ice Age waned. I leave the road and railway to drop right towards the Eden, passing the cosy and tidy little Drybeck Farm and its quite exquisite campsite. What a lovely place it would be to prise kids away from their screens.

From here to Wetheral I shall be close to the river all the way, on a waymarked route. Sometimes I'll be on the riverbank, at others I shall be atop the gorge or clambering up steps or slithering down slopes between the two. What I shall not be doing is resting on my laurels, as it quickly turns out that the presence of waymarks brings with it no guarantees, either of accurate direction posts, or as to the condition of the path itself.

But, to start with, it's easy walking on a pleasant track, then through woodland by the river. My route alternates between woodland, meadow and fields of barley. It is punctuated by the occasional smartly kept anglers' hut, on river stretches where signs nailed to the trees proclaim ownerships as distant as Yorkshire. At one, I share the time of day with a couple of fishermen, now returning to the banks after lockdown. The Eden is a fine angling river with lazy ponds permitting the waters to pause briefly ahead of successive rapids that might tempt a raft journey, though this might displease other users. Soon I find myself at an area of rein-forced riverbank, with large granite boulders at the water's edge.

I have reached Eden Brows – a location of some notoriety among S&C cognoscenti. During Storm Desmond, in December 2015, the raging river undermined its banks here, at the point at which its flow quickens as it is constricted by the gorge. The Victorian surveyors, unable to thread the railway through the winding gorge of the lower Eden, picked a route at times atop and at others on the flanks of the gorge. At Eden Brows, the line is a full 60m above me. In the wake of Storm Desmond, Network Rail engineers detected movement of the trackbed and a speed limit was introduced. But then the movement became more severe (one track dropped a full metre) and the line was closed, and remained thus for more than a year.

The Network Rail solution was radical – because the land was slipping all the way down into the river, there was no option but to tie the tracks to the bedrock, below. Huge piles were sunk and a concrete slab attached on top, effectively creating a submerged 'viaduct'. An extensive drainage system was installed on the steep valley side. But this solution was not cheap, coming in at a cool £23 million for what Network Rail described upon reopening the line in March 2016 as 'the most challenging railway repair ever'. More challenging, presumably, than repairing the sea wall at the notorious Dawlish, in Devon. Martin Frobisher, Network Rail's most senior person in the region, said: 'I am beyond thrilled that customers and goods are moving again on this vital economic artery through Britain's most beautiful landscape. Our orange army has ensured that even if the ground gives way again in the future, the railway will not.'

I quote Mr Frobisher in full here, because we do need to remind ourselves what a difference three decades can make… for S&C aficionados know well that £23 million is three to four times the various estimates for repairing or replacing the supposedly terminally decayed Ribblehead Viaduct, back in 1983, when closure of the railway was first proposed. That the former 'basket case' of a railway merited such spending (alongside a similar amount in track renewal and other works) is a measure of both the short-sightedness of the original closure plan and of the line's new-found purpose. It is today both an important route for freight that cannot be accommodated on the busy West Coast Main Line, and a popular passenger route for commuters, sightseers and those travelling between Leeds and Carlisle and points beyond.

I can see the stabilisation works on the wide scar of this reactivated old fault line, which leads my eye to the railway, high above. Tele-monitoring stations are there to report any future movement. Seeing the entire repair from below, it is far more impressive than I had ever imagined or been able to witness from a train window.

Eden Brows makes for fast progress, for a short distance at least, but both waymarking and the path itself quickly decline: I pick my way through the forest floor at the river's edge, with giant coltsfoot and Himalayan balsam at my shoulder. At one point the way is blocked by a tree, whose multiple trunks are too high and complex to scale. I shimmy beneath it like the world's worst limbo dancer. My hands are now covered in mud and it is slippery underfoot. I manage to edge around a deep sludgy puddle and reflect that this is at least better than a poke in the eye with a sharp stick, only to then receive a sharp poke in the eye from a blunt stick, which draws blood but fails to blind me. This stretch should be fun, but neglect and lack of fellow walkers ensure that it is not.

I emerge into a succession of fields and, hoping for better conditions underfoot, stop for my elevenses, only to discover I have forgotten to collect my flask of coffee at the Duke's Head. The omens are bad. I call Tom, who kindly says he'll leave my flask on my car bonnet at the station. The fields are of barley again, and do not deliver the hoped-for improvements underfoot, for my shoes are now wetter than ever. The farmer has protected his cereal crop by erecting a series of surreal scarecrows, comprising rudimentary wooden bodies and 'heads' made from used plastic sacks that once held high-energy sheep feed.

From Armathwaite to Carlisle

Crossing the barley field, I encounter an angler coming in the other direction and we stop to talk, reflecting on the perceived flourishing of wildlife during lockdown, an observation mirrored, he says, in the number of some fish species caught and returned by anglers. I comment how many swifts, swallows and martins I have seen skimming rivers this summer, surely a sign of more insects being about, which will, in turn, help certain fish.

And so we get to talking about the salmon, that king of river fish, and he reinforces what I already know: that Atlantic salmon populations are in a parlous state. Once the Eden was a fine salmon river and, while it still is, this is very much a relative term, for the decline of the poor old salmon has been terrifyingly rapid. Figures for England and Wales show that salmon numbers in 2018 were a seventh of those 30 years earlier. While the precise reasons for the decline are not fully understood, it is acknowledged that the problems are out at sea, rather than on our rivers. Indeed, my angler friend tells me that the great majority of salmon actually caught are now returned to the water. In fact, you can't even buy fresh salmon these days unless it's net caught... or poached for the black market.

A few years ago I learned a bit about the poor salmon's plight from people on 'the front line' who really know about such things: ghillies on the River Tay. I'd been invited to try my hand at salmon fishing on the UK's most celebrated river for the salmon. We were 'spinning', using a variety of lures to tempt the fish, and I learned that artificial flies and shiny lures tempt salmon, not because they look like food, but because the fiercely territorial salmon thinks someone, or something, is invading its space.

We were a bit out of season and didn't catch a great deal and what little we did was returned. But the conversation turned inevitably to reasons for the decline in salmon stocks, in which regard my ghillie friends cited too many seals in the Tay estuary, cormorants and goosander. Over lunch with two other ghillies, they produced a longer list of remedies. The netting of salmon on some estuaries should be stopped, they said. Haaf-netting on the Solway, to which the Eden is the major contributor of fresh water, is already on the wane, as those fishing on the Scottish side must return their catch. Using hatcheries to help restock rivers works, and has done so particularly well on the Tyne. Those films of cute baby seals being clubbed to death in Canada years ago, or closer to home on the Farne Islands, created a lasting legacy defined by a reluctance to control seal numbers, which verges on impossibility. And scientists and ghillies should sit down together to share their knowledge.

And they also told me about Orri Vigfússon, an Icelandic entrepreneur and conservationist who, they said, knew more about saving the Atlantic salmon than anyone. He was the founder, in 1967, when just 24, of the Atlantic Salmon Trust. Sadly, it now turns out that Orri died of lung cancer in 2017, aged 74. However, a speech by HRH Prince Charles at the Trust's 50th anniversary dinner, just a few weeks before his death, addressed succinctly many of the issues facing the wild salmon and what Orri's trust was doing to combat these. The Prince described the Atlantic salmon as 'the ultimate aquatic canary'. 'When all is well with the salmon, all is well with the world!' he said.

This was not by any means an event for just anyone, but it would be hard to imagine the 50th anniversary of the Stickleback Foundation attracting such as the Prince, King Harald of Norway and 500 other eminent guests, all at the Duke of Northumberland's little London pad, Syon Park House. Prince Charles said: 'We cannot continue to lose 95% of our salmon on their epic journey to and from our rivers. It is quite simply unsustainable. So we urgently need to know just what is happening to them along the way.' He spoke of the Trust's 'uncanny ability to sense well in advance the key issues which need to be tackled' and said it had established 'an outstanding track record' through the practical, management-orientated research it had commissioned or supported.

I think it is worth also reproducing more of the words of Prince Charles, in which he linked the fate of the salmon with climate change issues – not because there aren't enough people talking about the subject, but because what he said does give an insight into the multitude of different ways in which different species may be impacted:

Whilst the impacts of climate change, now and in the future, on salmon stocks is still the subject of much research, it is understood that factors such as warmer and acidifying waters, drought and flooding, scarcer feeding opportunities and invasive species are all affecting survival rates of salmon, both in the marine environment and in our freshwater ecosystems.

For example, it seems that there is evidence that the plankton that salmon rely on to feed at sea, as well as other species, are moving north, owing to warming temperatures. Similarly, it would appear that more frequent storms, leading to changing currents at sea, and flooding in rivers, are impacting migratory routes, feeding patterns and [the] survival of salmon eggs in rivers.

So, in the greater scheme of things, a few more flies and moths in the air (and on my car windscreen) during lockdown count for little…

* * *

Walking the Line

As I make another steep climb up and away from where the river divides around Coathouse Island, I hear the unmistakable cry of a buzzard. I wonder how best to describe this to someone who may not have heard it before. It's not the harsh screech of a barn owl, but nor is it in any way melodic. Some describe it as a mew, others as a keening cry, and some seek to render it into letters, like 'peeee-uu'. Rather unsuccessfully, I'd say. I suggest that it's a soft-edged shriek delivered at a distinctive unchanging pitch. Once heard it is not to be forgotten and so, as I look up on emerging from the trees, there it is, circling no more than 50ft above my head and landing at the top of a nearby oak.

Soon the bird is in the sky again, circling as a thermal drifts up from the tree canopy. They are such graceful birds and such a pleasingly common sight in our skies compared with when I was a young lad. Salmon may be struggling, but some bird of prey species have been doing quite well, since the end of DDT and the advent of stricter, if oft ignored, regulation.

I descend the slippery, eroded wooden steps towards the river and, entering Wetheral Woods, know that my lunch stop is now within reach. I look out for steps down to St Constantine's Cells, but somehow miss these: I must have taken a higher path than the one suggested by Viv. On reaching the shoreline, a woman is sitting on a rock watching a large group of kids splashing and swimming in the river. On the opposite shore I can see the caves in the Corby Castle gardens. One of these is, I understand, inscribed with the verse from Milton at the start of this chapter. I might have stopped at this pretty spot, but there are too many people, so I press on and arrive at Wetheral. Spearmint beside the path sweetens the air and, in front of me, downstream, the red sandstone of Wetheral Viaduct, on the Newcastle–Carlisle Line, frames the view perfectly.

From Armathwaite to Carlisle

There are benches, but all are occupied. One is surely the 'most benchy' of all the Eden Benchmarks, for Tim Shutter's 'Flight of Fancy' actually is a bench… A man of maybe 60 is sitting eating a bag of crisps, with his two dogs, perhaps a spaniel-poodle cross and a hunter-spaniel. I ask if I may perch two metres away at the opposite end of the artwork, and we get chatting, as two dippers skim the surface of the waters. A pair of oystercatchers joins the scene as my new companion tells me one of the sadder lockdown stories I have yet heard.

He recounts how he and his wife so fell in love with the Kintyre peninsula, in the west of Scotland, that, upon her recovery a few years ago from breast cancer, they decided to waste no more time and moved permanently to the holiday home they had bought there. Then, 18 months ago, she contracted an unrelated kidney cancer and died in February, just before lockdown. The only saving graces in this tragic story are that his son and his American wife ended up locked down with him, and so he did at least have family around him, and his other son and wife, in Somerset, have had a baby boy, again during lockdown. He's travelling down there now and has parked his camper van overnight in the Eden Valley, not far from Wetheral.

From Somerset, he'll return north, catching his parents in Derbyshire while en route. 'I just don't know what to do next,' he says, despairingly, and my heart goes out to him. The best I can manage is to urge him to pause and reflect before doing anything precipitously.

He leaves me to my lunch and I contemplate the tall façade of Corby Castle, towering over the opposite bank of the river, and high above the steps that tumble down to its estate's various water-side features. Like those at Pendragon, Lammerside and Wharton, this has at its core a 13th century fortified tower house. However, reflecting the turbulent Borderland times before this, it probably began life as a humbler pele tower, like those common both sides of the border in the centuries following the departure of the Romans. They comprised a safe store for cattle below, with sanctuary for humans on the higher floors, and were built to protect their occupants from the marauding gangs of Reivers, or robbers, who rode malevolently across the so-called Debatable Lands, on the fuzzy border between England and Scotland. These Reivers are very much part of Borders folklore, and feature in many a local ballad or poem, such as Sir Walter Scott's *The Lament of the Border Widow*, which begins:

My love he built me a bonny bower,
And clad it all wi' lilly flower
A brawer bower why ye ne'er did see
Than my true love he built for me.
There came a man by middle day
He spied his sport and went away
And browt the kin that very night,
Who broke my bower and slew my knight.

In his excellent book *The Steel Bonnets*, George MacDonald Fraser describes how, when the war for Scottish independence began, 'the Borders had been moving towards civilisation'. The scorched-earth guerrilla warfare waged by Robert the Bruce and William Wallace against Edwards I and II had inevitable consequences for that tranquillity, however. 'When they ended, the people of the Marches had returned to something like the cave ages,' observes Fraser. Addressing some of the more romantic myths surrounding these families and their reiving men, he observes: 'The fact remains that the records of Border reiving show a deplorably high killing rate, and not much evidence to suggest that the Borderers were, for robbers, unusually humanitarian.

When [Sir Walter] Scott says that they abhorred and avoided the crime of unnecessary homicide, one can only comment that they seem to have found homicide necessary with appalling frequency. Yet the myth has grown, in spite of all contrary evidence.'

The tower house at Corby was sold by the Salkeld family to the Howards (one of the great noble Cumbrian families) in the 17th century. Early in the following century, Thomas Howard created extensive pleasure gardens, including the riverside caves, or wine cellars referred to earlier. The house itself was remodelled in the 19th century, to give its main walls a neo-classical look.

Corby Castle has not faded from public eye with the passage of time: on the contrary, it seems to have popped in and out of public consciousness with a certain regularity since before the turn of the century. If we go back to 1994, that was when Sir John Howard-Lawson sold the castle and its estate. All well and good, except that his son, Philip Howard, a business consultant (not, so far as I can determine, closely related to the Howards of Naworth Castle), decided it was not his father's to sell and took his claim to the High Court. He argued that his father had forfeited his right to inherit in 1962, by allegedly failing to comply with certain rather arcane stipulations in his great grandfather's will. Philip wanted £1.5 million from the £2.5 million proceeds of sale, arguing that this was his rightful inheritance, but he lost. Undeterred, he took his claim to the Court of Appeal, where he won. But it was a decidedly pyrrhic victory, as he was awarded the princely sum of just £5.60 a year in ground rent and a very much more consider-able sum in costs.

But over to the man who bought the castle and its lands for what seems like – even given the passage of more than a quarter of a century – a bit of a snip. However, Edward Enda Haughey, as he then was, did not get where he was by not driving a hard bargain. Born near Dundalk, in the Irish Republic, Haughey was

nonetheless an Ulster Protestant and Unionist. An astute businessman, he began a career in pharmaceuticals in the USA, before
moving to Northern Ireland, where he established Northbrook
Pharmaceuticals, which he developed into a worldwide business,
supplying veterinary medicines. It made him very rich: he became
the second richest man in Northern Ireland and the ninth richest
in all Ireland. He left £339 million in his will after being killed,
aged 70, in a helicopter crash, having taken off in dense fog from
his Gillingham Hall home, in Norfolk, in 2014. An inquest heard
it was a flight that should never have happened, and would not
have happened at a public airport. The aircraft took off 20 minutes after the 'safe' weather window agreed by the pilots, because
Haughey was still busy hanging pictures in the house. The crash
happened because the pilots became disorientated in the poor
visibility.

Haughey had a liking for big houses and, besides Corby and
Gillingham Hall, also owned Ballyedmond Castle in County
Down, a £12 million home on London's Belgrave Square, a fashionable Georgian house in Dublin, as well as land in Uganda and
several islands on Lake Victoria. At one point he also owned an
expensive shooting estate in Scotland.

He was nominated for a peerage by the Ulster Unionist Party in
2004, sitting as a crossbencher as Baron Ballyedmond of Mourne.
He was also one of only three politicians ever to sit in both the
Lords and the Irish upper house, the Senate, and he was a member
of the Forum for Peace and Reconciliation. In 2010 he joined the
Tories and is recorded as having donated more than £1 million to
the party since 2001. He collected numerous honorary awards,
including a doctorate from the University of Ulster.

However, it is rare that people rise from little or nothing to
accumulate such wealth without treading on the odd toe here
and there, and some of those owning said toes dared to challenge

Baron Ballyedmond in court. In 2003 he lost in an industrial tribunal with Linda Heaton, his housekeeper of three years at Corby Castle. She was awarded more than £7,000 in compensation after she was reduced to tears and walked out, following a succession of public humiliations, having worked a 76-hour week. She told the tribunal: 'Dr Haughey seemed to be following me everywhere, and everything I did seemed not right for him. He upset several members of staff, reducing one to tears. He was in an awful mood and I couldn't take his manner any more. I had to go home.

'I had to go,' she added. 'I didn't walk out, I ran out. I couldn't get away fast enough.' Four days later, she received a letter saying she had resigned from her post, when she claimed she had, in fact, been on sick leave.

Then, in 2006 he lost a lengthy legal battle with a Scottish fisherman over the ownership of a derelict cottage on land adjacent to his Irish estate, at Rostrevor, with views across Carlingford Lough. He had tried to claim ownership by putting cattle on the land and erecting a fence and no trespassing signs. He argued in court that the cottage had been unoccupied for 12 years. He lost the case when the rightful owner presented his title to a court in Belfast, but the latter had only been able to make his legal challenge years later, after he had saved sufficient funds. It was a clear case of a rich man using his wealth as a bulldozer.

I mention these documented cases only because they give context to other behaviours that never got anywhere near a court of law or an industrial tribunal. There was his row with local walkers who, by custom and practice, were used to walking the paths of the Corby estate. I recall that he closed these summarily after he acquired the estate, causing much local bitterness. Then in its infinite wisdom, Carlisle City Council sold the city's airport to him in 2000. The then Conservative administration was only too happy to find a willing buyer for the loss-making airport – and one who was promising to really make things happen there.

After the events of September 11, 2001, the airline I was working for had its finance withdrawn and had to close, but a close colleague was, it seemed, fortunate enough to walk straight into a new job with Haughey, charged with coming up with a commercial plan to developed scheduled air services at Carlisle. It didn't last long, as my colleague was one of two respected figures in the aviation industry who walked out, citing the 'impossibility' of working for the man.

At his funeral, in Belfast Cathedral, the priest described him as 'a self-taught, hard-working, determined individual who had a thirst for knowledge'. It would not necessarily have made him a nice man who was easy to rub along with. So far as I can determine, his widow and heirs still own the castle, although both home and gardens have an air of neglect about them.

Haughey tired of his flirtation with Carlisle Airport in 2006, when he sold it to the group that owned Eddie Stobart, the lorry people. There then followed a protracted period of negotiation. Stobart wanted to build a logistics centre, or giant lorry park, at the airport but said it would also upgrade the airport and seek to start scheduled services. Stobart did have other aviation interests, having acquired the failing Irish regional carrier, Aer Arann Express, which it later renamed Stobart Air. In 2008, it acquired Southend Airport and its plans for Carlisle included a new terminal building and a realigned and longer runway.

After running into various planning obstacles the latter part of the plan was abandoned in favour of simple resurfacing of the runway. However, a smart new terminal was built and the airport was renamed Carlisle Lake District; there were also plans for a new hotel. Eventually, after successive delays, scheduled services by Loganair began in 2019, but the scheduling of flights to Belfast, Dublin and Southend was not hugely attractive and the fundamental issue was that, having not rebuilt the runway, an operational weight limit meant only small 36-seat aircraft could be used. Then COVID hit and passenger services were halted at the airport; at the time of writing there are no plans to resume scheduled flights. It joins a growing list of municipally owned airports that have struggled or closed following sale to private interests.

* * *

Back to the river's left bank, I find that Wetheral is another lovely village. I haven't really seen this side of it, down towards the river, as previous visits have been to its pubs or restaurants, up on the green. For this reason, the church, with its attractive lychgate, through which I can spy the unusual, octagonal, crenellated tower, is also new to me. Now the Church of the Holy Trinity, it was once the only CofE church dedicated to St Constantine. I don't know why the powers that be at some time chose to follow the crowd and relegate Constantine to the status of cave-owner only. The church and a mausoleum in Gothic style are the final resting place of several members of the aforementioned Howard family.

A few minutes' walk from the village is what is left of Wetheral Priory, namely its gatehouse, which is, effectively, a modest pele tower in the care of English Heritage.

As I leave Wetheral behind me, I feel I am now very much on the home straight. Indeed, there is now just one remaining stretch of open countryside to cross, to reach the next village, Scotby. To get there, I first pass a farm, where another change of gate type has me wandering in circles for a while and twisting my ankle in a rut. Then, having got back on course, I reach the end of the track to find a notice pinned to a post, its lettering severely smudged by the elements. It reads:

Walking the Line

Due to the current COVID-19 virus outbreak, this footpath has been temporarily closed, in line with government guidelines. STAY AT HOME and prevent the spread.

A second, larger and better-made notice proclaims:

Please Use an Alternative Route. Prevent the spread of COVID-19.

I feel I need to point out that there never was any official advice to close public rights of way, even though this could doubtless have been done under the powers assumed by the government. This kind of notice is no more than opportunism by landowners nostalgic for the days of foot and mouth, when they could keep everyone off their land legitimately. No one using this path would pass anything like as close as two metres to the nearest farm building, which, in turn, is many more metres away from the farm itself.

Soon afterwards, I cross beneath the S&C then follow it towards Carlisle, recrossing over it to a pleasant country lane that soon delivers me into Scotby. Now a desirable commuter location just beyond the edge of the city, this village once had two stations. The Midland station on the S&C closed in 1942 and the one on the Newcastle line, maybe 500m to the north, followed in 1959, thereby depriving Beeching of the honours.

Scotby is a pleasant village and one I know reasonably well, but it already has the feel of encroaching suburbia and it is along a very suburban road, with new housing, that I approach the bridge over the M6, atop which a young man in an anorak and bearing camera and notebook, is sitting watching the traffic. I might give him the benefit of the doubt and suggest that he has some official or semi-official function, but, to be honest, I think it's his hobby. I shall leave him to it.

From Armathwaite to Carlisle

Beyond the motorway, there is much new development, which may just about be high enough not to be on the flood-plain of the Eden. Carlisle has suffered terribly this century in floods that are supposed to be 'once-in-a-lifetime events', at most. The first big flood was in January 2005 and I couldn't possibly forget it. We had just arrived on holiday at Sharm El-Sheikh and switched on the telly, to be confronted by pictures of water. We casually assumed it was further coverage of the Boxing Day tsunami in the Far East, until the sight of Carlisle Civic Centre rising from an apparent lake told us otherwise. Linda is from Carlisle and so immediate thoughts turned to which areas of the city were affected. It turned out her brother's home, on Warwick Road, the main thoroughfare from the east, was under five feet of water. He'd escaped to move in with his girlfriend, who only had water up to her doorstep.

As if that was not bad enough, there was a full action replay barely a decade later when Storm Desmond struck, only this time the water reached head-height. The city is still awaiting delivery of a £25 million plan to contain future flooding, amid continuing claims that these schemes will not work. In both inundations, it was a combination of factors that made the flooding so bad and, while some of the factors were naturally occurring, others were exacerbated by human activity. In the broadest sense, we might of course include the human contribution to climate change among the latter, as there is a clear increased incidence of extreme weather events as global temperatures rise. But at the more local level, who on earth thought it would be a good idea to permit the building of a Tesco superstore with large car park slap-bang on the flood-plain?

The main plan for Carlisle's flood defences is really just 'more of the same': higher defences and more of them. But other works in the catchment – right up where I first entered the Upper Eden Valley, at Mallerstang – are designed to slow run-off into the river.

Tree planting is the most obvious among these actions, but work is also ongoing to reintroduce meanders to some of the Eden's tributaries. However, I do sometimes wonder about the practicality, and environmental sustainability, of what would be the ultimate flood defence: a barrage across the Solway to create a giant safety valve, while also generating green energy. Of course, any such scheme would have to maintain the daily draining of the Solway sands and the habitats that depend on this movement of water. I am neither a civil engineer nor an expert on these habitats, but I would like to know if such an ambitious project might be feasible.

Today, I cross Warwick Road right beside the aforementioned Tesco after a less than inspiring stretch through the big Rosehill industrial park, and immediately head north-east, away from my final destination, along a wooded lane. But for the sound of the M6, it might be in the countryside. Soon I reach the riverbank, which does offer as rural a setting as you're likely to find in any city, and the walk along the river's edge is enjoyable in the afternoon sun. Soon I reach Stony Holme golf course, which is very busy with a nice mix of casually dressed golfers. I know that golf courses are a manicured, artificial environment, but I do find today that the neat fairways and nicely dressed bunkers are sitting in perfect harmony with the trees and the rough.

In our original Settle–Carlisle Way, the route stuck to the riverbank all the way to Eden Bridge, where Scotland Road heads north out of the city. In an ideal world, I would take this route today, and come into town by way of the castle and Tullie House Museum, but the 'official' route in Viv's book permits me to make a more direct approach to the station, via Strand Road and Warwick Road. Having loosely flirted with the idea of catching a bus at Tesco and wary of missing my train, this proves an easy decision.

From Armathwaite to Carlisle

∗ ∗ ∗

Those arriving in Carlisle in 'better times' may think of Citadel station as something of a metaphor for the wider city. It's not that Carlisle isn't an important sub-regional centre for Cumbria and the Borders, but it was once a town at an international frontier: a frontier whose existence we can really trace to the Romans. Citadel station is a product of the height of the so-called era of Railway Mania, when it sat at a hugely important junction of several railways, only some of which remain. Archaeologists and historians still argue as to whether Hadrian's Wall was defensive, against the unruly tribes to the north, or more of a control point, a customs post, even. Perhaps they were protecting the mineral-rich North Pennines and Cumbria for themselves. What is without dispute is that the Wall passed through Carlisle on its way from Wallsend to Bowness-on-Solway, beyond where, the fortifications, but not the Wall itself, continued down the coast as far as Ravenglass.

The Roman fort of Luguvalio is buried beneath the intrusive dual carriageway, thoughtfully built for the purpose of dividing the impressive castle from the city centre. Despite this and other such burials, there have been numerous significant Roman finds in Carlisle, the site of two Roman forts, and from where the Wall was administered by the Romans. Most recently, excavations when the pavilion at the cricket club, just over the river, was being moved because of Storm Desmond damage, uncovered a Roman bath house. When the remains were discovered in 2017, archaeologists described the find as 'of national significance', and work is ongoing, with the cooperation of Carlisle Cricket Club, to open the site up for public access.

Tullie House Museum, just across the busy road dividing it from the castle, houses many important Roman artefacts, mostly reflecting finds from the western portion of the Wall and complementing those from the eastern portion, exhibited in the Great North Museum, in Newcastle. The Roman Wall and the various museums along its length are all dear to my heart, not just because I grew up with trips to Housesteads, Chesters and other forts, but because my wife, Linda, for some years ran Hadrian's Wall Heritage, latterly becoming Hadrian's Wall Trust, in what was a pioneering venture, brining together all aspects of the management of the World Heritage Site under one roof, near Hexham.

As she was born and raised in Carlisle and we live in Durham, this was a dream job for her, drawing upon all her skills in tourism management and promotion, capital development, the arts and conservation. Among her achievements while chief executive was assembling the finance and the respective visions for the various museums and forts along the entire length of the Wall, to tell the compelling stories of the Wall in distinct and diverse heritage attractions. This freshened up existing sites and ensured that they all complemented each other rather than competing. All the museums and forts are run by a variety of organisations, from English Heritage and the National Trust, to regional museum consortia, local authorities and private concerns.

The Hadrian's Wall National Trail was also a source of pride, as too were some of the spectacular events she organised, including 'Illuminating the Wall', in which the idea of lighting beacons at intervals along the Wall, just as the Romans had done, really captured the public imagination. It attracted volunteers from all over the world, who worked alongside the communities on and around the Wall to deliver a spectacular event.

'Hadrian's Wall was a World Heritage Site at which visitor numbers had been underline for more than 30 years,' she says. 'Through a coordinated approach to management, conservation and marketing, we not only reversed this trend but turned the Wall into one of the most potent symbols of the UK's visitor economy.'

What was innovative about the entire concept was that it brought together all the different disciplines associated with managing a World Heritage Site and the model was admired way beyond these shores. Linda did presentations on heritage management in places from Portugal, to Germany to Belarus and Moscow, earning a certain amount of prestige for the UK amid conservation circles.

'New businesses have sprung up all along the Wall – accommodation, cafés and pubs offer interpretation of the great story of this linear defence and the people and communities who lived and live along its length – it truly offers a world-class experience for visitors who now stay longer and experience so much more,' Linda says.

But what would all that matter to a novice government wishing to make its mark? Hadrian's Wall Heritage was substantially funded by the Regional Development Agencies in the North-East and North-West and when these were abolished by the Cameron-Clegg coalition government, with other partners under severe cuts and pressure themselves, the organisation was left to fund itself by other means. Ultimately it became too difficult to sustain.

This was all part of the coalition's social experiment – austerity – in which we were all supposed to be 'in it together' for the good of the country. Except that austerity, by all economic measures, made things worse and failed to reduce the national debt, as had been promised. In fact, it was no more than a dogmatic political strategy to erode the power and influence of local authorities and other public services. We should, as citizens, be very wary indeed of people who talk about us being 'in it together' or making sacrifices 'for the national good'. In reality, while the poorer – and even the not so badly off – will undoubtedly feel the pain, the rich will scarcely notice.

The truth of this is most recently echoed in the governmental response to COVID, in which those left behind include people in the so-called 'gig economy' – a sector which only really began to grow with austerity – children in less advantaged schools, and those on income support. Meanwhile, it is only we plebs who are required to adhere to the rules designed to stop the spread of the virus; rules from which aides to the Prime Minister and the family of the same appear to be exempt. One rule for them and one for all the rest of us, as it always was.

* * *

After the Romans left (or while they were even in the process of leaving), around the fifth century, the native tribes of Britons and Picts snaffled whatever they could from the former riches of the occupiers. However, the popular conception that the country collapsed into chaos is probably not correct. In this part of the world, there was certainly a period of relative stability as the Brittanic Kingdom of Rheged held sway across what is now Cumbria, Dumfries and Galloway and even as far south as Cheshire.

These Celtic people called themselves *Kombroges*, or 'comrades', giving rise to the names of Cumberland and Cumbria. It's also the derivation of Cymru, the Welsh for Wales. But to the east, there were new arrivals, who termed the inhabitants of Rheged as *Wealas*, or foreigners, which, curiously enough, is the root of the words 'Wales' and 'Welsh'. Traces of the old Brittanic tongue still survive in place names across the North and in Scotland, like Pen-y-ghent (hill of the winds) or Caerlaverock (walled fortification) and in the old sheep-counting system common in Cumbria and the Dales – *yan, tan, tethera, methera, pimp...* Rheged enjoyed the odd victory over these Saxon arrivals, most notably over Bernicia (modern North East England and south-east Scotland), but then Bernicia and Deira (lands north of the Humber) merged to form Northumbria, which annexed Rheged, some time before 730, to become the most powerful kingdom in the isles.

These were also good times, for Northumbria became a seat of learning, producing such great tomes as the *Lindisfarne Gospels* and the *Codex Amiatinus*, and let's not forget the remarkable work of the early and great scientist the Venerable Bede, and fine artworks, such as the Rothwell Cross, in Dumfriesshire. But the so-called Golden Age of Northumbria, or the Northumbrian Renaissance, only really lasted about 100 years, between the mid-seventh and mid-eighth centuries. With the decline of Northumbria, areas west of the Pennines – including Carlisle and Cumbria – were ruled relatively peacefully by the Scottish Kingdom of Strathclyde, until William II took Carlisle for the Norman colonists in 1072, establishing a fortress in the city. Then David I of Scotland took it back in 1136 – only for Malcolm IV of Scotland to return it to English rule 21 years later, after David died at Carlisle Castle in 1153.

During the ensuing wars between England and Scotland, Carlisle yo-yoed between the two countries – a situation that endured till the 17th century, with the unification of the English and Scottish Crowns in 1603. Then the rebellion of 1745 saw Carlisle Castle taken by the Jacobites and subsequently retaken by the Duke of Cumberland. The 'modern' castle, which stands proud today, is largely 19th century, though much of the original building's materials have been recycled more than once. You can, courtesy of English Heritage, visit both the 'modern castle' and its medieval rooms, while its museum tells the story of the bloody history of the border. It is a visit that I truly recommend – many castles invite one to imagine bygone years amid their ruins, but Carlisle is a full-blooded intact and large fort, in which times of turmoil seem realistically recent.

It was the squishiness of the Anglo-Scottish border, against the backdrop of its repeatedly changing hands, that provided fertile ground for the rise of the Reiver bandit families in the so-called Debatable Lands, or Border Marches, where the border was imprecisely drawn, or not drawn at all.

These days, there's a certain local pride attached to bearing a Reiver surname: my mother was a Dodds, and Linda boasted both Musgraves and Irvings on her mother's side. The Dodds' roots are in the North Tyne valley, the Musgraves', just across the fells around Bewcastle, and the Irvings were centred around Lockerbie, on the Scottish side of today's border. These Reiver folk even extended their influence across the world: we once found ourselves marooned in St John, New Brunswick, in the wake of an Atlantic hurricane, and chose to go and witness the huge tidal range in the Bay of Fundy. We could not fail to notice that the name Irving was everywhere – it festooned filling stations, haulage yards, railway wagons, shipping containers… it was as though being called Irving was a prerequisite of being in business. We stopped for ice cream at a little shop over the road from an Irving garage, where we commented on the ubiquity of the Irving name and its links with our side of the Atlantic. We were then told a little bit about the Irvings: the Irving filling station was only there because the ice cream seller's own family had been bold enough to open its own gas outlet. 'Irving's set up over the road and undercut us until we were forced to close,' she said. 'It's what they do.' Well, once a Reiver, always a Reiver, I guess.

Carlisle's 12th century cathedral has some links with the castle, though for somewhat negative reasons: stone from the nave was stolen by the Scottish Presbyterian Army during the Civil War, to reinforce the castle. Partly for this reason, it is the second smallest cathedral in England, though it does boast a very beautiful blue and gold ceiling in what remains of said nave, and a fine Gothic stained glass window. Also worth a visit are the surviving city walls, though sadly carved asunder by the aforementioned dual carriageway, which is now crossed by a modern bridge of steel.

Carlisle still retains the feel of a border town: accents really do change the moment you step across the invisible line near Gretna Green, and many people commute in and out from the Scottish side, so you will hear English in Scotch Street and Scots in English Street. As the largest place for some distance, it's also a bit of a night-time magnet and Botchergate is no place for the sober on a Friday or Saturday night.

* * *

I head towards the top end of Botchergate via The Crescent, the autological name for the potentially graceful arced road that girdles the Citadel – the twin 19th century round red sandstone towers that once guarded the southern approach to the city. But here, I begin to feel a slight sense of anti-climax. Surely my approach to my final goal should be met with a modest fanfare, at least – a few socially distanced Northumbrian pipers, perhaps, or a modest blast from a bugle or two. In less unusual times, perhaps Simon Armitage, the poet laureate, would have composed a short verse for such auspicious occasion?

Perhaps something like what follows, entitled simply 'Poem', though with heartfelt apologies to Mr Armitage for the massacre of his original.

He here comes, as he strides into town
He's hiked up from Settle and covered much ground
And walked up the hills and down all the dales
And climbed wire fences and rickety stiles.
And kept his eyes open for other folk as he walked.

And minded his distance when with others he'd talk.
And eat in a pub bar of fish or of pork.
And once, for a change, drank Romanian wine.

And on some days he might fall in a ditch.
And occasionally encounter a similar glitch.
And wringing his socks out declare, 'Ain't life a bitch?!'
And though some may think that praise is too rich.

Here's how they rate him at Citadel station:
He's walked here from Settle – the pride of our nation.

However, I am by now swimming in the Sea of Surreally Disappointing Disappointment; lost in the forest of forgotten fanfares; locked in the Forbidden City of missing sympathies long after the gates have closed. I enter a Costa coffee shop close to the station, as my fluids intake is down by one flask of said drink today. Under COVID rules, it takes three people to serve me an iced coffee: one to ensure I follow the distancing rules, one to take my order and one to pass me the drink and take payment. I hesitate to 'do the math', as the Americans would say, as I fear the answer would be the wrong side of zero from a Costa perspective. Returning outside to the square that fronts the station, there is no one; only the odd crisp packet blowing in the breeze, and it's not going to buy a flat white any time soon.

Citadel station is a fine Grade II listed building. Like the station at Crewe, its size reflects not so much the scope of the city it serves, but the number of different railway lines that once converged here. When the Midland Railway completed the S&C, it was the seventh railway company to serve the station and the ten or so routes radiating from it. Were you to represent the station as the hub of a wheel today, there would today still be six remaining spokes – north and south on the West Coast line to Glasgow and London; north-west to Dumfries and Ayrshire; south-west to the Cumbrian Coast and Barrow; east to Newcastle and, of course, south-east to Settle and Leeds.

Once there were four more spokes, though there are now hopes that, in time, the Waverley route through the Borders to Edinburgh, may be restored all the way from Carlisle – at present you can travel from Edinburgh only as far as a terminus near Melrose.

Even this mighty edifice is near empty in these curious times, though – unlike on my previous journeys – I am this time asked for my ticket at the barrier. I struggle to locate it on the Northern Rail app and have to retreat and try again. When I return to the barrier there is no one there. There's a nice area where you can sit and wait for trains on the S&C or to Newcastle. A solitary Newcastle-bound passenger is also there. I take a selfie next to the board promoting the delights of S&C Country and that is the full extent of my muted celebrations.

I had, back in the other world that was 2019, anticipated downing a pint or two at the Howard Arms (how appropriate today!) then rounding up a few friends for a celebratory curry at the Viceroy, on Dalston Road. But, in July 2020, my most exciting option is to get to Armathwaite, jump in the car and head for home, in Durham, where I shall immediately sink into a hot bath with a gin and tonic. On the ride to Armathwaite, I gaze down the 'scree slope' at Eden Brows and marvel at this solid endorsement of the right to life of 'my railway'. At Armathwaite, I allow the train to leave before slipping, illegally, across the tracks: it is a long way down and up again if you take the correct route. Tom has been as good as his word and at least I can enjoy a coffee: better, the sun has baked the flask and the drink inside is still nice and hot.

Walking the Line

It is July and there remains time enough for the day to gently wind down and take itself to bed. But it is the sunset of my journey from Settle to Carlisle, and, on this cue, I think of all those whose paths I have crossed on my unexpectedly disjointed journey, and of their various literary inspirations. Baron Hothfield and his treasured diaries of Lady Anne; John Bucknall and his oh-so-apt quotation from *The Sword in the Stone*; Diane Lawrenson and her love of the Brontë sisters, and most especially, Emily.

As I point the car towards Brampton and the A69, I choose to leave the last few words to Emily:

I know not how it falls on me,
This summer evening, hushed and lone;
Yet the faint wind comes soothingly
With something of an olden tone ...

Postscript

Standing it All on its Head

As I said in the Introduction, the story, or stories that you have just read do not comprise a guidebook. Rather, my journey from Settle to Carlisle provided a scaffold upon which to hang a wider narrative, which I hope may have not only given the reader a greater insight into the life and ways of the Pennine country traversed by a great Victorian railway, but also stimulated wider thought about… well, life, the universe and a little bit of everything.

When I began the project I could not have predicted the way the world would look as it drew to a close. Writing a book is not the same as writing a news story for a newspaper or, indeed, a longer feature for a magazine. Both of these are anchored to a particular point in time, but a non-fiction book needs to be able to endure well beyond the brief moment of its publication. Ideally, it should remain worth reading, just like a good novel, years into the future.

So, when COVID barged into our lives, my initial thoughts were along the lines of how I could best ignore it and get on with writing my book. That knee-jerk reaction progressively subsided as time dragged on through lockdown and the epic scale of the pandemic became more evident. When I resumed my journey, the day after lockdown rules were eased, I faced the reality that this event simply could not be ignored. But it was only when curiosity drew me deep into the pages of Alfred Wainwright's *A Pennine Journey* that I realised that COVID was more than just an irritating inconvenience, but was actually a significant part of the very scaffold to which I referred earlier – just as was the uneasy peace that punctuated preparations for war in Wainwright's narrative.

Some 67,000 British civilians died in the Second World War. As I wrote this, the COVID death clock was ticking up towards a similar figure (and at the time of going to press, that death toll has almost doubled after the second wave). It requires no feat of genius to spot the correlation and, so, reading Wainwright's longest, yet earliest, work acquires new significance. The Second World War was the most significant event of Wainwright's adult life and we shall come to appreciate in due course just how great a watershed COVID shall be in the modern world.

Of course, society now is very different from the one that Wainwright describes – no writer today could get away with his sweeping societal generalisations; his casual sexism, erring too often towards misogyny; his stereotyping of some of those, like Gypsies, whose lives he briefly brushes against; the persistent smoking, even while 'suffering from flu' and without heed to the health consequences. Yet all this is integral to the work, which is as revealing of the times in which it was written as some of the finest novels written in or about this period – the anticipation of impending war in Ian McEwan's *Atonement*; the social commentary of Stella Gibbons's *Cold Comfort Farm*; the descriptions of farm life privations featured in James Herriot's factually based *All Creatures Great and Small*.

I'd like to think that, 50 years from now, someone might casually pick up a printed copy of my own book (in itself most likely a rare object by 2070), blow off the dust and find it a fascinating reflection of the notorious COVID Years; find my own societal commentaries an intriguing mirror to hold up to received interpretations of those distant past times.

I take few positives from the COVID year, which laid bare the failings of an amateur one-trick government for all to see what many of us already suspected or knew. Such initial social cohesion as there may well have been was ultimately discarded on the altar of saving the skin of a government adviser; online shopping drove another nail into the high street's coffin and a great many people suffered or died, many of them quite needlessly. We got a taste of just how easily a future government so minded might impose martial law should such action ever be called for, and just how eagerly some members of the public might slip effortlessly into the role of the Stasi. And we learned just how very badly people who had never before been there, could behave in our countryside. Having once explored every corner of our localities, we learned to live in a nether world of endless TV repeats and stultifying *Archers* monologues. My greatest personal lockdown bright spot came in a medical consultation conducted by telephone, being formally excused any further such requirement by my cancer consultant, it now being more than six cancer-free years since my operation. I had not just recovered from cancer, but I had *officially* recovered from cancer.

And of the journey itself, as opposed to the journey through life and a pandemic? Well, the highlights I take from it are the wonderful trad jazz band in Settle, as a reminder of how much live music means to us; my first ascent of Blea Moor; the incessant fortitude of Eden Valley villages in being perpetually beyond loveliness; the outpourings of enthusiasm I witnessed from the likes of Hester Cox, with her butterflies, John Bucknall and his castle, Anthony Hothfield and the Lady Anne legacy, Diane Lawrenson and her evocative Brontë bronzes; the stoicism of those getting back to providing us with hospitality against the odds; my journey deep underground at Long Marton; the riverside at Wetheral as my fond farewell to open country.

Bleaker moments were few, but finding myself knee-deep in freezing cold water comes near the top, followed by the anti-climax of arriving in a near-dead city in the midst of lockdown.

On the physical side, the apparent 'cure' enjoyed by my dicky right knee ligaments was a quite unexpected bonus; but the bruises on my toenails remained for months an enduring reminder that it is a bad idea to wear boots that are too small.

The adventure provided me with the novel opportunity to take a dip in the waters that lie between the presentation of fact and the liberty of fiction and has whet my appetite for more, as I hope it may also have tempted you – if not to make this particular journey, then to plan your own as a means not just of making new discoveries but also of digging a bit deeper into yourself, and rearranging a few bits to create a more inspiring path to your future.

There is a received wisdom that, on a long walk in Britain, you always go south to north or west to east. This is so that the prevailing bad weather, which normally comes from the west or south-west, is on your back, and the sun, should it grace your presence, is rarely in your eyes. The Settle–Carlisle Way is inclined a bit to the north of south-east to north-west and so should, technically, be walked from south to north, or Settle to Carlisle. But it's a marginal case, as Carlisle is significantly to the west of Settle. And, of course, it should also be remembered that travelling in this direction also echoes the original raison d'être for the line – to forge a new route to the Scottish border.

So, some may find what I am about to suggest something of a heresy: if this small volume should tempt you to make your own journey, then I shall recommend that, instead of starting at Settle, you might perhaps begin in Carlisle and head south. This is not because my arrival in a near-deserted Carlisle city centre was prejudiced by the curse of COVID. No, rather, it's because the railway's woven course through the pastoral lands of Eden and then its steeper ascent of the upper valley is surely the best approach to the dramatic central 'mountain section' between Ais Gill Head and Ribblehead. You could preface your walk by mugging up on

Standing it All on its Head

Reiver and Roman history, the better to understand the back stories of pele towers and tower houses, or why the Romans built roads through Cumbria. Once across 'the mountain section', the descent of Ribblesdale will retain the mountainous qualities until your arrival – bursting from a narrow ginnel onto the bustling market square – in Settle itself. There might be few better places to end one's journey than in 'the perfect little town' so loved by Mark and Pat Rand in their converted water tower by Settle station.

But now another idea... the original Settle–Carlisle Way Speakman-Morrison route actually began in Leeds and followed the towpath of the Leeds & Liverpool Canal all the way to Gargrave, via Skipton, and on along the southern rim of limestone country, to Settle. So I shall go further: I venture that there is some merit in the idea of extending the walk from Settle, south to the magnificent station at Hellifield, at the southern end of the linear Settle–Carlisle Conservation Area, to then finish in Skipton. This could offer an even greater sense of arrival than Settle, while also chiming loudly with the repeated journeys of Lady Anne Clifford, from her seat at Skipton Castle, to Brougham, near Penrith.

All that's needed is for someone to rewrite the guidebook 'back to front'... to reiterate earlier protestations on the subject of writing guidebooks, that person is unlikely to be me!

Notes

[1] An updated version of this account is being published by Saraband in 2021, under the new title of *Settle & Carlisle: The Enduring Life of the People's Railway.*

[2] The interactive map is also available online: https://bit.ly/2Et9KRd

[3] See:www.northernarchaeologicalassociates.co.uk/ribblehead-navvy-camps-earthwork-survey

[4] *George Gibbs: The Life Of A Railway Tunneller*, by Sarah Lister, a tour guide and local historian, from Settle, March 2019. Research by Ken Lister as part of the Settle Graveyard Project, which looks at the lives of those buried in the church graveyard.

[5] See:www.seren.bangor.ac.uk/features/2012/05/23/wuthering-height-a-truly-original-story/

[6] See: http://janetandstephen.info/publications.html

[7] The Dales Countryside Museum was closed throughout the initial COVID lockdown, and Hester's beautiful exhibition arrived somewhat later. We visited it in October 2020 and loved the work.

[8] Dick Capel explores the River Eden and the Benchmarks in *The Stream Invites Us To Follow*, also published by Saraband.

[9] My return to the location in August 2020 tells me that, because someone has laid a track that is not marked on the map, I did indeed turn too soon. This is a shame as I discover that the 'correct' track makes for excellent walking. It is a mistake I should not have made and would not have made, had I taken more

care map-reading, for the absence of a house at the track-end should have made everything more than clear...

[10] Sabaratnam, J (2018). 'Lady Anne Clifford: From Idealized Gender Warrior to Exceptional Literary Bureaucrat', *Berkeley Undergraduate Journal*, 31(2).

[11] Once again I return to the scene of any possible crime, in August 2020, and follow the route backwards, from Culgaith. The path has not been obstructed and, therefore, either the directions were misleading, or I misinterpreted them. Moral of story: always check everything against the map!

[12] A local resident later tells me that this sign appeared 'around the time of COVID'. However 'official' it may have looked, it seems this was just another bit of farmer or landowner muscle-flexing.

[13] St Cuthbert's journeying is symbolically remembered through the creation of the St Cuthbert's Way long-distance footpath, from Melrose to Lindisfarne – an excellent five-day walk, which I strongly recommend.

Bibliography

Abbott, Stan (L) and Whitehouse, Alan, *The Line That Refused To Die*, 1990 and 1994.

Abbott, Stan (L), *To Kill a Railway,* Leading Edge, 1985.

Abbott, Stan L, *Settle & Carlisle: The Enduring Life Of The People's Railway*, Saraband, 2021.

Brontë, Emily, *Wuthering Heights*, with commentary by Christopher Heywood, Broadview Press, 2002

Capel, Dick, *The Stream Invites Us to Follow*, 2020.

Cardwell, Peter, Ronan, Damien, and Simpson, Roger, *An Archaeological Survey of the Ribblehead Navvy Settlements*, Northern Archaeological Associates, 1995.

Clifford, D.J.H. (David), *The Diaries Of Lady Anne Clifford*, Sutton Publishing, 2003.

Coleman, Terry, *The Railway Navvies*, Hutchinson, 1965.

Crow, Vivienne, *Settle to Carlisle Way*, Rucksack Readers, 2012.

Forder, John and Eliza, with Arthur Raistrick, *Open Fell, Hidden Dale*, Frank Peters Publishing, 1985.

Fraser, George MacDonald, *The Steel Bonnets*, Harvill, 1986.

Gordon, Ian and Andrew, *Settle to Carlisle Walk*, Dalesman, 1990.

Gordon, Sheila, *Lady Anne's Way*, Frank Gordon, 2019.

Jackson, K C, 'The Construction Works Between Batty Moss and Dent Head', Yorkshire History Quarterly, 2000.

Jenkins, David, *The History of BPB Industries*, BPB Industries, 1973.

Jenkinson, David, *Rails In The Fells*, Peco, 1973.

Bibliography

Lyons, Kim, *The Dentdale Brontë Trail*, Kyon Equipment, 1985.

Mitchell, Bill, *The Lost Shanties of Ribblehead*, Castleberg, 1996.

Morrison, John and Speakman, Colin *Settle–Carlisle Country* (featuring the Settle–Carlisle Way), Leading Edge, 1990.

Northern Archaeological Associates, The, *Batty Moss Navvy Settlement*, Yorkshire Dales National Park, 1995.

Page, Lewis, *Lions, Donkeys and Dinosaurs: Waste and Blundering in the Military*, Arrow, 2007.

Ratcliffe, Dorothy Una, *The Cranesbill Caravan*, Dalesman, 1961.

Salveson, Paul, *The Settle–Carlisle Railway*, The Crowood Press, 2019.

Trueman, Michael, Isaac, Susan, and Quartermaine, James, *The Langcliffe Quarry Limeworks*, Settle, Lancaster University Archaeological Unit, 1989.

Wainwright, Alfred, *A Pennine Journey*, Michael Joseph, 1986.

Maps

Settle to Carlisle Way, Harvey Maps, 2012.

Ordnance Survey Explorer, sheets OL2 (South and Western Dales), OL19 (Upper Eden Valley), OL5 (Penrith), 315 (Carlisle).

Acknowledgements

Averil King-Wilkinson's 'Chapel-le-Dale Churchyard' was first published by the Friends of the Settle–Carlisle Line in its journal, *Track Records* (date unknown). It is reproduced with the kind permission of Averil's family.

The verse at the start of Chapter 3 was written by T. H. White and first published in 1938 in *The Sword in the Stone*, part one of his Arthurian tetralogy. Thanks to HarperCollins for kind permission to reproduce these words.

The extract from 'George Gibbs, The Life of a Railway Tunneller' was first published online as part of a project by the Settle–Carlisle Railway Conservation Area researching the lives of the railway navvies. It is reproduced with the kind permission of Ken and Sarah Lister.

Mick Yates' 'Appleby Horse Fair' is reproduced with the kind permission of the author and publisher, Indigo Dreams.

The four lines of verse by Dorothy Una Ratcliffe quoted in Chapter 5 are the final lines of her poem 'Requiem', originally published by John Lane, at The Bodley Head, in 1922, in a collection entitled *Singing Rivers*. The prose by the same author comes from *The Cranesbill Caravan*, published by Dalesman in 1961. Every effort has been made to locate the current holder of the copyright of D.U. Ratcliffe's writings.

Among the many people who have contributed to my writing this book, special thanks are reserved for those who gave gladly of their time and resources to help me to create a more rounded picture of my journey through some of England's finest countryside.

Thanks to Mark and Pat Rand for sending me on my way from Settle, secure in the knowledge that help with facts about the line

Acknowledgements

would always be just an email away. I thank David and Chris Stewart for their hospitality (plus walking company, curry, dry socks and a set of dice to amuse me on my travels) in the days just after lockdown – and the staff at the Shepherds Inn, Langwathby, and the Duke's Head, Armathwaite, for providing a secure environment in which to stay during those same difficult days. Similar thanks to the teams at the Falcon, in Settle, and the Ribblehead Inn for their assistance in an earlier time, when life seemed so much simpler.

I thank the irrepressible John Bucknall for his generosity in gifting me a lasting memory of my visit to Pendragon Castle and Baron Anthony Hothfield and Diane Waterson for inspiring my enthusiasm for Lady Anne Clifford and her important legacy. The scope of my welcome at Saint-Gobain's Birkshead Mine and Kirkby Thore works was beyond all reasonable expectations and provided me with a view of the Eden Valley from a wholly different, and much 'deeper', perspective. That I was able to make this visit in such difficult times is down to Emily Atherton, at the resurgent *Cumberland & Westmorland Herald*, to which I extend my sincerest hopes for a prosperous future.

I thank Miles Johnson and Debbie Allen for facilitating my research on the social history of the Yorkshire Dales; Hester Cox for tea and inspiration; and my sister June, and Carol Cross, for their company while walking. Last but by no means least, my thanks and appreciation to my wife, Linda, for understanding so well what drives me, for braving COVID to join me from Langwathby to Lazonby, and for her insightful critique when I stray too close to my subject.

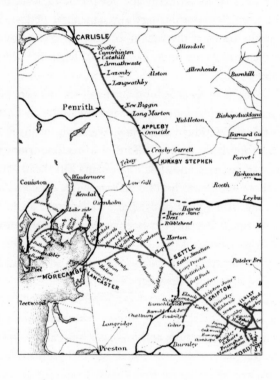